Land of the Permanent Wave

Southwestern Writers Collection Series
CONNIE TODD, Editor

Land of the Permanent Wave

An Edwin "Bud" Shrake Reader

Edited and with
an introduction by
STEVEN L. DAVIS

Foreword by
LARRY L. KING

UNIVERSITY OF TEXAS PRESS, AUSTIN

Requests for permission to reproduce material
from this work should be sent to:
   Permissions
   University of Texas Press
   P.O. Box 7819
   Austin, TX 78713-7819
   www.utexas.edu/utpress/about/bpermission.html

(∞) The paper used in this book meets the minimum requirements
of ANSI/NISO Z39.48-1992 (R1997) (Permanence of Paper).

Library of Congress Cataloging-in-Publication Data
Shrake, Edwin.
   Land of the permanent wave : an Edwin "Bud" Shrake reader /
edited and with an introduction by Steven L. Davis ; foreword by
Larry L. King. — 1st ed.
     p.   cm. — (Southwestern writers collection series)
   ISBN 978-0-292-71804-3 (cl.: alk. paper)
   I. Davis, Steven L. II. Title.
   PS3569.H735A6   2008
   813'.54—dc22
                              2007045365

*The Southwestern Writers Collection Series originates from the
Southwestern Writers Collection, an archive and literary center
established at Texas State University–San Marcos to celebrate
the region's writers and literary heritage.*

For Jody Gent—Bud Shrake

Para mis tres hermanos:
Jeff, Joe, Don—Steven L. Davis

Contents

PART 3
Mad Dogs and Outlaws

PART 4
Night Never Falls

Foreword

I felt like I knew Bud Shrake before I met him. Mutual friends in Texas and New York had recommended us to each other, and I had read his first novel, *But Not for Love*, about a period when our home state was shaking off much of its rural dust in becoming more urbanized, more varied, more political, and more corporate.

Shrake called me unannounced when he arrived in Washington, D.C. in 1965 on a job for *Sports Illustrated*. I invited him to my tiny apartment—a one-room "efficiency" plus a bathroom and a kitchen so small two people couldn't occupy it. We began drinking and inhaling Mexican Boo Smoke almost before exchanging howdies. In ten minutes we were brothers.

In time there was a knock on my door. Shrake hissed, *Don't answer it. Don't answer it.* I looked through the peephole and saw a young man. "Who is it?" I asked. "Telegram for Mr. King" was the response. Shrake said, *No! It's a trick!* He leaped from his chair and made a clatter near my writing desk and the bookcase behind it. I turned back to the door. "Slide the telegram under the door," I said. The young man hesitated. "You can't come in," I said. "My wife and I are naked."

It was, indeed, a telegram that came in under the door, one asking me to review a book for the *New York Times*. Shrake by that time was fumbling around my homemade bookcase, where he had deposited his dope stash when he thought the narcs had come calling. I began to help him look for his stash, and in doing so removed my copy of *But Not for Love*. "Aw, hell no!" Shrake said. "I wouldn't have hidden it behind *my own* book."

Weird things have a way of happening to Bud Shrake. On assignment to cover a chili-eating contest for the *Fort Worth Press*, he became the accidental winner by eating more chili than any true contestant.

For years, Shrake and writing buddy Gary Cartwright, when well oiled, talked broken English and a few words of Italian in getting it across that they were a famous acrobatic team touring the United States. To sell that story, they sometimes wore capes and other items not normally associated with the sane. Often they were asked to perform one of their routines. "The Flying Punzars" were happy to oblige. Their performance at a Dallas country club was typical. Shrake positioned himself near the house band in the dining room and made a cup of his hands, the better to flip Cartwright into the air for an unannounced "triple somersault."

Cartwright ran at Shrake full speed, launching himself airborne so as to hit Bud's cupped hands. There was a slight miscalculation: he kicked Shrake in the chest, knocking him back into the band amid a noisy clatter of musical instruments that suddenly became the worse for wear, and he himself flopped atop Shrake. While the diners in the country club gasped, the Flying Punzars bounded up, bowed to the crowd, threw kisses, and then departed at maximum speed. "We were always persuaded that we'd get it right," Bud Shrake once told me. A shrug. "But . . ."

Once in a Manhattan bar Shrake noticed a young woman, "very attractive and sensual-seeming and pleasant with a nice laugh," and managed to manipulate his way onto a barstool beside her. They began to chat and got along famously, so well indeed that Bud began scheming how to cut her out of the herd and have his way with her. Only when two bearded suits with the young woman said she must leave with them did Shrake realize that she was Gina Lollobrigida.

Shrake later wrote several screenplays that were actually made into movies, and associated to varying degrees with Steve McQueen, Dennis Hopper, Warren Oates, Willie Nelson, and Peter Boyle, among others—but, alas, no Gina Lollobrigidas. Ham that he is, Shrake managed to play three small roles in his own movies.

This book contains some scenes from Shrake's various screenplays—and stories about the filming of a number of them. Shrake has, indeed, written just about everything but TV documentaries and, perhaps, poems: novels, nonfiction books including an as-told-to bio of Willie Nelson, magazine articles, and many funny letters. We get samples of all in this collection.

My favorite letter was one Shrake wrote in 1966 to Pete Rozelle, commissioner of the National Football League, in which he applied for an NFL franchise in Santa Fe and included a dollar of "earnest money" to show his good faith. Shrake admits he was a bit out of his mind during that composition.

He was clicking on all cylinders, however, when he wrote an article called "The Land of the Permanent Wave"—set in East Texas—that Willie Morris, the storied editor of *Harper's* magazine, called one of the two most memorable articles he had published. Over the years, many people have complimented *me* for writing that article, probably because I wrote many *Harper's* articles as a contributing editor, many of them set in Texas. I always say to those who compliment me for Bud's article, "Yes, it was one of my better efforts and I treasure your comment." Or, "Thank you *so* much! You would not believe what I went through to write that piece." ("Our" article is in this book, of course.)

Shrake wrote what I thought a brilliant novel, *Blessed McGill.* When I asked how it was doing, he reached in his pocket and handed me two short newspaper clippings from—as I recall—Idaho and West Virginia. Neither review was over a dozen sentences long. One indicated that *Blessed McGill* might be the best novel ever; the other stopped just short of recommending the death penalty for its author. In time Shrake became frustrated that few among his critics, including some personal friends, understood that the book was a commentary on religion, its misuses and consequences. Most thought it an offbeat cowboy yarn or didn't have a clue what it was. It was almost too much for Shrake when a Hollywood type who professed interest in turning *Blessed McGill* into a movie said, "Of course, we'll have to take out all that religious crap."

It was Shrake's frustration over the reception of *Blessed McGill* that caused him to write me a letter about our mutual calling, in which he described writing as "the freakiest most utterly egotistical endeavor a man can undertake."

Fortunately, for those who care about literature, Shrake's urge and need to create allow him to often forget such concerns. The results are richly on display in this collection. I love and appreciate Bud Shrake's work. He has few equals, and even fewer superiors.

—LARRY L. KING
January 21, 2007

Larry L. King, the author of numerous books and stage plays, is the only writer to have been nominated for a National Book Award, a Broadway Tony, and a TV Emmy.

Land of the Permanent Wave

INTRODUCTION

Edwin "Bud" Shrake is one of the most intriguing literary talents to emerge from Texas, although his best work is too little known among most readers. He is primarily viewed as a sportswriter and the coauthor of *Harvey Penick's Little Red Book*, which became the best-selling sports book of all time. Shrake has also been a successful screenwriter, working for Hollywood while remaining rooted in Texas. Yet his enduring legacy is found in his novels. He has not enjoyed the commercial success of contemporaries Larry McMurtry and Dan Jenkins, but his work has a lasting resonance. His novels, highly praised upon their release, have retained their vibrancy over the years. Three of his books are ranked by literary scholars as among the best ever written about Texas.

Shrake is one of those rare Texas writers who describes his home state in the manner of a national writer, rather than a regional one. His prose strides confidently through the pages, comically subversive, yet with a heightened regard for the abundant mysteries of human nature. In matters of style, Shrake has less in common with his Texas contemporaries than with other American novelists such as Ken Kesey, Walker Percy, and Kurt Vonnegut.

In his fiction, as in his best screenplays and journalism, Shrake has explored major themes while observing the world from odd angles. He's written compellingly about gender relations, civil rights, and the Kennedy assassination. He's created stories about the early days of the Texas Republic and the making of the atomic bomb, and he's brought to life Native Americans and octogenarian golfers with equal felicity. He's written of beatniks, buffalo hunters, German Jewish immigrants, country musicians, bisexual interior designers, and Tom Landry. He's collaborated with Willie Nelson, and he was the longtime close friend of former Texas governor Ann Richards. Indeed, Shrake was known as "The First Guy" during Richards's tenure in the governor's mansion.

Shrake has always been a serious novelist, despite his reputation for humor and his day job as a journalist. His friends and fellow sportswriters Dan Jenkins and Gary Cartwright wrote successful football novels, as did another friend, former Dallas Cowboy Peter Gent. Yet Shrake himself resisted that temptation. Instead, he used the access his sportswriting offered to win entrée into elite circles. While partying with Dallas's oil millionaires, he took

note of their social interactions, business interests, and political preoccupa-
tions. Fragments of these observations appear throughout his work, although
football itself has remained conspicuously absent.

Shrake's documentarian sensibility is amplified by his uncanny instinct
for finding the thick of the action. Many people, for example, have written
of Dallas in 1963, but only Bud Shrake was dating Jack Ruby's star stripper
at the time of the Kennedy assassination. Shrake's novel of that era, *Strange
Peaches*, captures Dallas's underground culture and also sheds light on the
city's vocal right wing—those whom Shrake had observed through his friendship with Dallas Cowboys owner Clint Murchison Jr. Few novelists can bring
such material to their work; no wonder *Texas Monthly* critic Don Graham
has written: "When anybody asks me what Dallas was like during the time
of the Kennedy assassination, I always refer them to one book: Edwin 'Bud'
Shrake's *Strange Peaches*."[1]

Shrake's fiction is inextricably linked to his experience as a reporter. Early
in his career, he was an integral presence at the *Fort Worth Press*. As his
friend Gary Cartwright has noted, Shrake "would write all the police stories,
most of the city and country stories, handle club news, obits, stock markets,
call-ins about five-legged dogs and eight-pound turnips. Then in the afternoon [the editor] would let him write features." Shrake estimates that he was
writing 50,000 words a week during that time—the equivalent of a novel. "It
was the greatest training I could have had, going to work for a paper that was
woefully understaffed and underpaid where I had to do about five different
people's jobs all at once. Even then I realized that I was learning a lot. I bitched
about it, of course, but then newspapermen bitch about everything."[2]

Later, during his fourteen-year tenure at *Sports Illustrated* (1964–1978),
Shrake traveled the world, reporting on the athletic contests of the day. Upon
joining *Sports Illustrated*, he had published a well-received novel, *But Not
for Love*, and his editor at the magazine, André Laguerre, considered him a
"literary" sportswriter. Because of that, Laguerre often assigned Shrake to
write "bonus pieces"—long feature stories that were only marginally, if at all,
related to sports. Reading these articles now, years after their initial publication, one is struck by the realization that Shrake was engaging in "the New
Journalism" every bit as much as his celebrated friends Larry L. King and
Gary Cartwright were. In Shrake's case, though, his articles appeared in a
sports magazine, and thus they were not immediately recognized for their

literary merit. But as with his fiction, time has been kind to Shrake's best journalism.

During his employment at *Sports Illustrated*, only one of Shrake's articles was rejected for publication. That was a story about the environmental despoliation of the Big Thicket in East Texas. *SI* editors worried that the article would offend one of the magazine's owners, who happened to be an East Texas lumber baron. Shrake eventually submitted the story to *Harper's* magazine instead, where it appeared in the May 1970 issue as "The Land of the Permanent Wave." *Harper's* editor Willie Morris, who had published such groundbreaking work as Seymour Hersh's My Lai story and Norman Mailer's "On the Steps of the Pentagon," later ranked "The Land of the Permanent Wave" as one of "two pieces among the many [that] gave me special pride." Morris wrote that Shrake's story "struck a chord in me that I have never quite forgotten, having to do with how clean, funny, and lambent prose caught the mood of that moment in the country and mirrored with great felicity what we were trying to do at *Harper's*. To me few finer magazine essays have ever been written."[3]

From his earliest days at *Sports Illustrated*, Bud Shrake had hoped to win a multi-book contract from a publisher so that he could strike out on his own as a full-time novelist. Yet the modest sales of his novels doomed that prospect. But *Sports Illustrated* proved fortuitous in other ways. Shrake's feature stories for the magazine often took him to the very same places, and had him writing about the very same people, that became the subjects of the novels he was working on. In 1966 he went to Chihuahua, Mexico, to write about the Tarahumara Indians. That same tribe figures prominently in his 1968 novel, *Blessed McGill*. In 1970, Shrake wrote about the richest family in the world at the time, the Hunts of Dallas. The similarities between his account of H. L. Hunt in the *Sports Illustrated* article and his character "Big Earl" in *Strange Peaches* are evident. As Shrake notes in this anthology, the excerpt from *Strange Peaches* "comes about as close to being a verbatim transcript of my lunch visit with H. L. Hunt as I could write and still call it fiction."

In the 1970s, Shrake began to drift away from sportswriting to write screenplays for Hollywood. His very first script was made into the film *Kid Blue*, starring Dennis Hopper, and the possibilities seemed tantalizing. As Shrake wrote to Larry L. King, "Writing a script is a lot more fun and far, far easier than writing a novel. Only bad thing is that everybody connected with movies thinks he's a writer, and you got to fight thru the thickets of their minds constantly."[4]

During the 1970s and 1980s, Shrake wrote about thirty screenplays. His film credits include *Tom Horn* (Steve McQueen), *J. W. Coop* (Cliff Robertson), and *Songwriter* (Willie Nelson and Kris Kristofferson). Shrake resisted the studios' entreaties for him to move to California, and instead maintained his home in Austin. He made a good living as a screenwriter, but the disappointments inevitably mounted, and a string of near misses left him feeling alienated. "The only time you can be absolutely sure your movies will make it to the screen," he once said, "is when you go to the theatre and watch it."[5]

Yet among his unproduced screenplays is some fine writing that ranks with his best fiction. One such script, "Pancho Villa and Ambrose Bierce"—written before Carlos Fuentes's novel *The Old Gringo* was published—presents Shrake's version of the mythical meeting between the Mexican revolutionary and the American writer. Although unfilmed, it later became a stage play, *Pancho Villa's Wedding Day*, which premiered in Austin in 1984. Shrake's best screenplay of all is "The Big Mamoo," an absurd, yet true-to-life tale of the making of the atomic bomb at Los Alamos. Director Jonathan Demme considered "The Big Mamoo" his dream project, but to date the film has not been made. Excerpts from both scripts appear in this anthology, along with a scene from *Kid Blue.*

In the late 1980s, Shrake began co-writing "as-told-to" biographies of famous friends, publishing best-selling books with Willie Nelson and Barry Switzer. In 1992 came *Harvey Penick's Little Red Book*. That volume's astounding success, and the cottage industry it spawned, finally gave Shrake the creative freedom he sought. "With the money from the Penick books," Shrake said, "I could finally become what I had hoped to be twenty years before—a former newspaperman who writes novels full-time."[6]

In the years since, Shrake has been extraordinarily prolific. In 2000 he published his long-awaited historical Texas novel, *The Borderland*. In 2001 came *Billy Boy*, a coming-of-age novel set in 1950s Fort Worth. He has also co-written two plays with Michael Rudman, *Benchmark* (which premiered in London in 2002) and *Jack* (set in the Carousel Club the night before Ruby murdered Oswald). In 2006 Shrake completed a new stage play, *The Friends of Carlos Monzon*, based on the time he was briefly held in an Argentine prison during the 1970s while on assignment for *Sports Illustrated*. He finished another novel, *Custer's Brother's Horse,* in 2005. Also in 2005 he wrote a short story, "How to Live Forever," that is included in this volume. Shrake once told an interviewer that he measures time the way American Indians do: child, young, prime, old. Bud Shrake has remained in his prime for a very long time.

This anthology highlights much of Shrake's best writing, and it also explores the connections between his journalism and his novels, between his life and his art. Much of this "behind-the-scenes" material is drawn from the extensive Edwin "Bud" Shrake archives housed at the Southwestern Writers Collection at Texas State University–San Marcos. Within these literary papers reside correspondence, manuscripts, screenplays, ephemera, and personal materials documenting Shrake's life in writing. However, Shrake did not always keep a copy of his outgoing correspondence. Fortunately, several hundred of his letters to Larry L. King are preserved in the King archives, also housed at the Southwestern Writers Collection. Shrake's letters to King are among his funniest and most playful, testifying to the two writers' longstanding friendship.

The Southwestern Writers Collection Book Series is intended to showcase the region's important writers while highlighting the rich holdings in the collection's literary archives. I can think of no better book to fulfill that purpose than this collection of Edwin "Bud" Shrake's work. This anthology charts the life and career of a significant Texas writer—one whose talent rivals that of the best American writers of his generation.

STEVEN L. DAVIS
Southwestern Writers Collection

Notes

1. "Strange Days," by Don Graham, *Texas Monthly,* November 2000

2. Gary Cartwright, *Confessions of a Washed-Up Sportswriter* (Austin: Texas Monthly Press, 1982), p. 351. Shrake, interview by Steve Davis.

3. Willie Morris, *New York Days* (New York: Little, Brown, 1993), pp. 325, 326.

4. Letter from Bud Shrake to Larry L. King, April 7, 1971. Larry L. King Archives, Southwestern Writers Collection, Texas State University–San Marcos.

5. Shrake interview.

6. Ibid.

PART 1

Strange Peaches in the "Land of the Permanent Wave"

Is He Edwin, or Is He Bud?

The best thing about being a writer of fiction is you are never alone.

Fiction writers live with a head full of voices, landscapes, scenes, and characters and hear a full symphony playing the background music.

Sometimes it's like Cirque du Soleil is going on in there. Other times it's just a quiet chat while strolling along the beach. But at no time are you ever alone.

Isabel Allende says the art of writing fiction is the act of remembering things that never happened. J. M. Coetzee calls himself a stenographer to the invisible. Rudyard Kipling explained how to write fiction: "Wait, listen for the voices, and obey."

Some would say this means fiction writers are nuts.

The famous serial killer Son of Sam heard voices that told him to go to lovers' lane and shoot people in the head, and he went and did it. If he'd had a different twist to his makeup, he would have written about a murderer creeping through the dark instead of actually doing it, and instead of ending his life in prison he would have written a string of best-selling thrillers and be living in a villa in the Hamptons.

It's not just a matter of fiction writers' having what used to be called multiple personalities. Everybody has different faces they put on. Nobody really knows what the personality at the core of their being truly is. The personality that people call "you" is the one that is most often on public display. But fiction writers are driven by the obligation, or curse, or blessing of being open to tuning in to the voices and turning these imaginary characters into some kind of art on some kind of level.

So a fiction writer is never alone and never has nothing to do.

Introducing me at a banquet one evening, the master of ceremonies said, "When he writes something he is serious about, he is Edwin. When he's writing about sports, or just having fun, he is Bud."

This sounds reasonable. But it is not true.

I have never been more serious about or worked harder on anything than I did on the novel *Night Never Falls,* which was written by Bud. For fifteen years at *Sports Illustrated* in New York, my byline was Edwin, and nobody could have had more fun at a writing job than I had at that one.

The voices tell me who wrote what.

It says Edwin on my birth certificate, but my father started calling me Buddy when I was in the crib, and immediately the personality went splitting off in uncharted directions.

In school I was Bud. My newspaper bylines were Bud. Then I wrote a novel and got a New York agent who had the impressive name of Annie Laurie Williams. I was humbled that she would put me on her list of real writer clients. The first piece of advice she gave me was: "Bud is a perfectly good newspaper byline, but you can't put the name Bud on a novel. Nobody will ever take it seriously. The critics don't like Buds, and especially they don't like Buds who ever wrote about sports. On this novel you are Edwin."

The novel we were talking about was Edwin's *Blood Reckoning,* which nobody took seriously, anyhow, except in Italy, where it was a big seller for years as *Vendetta de Sangue.*

The second novel that Edwin wrote, *But Not for Love,* came out weeks before I moved to New York to write for *Sports Illustrated,* which was a very classy magazine where Edwin put his name on the stories but everybody called me Bud.

My first two movie bylines are Edwin. The rest are Bud.

The only people who have ever called me Edwin are people who either don't know me or else know me so well that they use Edwin as a sort of nickname.

The awkward thing is when I am identified as Edwin (Bud) Shrake, so as to be sure that you're getting the whole package.

Someone in Hollywood suggested that to be taken seriously I should spell Bud with two *d*'s, like Budd Schulberg, but I didn't see how adding a third party would solve the problem.

And it is a problem, always has been. But I'm not totally in charge here.

Cops Eat Kid's Pet

Texas Observer, July 25, 1975

It was a dirty old building with exhaust fans that blew clouds of black soot on hot summer days in a time when reporters wore white shirts and neckties. Prostitutes worked the narrow alley between the *Press* building and a ramshackle hotel called the New Gem, where Delbert McClinton, a white boy barely twelve years old, was playing in a black jazz club. On Saturday nights printers in the back shop of the paper would peer across the alley into the open windows of the bedrooms on the second floor of the New Gem, where romance was usually in the air. Nearly every hotel south of Tenth Street was a walk-up whorehouse. Bookies with names like Circus Face, Little Mac, and Puny the Stroller operated openly out of bars where it was illegal to serve a mixed drink, so if you stopped in for a drink you brought a whole bottle in a brown paper bag. There were so many slot machines and pinball machines that gangsters from Dallas tried to move in and take over, setting off a war of shootings, strangulations, car bombings, bombs planted in mailboxes and under telephones, and even bombs dropped from Piper Cubs. Preachers and civic leaders accused us of tabloid excesses in the vivid stories we published at our dingy domain at Fifth and Jones Street in Fort Worth, but the fact is we didn't tell half of it.

I never saw the books, but I never doubted that the *Fort Worth Press* was on the down side of broke. They told us that every day. You had to turn in an old stub to get a new pencil. Sometimes you would go to the back for more copy paper to write stories on, and find stacks of it cut in the shape of pennants, reject stuff. But if you rolled the paper into the typewriter with the pointy side up, it taught you to write a quick, crisp Scripps-Howard style first paragraph, preferably no more than four short words, like, "'Help!' cried the Queen." The pyramid idea of how to write a news story, punching it at the top and broadening it as you went down, became for us as much of an obligation as a device.

But those things made us search for glamour in the dirt and outright stinginess of the place, and we worked to produce stories that were in their own class great—by that I mean news stories that were ingenious and diligent

Shrake as a young reporter at the *Fort Worth Press*, 1957.
Photo by Gene Gordon.

pieces of reporting, with a fair amount of accuracy under the conditions. Even stories that were dull and ordinary, except to the victims, like traffic fatalities, one could occasionally turn into a front page lead for the street edition with a headline that said BLIND EVANGELIST MOURNS HIT AND RUN BABY.

Some of the stories we did could hardly be justified except as tabloid show business. I interviewed a woman who had raised a seven-foot hollyhock and detoured this event into a whole *Press* page of creepy fiction. One Saturday night on the police desk I was called by the night city editor—Mac Williams, bless him, whose notion of the perfect lead would have been "Jesus wept," if you could just cut out one word in there someplace—and told to go out on the North Side and talk a woman out of killing herself. She had phoned up the paper, as do a lot of lonely people, and laid her tale on Mac. For me to go to the North Side meant leaving the police beat open for a couple of hours and I argued, and I went. Down a dirt road was a little frame house with three junk cars in the yard. I knocked on the door. A dog crashed through the screen and bit a rip in my pants. In those days we wore suits and ties and snapbrim hats on the police beat, so as to pass for detectives, and I kicked that dog about 18 feet through the living room into the kitchen where the dog slammed his head against the refrigerator and commenced howling.

An old man with a shotgun stumbled out of a bedroom and said, "That's the one that wants to kill herself over there, it's not Spot that wants to die." On the couch a woman lay in the heap of gin bottles. I nudged her and asked if she wanted to kill herself. "Betcha goddamn ass," she said and went back to sleep. "Nearly ever Satdy night she says that," explained the old man.

I drove to a gas station and phoned Mac and said if the woman killed herself I would hear about it back at the police beat, where as it happened I should have been reporting about a local gangster who had just been blown up with a bomb. Sunday morning I picked up the paper and saw my by-line with a big headline on it that said I SAVED HER FROM SURE DEATH.

We were trying to sell newspapers, and there was a theory that was how it was done, although that theory seems not to be have proved out in Fort Worth. If there wasn't a tornado we could dress up with a big front-page headline (never mind that the tornado was in Oklahoma), we would find a banger of a first-person story that was supposed to grab people at the news rack on their way out of the office, the *Press* being an afternoon paper five days a week. Or we would twist a small event into an ejacorama. Like when a policeman ran over a deer in Trinity Park and, not knowing what else to do, brought the carcass down to the station, where the deer was slaughtered and handed out as venison. The policemen didn't know who the deer belonged to, but anyhow it appeared in the *Press* as COPS EAT KID'S PET.

Fort Worth was not a subway audience 20 years ago, when the *Press* went tabloid, and Fort Worth still isn't, but the *Press* struggled along as a subway-minded version of the *Star-Telegram*, going after targets like pinball machines and especially flagrantly crooked public officials. The main reason to read the paper was the personalities of its writers—like the Christian coun-sel dispensing Edith Dean, and some of the stars of the sports *department*, foremost of whom have been Pop Boone, Blackie Sherrod, Dan Jenkins, Gary Cartwright, and Andy Anderson.

A number of odd people, including me, did time in that sports depart-ment. There was Sick Charlie Modessette, who beat Hodgkins disease and remembered everybody's batting average and played honkytonk piano and knew last night only as a mystery. Jerre Todd, whom we called Spanky the Child Star, would charm his way out of disfavor by doing hook slides and movie star impersonations. Before he covered the Rose Bowl game in Pasa-dena one year—a plum assignment—Todd worked for days on several first paragraphs, each of them gorged with puns and similes, to assure himself that however the game turned out, he would find glory in that grandest of accomplishments—a flashy, quotable lead. Puss Ervin, who had saved up a fortune while working as a postman, got down to the office about 5 a.m. and

Gary Cartwright and Bud Shrake at the *Dallas Times Herald*, 1961.
Courtesy of Gary and Phyllis Cartwright.

took off his shirt but not his hat and drank bourbon while with one arthritic finger he poked out enough letters to fill up his bowling column, which drew him an outstanding amount of groupies. Puss had a piece of advice for all his friends. He would jab you in the chest with that bent, knobby finger and say, "Give up, son, you ain't ever gonna make it."

The real stars of the sports department were Blackie Sherrod and Dan Jenkins. Blackie wore his hair long and combed back and was known as being very funny and smooth, as well as being a smart editor and reporter, and he has written what I believe to be consistently the best daily sports column in the country for more than 20 years—a feat that is purely staggering. Dan was also known as being quick with his mouth, and he was a fair hustler on the muny golf courses, and his writing took him on to Dallas (where Blackie had moved to the *Times-Herald*) and then to New York. Dan now lives in a duplex penthouse with five terraces on Park Avenue, works for *Sports Illustrated* and writes a best-seller novel (*Semi-Tough, Dead Solid Perfect*) every year or two. I have left out Cartwright as the real star of the old sports department of the *Press*—a department where the so-called "New Journalism" was practiced to such an extent that if you had a few extra hours on a story you might turn out something that nobody knew what the hell it was about—only because he didn't stay there long before he followed Sherrod, Jenkins (and me) over to Dallas.

For a while, under Blackie, with Jenkins and Cartwright and others, I believe the *Press* had the best sports department in the country.

Priest Taunted at Mansfield

Fort Worth Press, September 4, 1956

I dictated this story for the noon edition (news rack street sales demanded a big headline) on a phone in a house near the school that was being besieged. The way you found a phone in a rural area was to look for the wires coming down from the poles. You followed a line down to a house. Then you knocked on the door and usually they let you in.

In the time of this story, Mansfield was a small town way out in the country. My family had owned a farm in Mansfield. Our place was constantly alive with the movement of horses, cows, pigs, chickens, ducks, and my carrier pigeons. I lived on the farm during my fifth-grade year. If I missed the school bus, I would ride my horse, a cow pony named Pet, seven miles to a two-room frame building called the Little School. First grade through sixth was in one room, the rest in the other. The bathroom was a shed divided between BOYS and GIRLS, with a partition that had several prominent holes drilled in it at various eye levels.

In the sixth grade we moved back into the big city—Fort Worth, where we kept a few cows and a lot of chickens and had a fruit orchard, yet we could see two fairways of Glen Garden Country Club, where Ben Hogan and Byron Nelson had caddied for my father as kids, across the street.

The next time I went back to Mansfield was to cover the integration story.

A young Fort Worth minister tried to bring peace to troubled Mansfield High School today, but was shouted down by a hooting, fist-clenching crowd.

At the same time the U.S. Supreme Court in Washington, D.C., turned down the last chance for keeping Mansfield a segregated school.

Texas Ranger Sgt. E. J. Banks, fearing the crowd might seize the Rev. D. W. Clark at any moment, quickly stepped in and led him to safety.

Father Clark, vicar of St. Timothy's Episcopal in Fort Worth, was spotted by reporters as he walked up the sidewalk toward the school. Asked the reason for his visit he replied:

"I'm pretty shocked at a situation like this. I'm surprised there hasn't been more Christian influence here. I come strictly as a peacemaker."

Noting the several hundred white townspeople assembled outside the school, he added with trembling lips:

"It looks like you need a peacemaker down here."

By this time a big crowd gathered around him.

"Somebody tell the preachers to stop backing the Niggers," shouted one man.

Rev. Clark, whose parish includes the Mansfield area, replied that he was following the teachings of the church. "God made man in his own image," he said.

A heckler asked why God made some men black.

The 30-year-old minister replied by taking note of the Negro effigy hanging atop the school flagpole.

"You've got an image of God hanging up there," he said.

The crowd grew angrier.

"You better get out of here, Mister!" one shouted. Another waved a clenched fist.

"I been raised up in the church, but niggers ain't my neighbors," another man shouted. "I tell you, Mister—you better get out."

At this point it became obvious that the crowd was getting worked up. "Do you want a nigger for a neighbor?" a voice said. "Do you want to sleep with one?" another voice yelled.

It was then that Ranger Banks, sensing danger to the clergyman, walked up and said: "I think we'd better get out of here."

"I don't think there's any doubt about it," Father Clark replied. They walked through the crowd without incident.

This is the third day that crowds of angry whites have gathered in front of the school, which is under federal court order to desegregate. So far the crowds have succeeded in scaring the eight eligible Negro students away.

This was the first regular day of school, and Supt. R. L. Huffman presumably would be under orders to register any Negroes who managed to get inside the school.

Supreme Court Justice Hugo Black received a petition at midnight from Atty. J. A. Gooch, local attorney acting for Mansfield.

The petition asked for a stay or order on the court's ruling.

About two hours later, Justice Black's office made the announcement that Justice Black refused to stay the integration order at Mansfield.

No reason was given.

Rev. David W. Crockett, pastor of Grace Chapel Baptist Church of Arlington, also arrived in Mansfield today. He said he came to see whether there was anything he could do as a peacemaker.

But he was wearing a pair of trousers and a shirt, in contrast to the Rev. Clark's clerical frock, and the crowd paid no attention to him.

Crockett disclosed that he was also at the school on Friday and he said he believes, as the Rev. Clark does, that: "Our people—the people at our church—are willing to accept Negroes at our church."

Letter: April 10, 1963, from the Navel of Mother Europe

I was deeply impressed by Paul Gallico, an ex-sportswriter who got into the ring with Jack Dempsey the way George Plimpton did with Archie Moore a generation later. What most amazed me was not his opulent living on the Riviera, where he wrote his best-selling novels, but the fact that he dictated all his stuff to his secretary. I told him I could never dictate a novel. He said, "Yes, you could if you had nerve damage in your hands and the alimony cops were after you."

Gallico took me into Antibes for drinks with an English writer who lived in Paris but was on the coast to pick up the new Cadillac he had delivered from the United States each year. Listening to their conversation, I realized this fellow wrote thrillers under three or four different names, a couple of best sellers per year, and spent money like a Texas oilman. I was reminded of the ancient truth that I have observed over the years: bankers talk about art and artists talk about money.

To: Dr. Billy Lee Brammer
Señor J. D. (El) Meelner

Dear El Señor and Mister Doctor:
I finished my new book [*But Not for Love*] the other day and got the last part of the manuscript off to New York so they can start printing up hundreds of thousands, and then I decided I better start on another one so the devil couldn't slip into my idle workshop. You know how I feel about the devil. I read in the papers where the Anglicans are doing away with Hell, which should make us all feel a lot better, but they may not get it done before all my ailments fetch me over the brink, and I want to keep the devil at a stand-off. Anyhow, work is the way to do it. And as Paul Gallico told me down in Antibes, if you're going to work you ought to make money. . . . First thing I want to tell you is about my visit to Gallico. I had just come from Rome, where them Italians breathed all over me and gave me a terrible case of the paranoia and a middling case of the angst and also a rattly cough, and it was raining when I got to Nice. I checked into a hotel near the railroad station

and phoned Gallico as I had been instructed to do via a letter from Gallico who wrote at the urging of Ken McCormick and Adela Rogers St. Johns. So I phoned him and he couldn't remember who I was and put me off. That didn't bother me a hell of a lot and I didn't blame him and I forgot it. But early the next morning he called me and apologized and said now I remember and can you come for lunch? I did, on the electric train that goes up and down between Monte Carlo and Cannes. Gallico has a 16th century house in Antibes, right on the water. There is a big, horseshoe bay and from his living room and the balcony on the third floor you can see across the blue water all the way to Monte Carlo, with Nice about midway, and the old forts and fishing boats and mountains. You can see even past Monte Carlo and see the snow-peaks of the Italian Alps. From the other side of the house you can see Cap d'Antibes and the villas. I was thinking what a great house it would be to have a party in and how we could wreck it in a night. Gallico is a big guy, a little bigger than El Señor Meelner, and looks younger than he is. He must be 60 or so, but his hair is still full and brown and he looks 40. A tall woman with an expression of smelling something bad came in and stuck out her hand. "This is the Baroness of Lichtenstein," said Gallico. I didn't know whether to kiss her hand or bite her fanger, but she grabbed me and give me one of those quick hard pumps that the Europeans use for a handshake. Gallico lives with the Baroness, or maybe it's vice-versa, and she can't get a divorce from the Baron but they get on swell. We all sat down to talk and had a big lunch with wine served by servants. Gallico dictates everything to a secretary, who then types it on an electric machine big as a phonograph. He said he used to type until a few years ago he got a pinched nerve and couldn't use his hands. "You better learn to dictate because bending over a typewriter will give you a pinched nerve," he said.

Gallico likes to talk. . . .

He asked me if my book could be serialized in Post and I said no. He asked why and I said because it is smutty. He looked a little irritated. I had dosed up on heart medicine and had a hard time keeping from interrupting him and making several speeches of my own. I wanted to tell him that we didn't look at things the same way a bit, but I manfully kept fairly quiet and ate his roast pork and drank his wine and listened. Then he and the Baroness drove me back to Nice. He said he was in Dallas a few years ago to do a 'Rediscovering America' series for *Readers Digest*. He said Dallas was great. I said it was in danger of being very crappy. We said farewell. But he was through all of it very nice and gentlemanly, much more so probably than I would have been if I was having my day wasted by someone I didn't know.

As I said in Rome them Italians had given me a terrible case of the paranoia, and then I went on to Barcelona and it didn't get much better, so I went to Paris . . . I fell in love with four identical midgets and got passing out drunk on Fundador (which costs 99 cents a quart in Barcelona) and wandered the streets yelling like a madman and got Billy Lee's letter. . . . Billy Lee had a suspicion that I had sneaked some literary talk into a letter to him, and he was right. It was the result and symptom of oncoming paranoia which the Italians finally give me. . . . I got some blessed medals which I am bringing you: medals of St. Jude, the Saint of Hopeless Causes, who should be the patron of all of us. I have worn a Jude for years; Joyce spotted the hopeless cause in me long ago. Now I've got some blessed ones for all of you. Rub them when the child support is due, or when you realize it is 6 a.m., or when you start to work, or when you are out of heart medicine, or on hundreds of other occasions. You still get screwed, but you survive.

My book came out 466 pages of m.s. and I did it in 52 working days (there were 20 other days during the interim from start to finish when I didn't do a damned thing, mostly in Rome) and even if it's not worth a shit that was a lot of work for me to have did. I am proud that I did all that work while I was busy falling in love especially with the four identical midgets. I got to looking through the carbon and it nearly made me throw up but anyhow Doubleday is going to publish it the end of October and we can have a mass throwing up. One big trouble was, I noticed there's no Indians in it. That's the thing about heart medicine: here I was going along furiously and finishing, and then I found out I had left out the Indians. What kind of goddamn book is that, without Indians? I will lose my reputation that was so dearly earned and so cherished. But I have lost other stuff. I am rubbing Jude. . . .

Jason and the Oui Oui Club

From *But Not for Love* (1964)

I was recently divorced for the second time from the same woman, Joyce, mother of my two sons. Joyce and the boys had moved back to Fort Worth, where she was teaching English lit at TCU. I was living in an apartment on Cole Avenue in Dallas. During a party one evening I walked into my bedroom and found a stranger sitting on my bed reading the 100 pages of manuscript of a novel that I had stacked on a shelf in the closet. The stranger was Ken McCormick, editor in chief of Doubleday. My friend Bill Gilliland, who ran the Cokesbury bookstore in downtown Dallas, had brought McCormick to my apartment and straight to where Bill knew I had hidden the first pages of what turned out to be *But Not for Love.* Ken stood up and shook my hand and offered me a contract for the book.

In short order I signed with Doubleday and headed for Europe early in what became known as the Cuban Missile Crisis. The United States and Russia were within one wrong move of going to war. I finished writing this novel mostly on trains, riding around Europe, typing on my little Smith Corona Skywriter, or in Dick Growald's apartment in Frankfurt am Main in Germany. Growald had been my close friend since junior high in Fort Worth. We had worked together as police reporters at the *Press.* He was boss of the Frankfurt bureau of United Press International, in charge of all UPI news bureaus in Europe and North Africa, while I was writing this book. He later ran the UPI bureaus in Moscow and in Saigon, and—Dick is dead now and there can't be any harm in me saying this—all the while he worked for the CIA. I finished the novel, dropped it off in New York, and returned to writing my column on the *Dallas Morning News* just in time for the murder of JFK across the plaza from my office.

When his wife left him, Jason Hopps thought he might kill himself. Willy moved out suddenly with the two children and left a letter Jason found when he came home from the Oui Oui Club at dusk:

> Mr. Rat: I am deeply ashamed that my two little girls have you for a father and I am going to try to get the court to keep you from ever seeing them again and causing me any more pain and heartaches forever.

("The court?" Jason said to himself as he was reading, and then he understood and he began walking back and forth on the living-room carpet.)

The letter continued:

You are a weak, unfit person. I feel sorry for you, but I can't live with you any longer. I'm tired of fighting with you and of my two daughters hearing you curse when you come home drunk at two o'clock in the morning and fall down trying to get your shoes off. I used to love you, Jason. You could really have been somebody important. When you were in the construction business for yourself I was so proud of you I would want to show everybody what you had built. But when you lost your courage I lost my respect for you.

("That's not fair," Jason said. "Twenty-seven days of rain wiped me out. Was that my fault?")

The letter said:

When you started drinking and staying out late and going around with other women—oh, yes, you thought you fooled me but I am smarter than you think I am, Jason—it broke my heart to see what you had become. Most people think you're clever and witty. I guess you like that. But I know what you really are, Jason, you're a scum of the very earth. If you were only scared and weak I would stick with you and try to take care of you and make you into something. But you're a bad person. It's not right that you can run around with other women night after night and make me pay for it. Last night after you came home I went out and looked in your car and found a pair of panties in the glove compartment and an earring on the floor. I think I know to who they belong. That's the last straw that broke my back. I still have my looks and I'm still young and I can find a man who is better than you who loves me. I'm going to my mother's house. I hate you. Don't ever try to see me or the little girls again. It will be hard on them not to have their daddy but having you is worse than having no daddy at all. If you try to see me or them again I will shoot you. Love, Willy.

"Gumbuckets," Jason said. "She's mad at me, all right."

He dropped the letter on the breakfast counter. Using the pink wall phone that Willy had insisted on having in the kitchen, Jason dialed a number.

"Hello," said Chub Anderson.

"Hi," Jason said. "Walter there?"

"He's watching television. Talk to me, hon."

"Can he hear you?"

"I don't think so."

"Is there a *chance* he can hear you?"

"Yes."

"Laugh like I said something funny," Jason said. He listened to her giggle. That giggle, very young and mirthful and accompanied by a wrinkling of the nose, had been her leitmotif at the University of Texas. "Now I'll really say something funny. Willy left me. You forgot some of your stuff in the car last night."

"I know I did."

"Was that a click?" said Jason. "Did somebody pick up the extension?"

"Of course not. Don't be so jumpy."

"I can't help being jumpy. Willy found that stuff. I don't think she knows it's yours. She says she knows who it belongs to, but she's bluffing. What a fool I am. What a low life. She's taken my little girls away from me. What'll I do?"

"I don't know," Chub said, as if he had asked what movies were playing on Seventh Street.

"Let me talk to Walter."

"What for?"

"I have to have a reason for calling, don't I? You going to tell him I called just to talk to you?"

"I'm not going to tell him anything. I hope you're not."

"All I'm going to tell him is I've been making it with his wife."

"Don't be crude."

"You know I'm not going to tell him."

"It would be mean. We wouldn't want to hurt him."

"Damn it, he might hear you. Put him on."

After a moment he heard Walter's voice: low, pleasant, amiable even though Jason knew he had got Walter up from a Western program. Walter was very fond of eating ice cream and watching Westerns on television.

"Lo Jason."

"Hey, stud. Did the guy from the church come see you again today?"

"Brother Chunk? Sure did."

"What did he say?"

"Said if I don't get on his team I'm through going to the legislature. Said all the Drys would solid vote against me. From the letters I've been getting. I think everbody in Fort Worth is a hard-shell Baptist."

"Anything I can do to help?" Jason said.

"Not right now. Thanks, though. Rand from the convention bureau called me. He kind of hedged around like he wouldn't want to really say anything but he let me know the big shots are saying anybody who tries to dry up the town is finished. Any politician, I mean. We've been losing a lot of conventions, Rand says, on account of the Liquor Control Board raids on the private clubs and our funny drinking laws anyhow. Then Morrison from the bank called me. He sort of let me know if I go with the Drys I can forget about that loan."

"That's tough."

"I've got to have that loan, Jason. I'm putting in two more hamburger joints. The one I got is going great, but I can't make it pay unless I got volume. With three joints I make money. With one, I have to go bust sooner or later."

"I can tell you this, Walter. If you come out for the Drys all the boys at the Oui Oui Club won't like you a bit. Not a bit."

"I told Brother Chunk I was still rassling with the problem. He said if I don't come out for prohibition inside of a week, ever preacher in town will get in the pulpit and tell their flocks I'm a no good antichrist. That's a guy who's against Jesus, isn't it?"

"Sort of."

"That's what I thought. Wow. I wouldn't want to have it come out that I'm against Jesus. Politically speaking, Jason, that wouldn't be very good."

"You could make a speech and say you're not against Jesus, you just don't agree with Brother Chunk."

"But Brother Chunk is a Jesus expert. Everbody knows Brother Chunk is for Jesus. People believe Brother Chunk. I think a couple of the legislators have given up and gone over already."

"Looks like I can quit worrying about the estimate on building that new brewery."

"Looks like it."

"I wouldn't worry too much," Jason said. "The Drys are organized and they do a good job of hollering about the evils of drink, but inside those curtains I think people will vote Wet."

"I wish I thought so. This is the most uncomfortable fence I ever straddled."

"Say, Walter, you still practice law?"

"Some. When I got time."

"I didn't tell Chub, but Willy has left me. I think she's going to court this time."

"Sorry to hear it. I really am. Maybe she'll cool off again."

"I doubt it."

"That sort of thing is out of my line, Jason. I haven't done any of that in years. Byron Williams would be a good man for you, if Willy hasn't already got him."

"I'll call him," Jason said. "Listen, Walter, don't talk it around, huh? I don't want it to get out about me and Willy unless it's absolutely definite. You know what I mean?"

"Yeah. Okay. I really am sorry."

"All right. See you at Ben's party."

"That's Friday night? I'll be there. Won't be any drinking, I hope."

"How could you think such a thing?"

Jason hung up and stared at the kitchen wallpaper. At least Walter didn't know. Jason made himself a cheese sandwich, washed the mayonnaise off the knife, poured a glass of cold milk, and then went out and sat in the patio to eat. The irony of it, he thought, was that this was the earliest he had been home in a week; it was only just now proper suppertime. He looked at the flower garden Willy had labored over. The flowers grew high against the stockade fence. Jason didn't know the names of any of the flowers, although he had helped Willy pull weeds a few times. He could hear crickets from somewhere, and kids yelling over in the next yard, and as it got darker mosquitoes began to bother him. The grass was smooth and thick and neatly clipped around the edges of the flowerbeds and the flagstone patio. At the rear, through a gap in the hedge, he saw a neighbor appear in the alley and then heard the clang of a garbage can lid. Jason got up and went inside.

He wandered through the house looking at things that had gathered in ten years of marriage: the furniture they had bought on installments, several paintings by Harry Danielsen and some prints from Paris that Jason and Willy had picked up when they were on leave from Germany during Jason's Army duty, an ash tray from the Stork Club, a towel from the Mark Hopkins Hotel, the machete with which he had cut off the head of a copperhead snake at Possum Kingdom Lake, tennis rackets, water skis. Framed on the wall in the den was a color photograph of Jason and Willy standing outside the bullring in Mexico City, both wearing dark glasses, looking gay and sophisticated with the bright posters in the background. It was a honeymoon photograph.

Willy was heavier then, and Jason was thinner. Jason examined the things with a vague envy, as if they were relics from the lives of two other people. Then he stuck an anti-acid tablet in his mouth, got his .32-caliber pistol out of a bureau drawer, and put on his coat. He felt used up, like a clown whose shabby tricks no longer amused, who performed to silence. He could sing harmony, imitate half a dozen movie stars, handle a big bass on a light spinning rod, shoot eighty at golf, do a soft shoe, estimate with great accuracy how much it would cost to build a thirty-five story building or a shopping center that covered forty acres (numbers on a pad, he thought: so much for steel, so much for glass, so much for labor, so much for plumbing and wiring, nothing for the wounds of the heart). He felt incapable of ever exposing himself again. And the house was empty.

Jason drove automatically. He went through the stone gates and down the hill past the softball diamonds into Forest Park, whose secret roads he had known since he was fourteen, the park whose trees and shrubbery had hidden the deflowering of so many high school girls that Jason's mind swamped at the thought. He went through patches of canary light from high lamps, beside the dark narrow fork of the Trinity River, past the field where Sunday people flew model airplanes on wires. At the bridge over the river, Jason turned left onto the wide boulevard of University Drive and went up the hill between the dark bluffs where big houses stood as monuments to dearer times. The zoo with its fearful noises and night odors was down below on one side, the golf course of Colonial Country Club down below on the other. He came to Texas Christian University, its yellow brick buildings as comfortably plain and ugly as old shoeboxes, and he drove beyond the university and into a parking space in front of the Oui Oui Club. The Oui Oui Club had a curling red neon sign against a plate-glass window covered by drapes. Jason walked unsteadily because he hadn't slept much the night before, and the tension of the events since he had found Willy's letter was pulling at his eyelids. The pistol hung like a rock in his coat pocket.

The inside of the Oui Oui Club was so familiar that Jason no longer saw it. A few years ago he could have described the rows of beer steins on shelves behind the bar, flanking the mirror, and the beer spigots, and the padded stools, and the cream-colored plaster walls upon which a university student had painted murals of his ideas of Paris streets (a sidewalk cafe with the Eiffel Tower in the background, another sidewalk cafe with the Arc d'Triomphe in the background, a third sidewalk cafe with Sacre Coeur in the background;

why, Jason had wondered, hadn't the artist painted Notre Dame and the Louvre with sidewalk cafes in front of them?) But now Jason had been in the Oui Oui Club so often that he had forgot almost every facet of its interior. The noise of the bowling machine came from the rear—a hard chink of bells. Jason sat on a stool in front of the Budweiser spigot, where he could see himself in the mirror, and tapped on the spigot when Harvey the bartender approached.

"How's stuff, Jason?" said Harvey, a soft pink man with the smooth complexion of a doctor.

"Nothing new," Jason said.

"Your wife called in here last night. I didn't know what to tell her."

"Doesn't matter," said Jason.

"I told her I'd just come on and that you might have been around and I'd try to remember to get you to call her. Hope that was all right. I'm not very good at lying to women. They see straight through me."

"It doesn't make any difference what you told her," Jason said.

"I've been having lots of trouble with my wife," said Harvey. "She nags the hell out of me about being a better man. She wants me to make more money. I get to thanking in another minute I'll either run off to Tokyo, Japan, or make her turn blue. Then she gets so nice and sweet for a couple of days I wouldn't trade places with the Sheik of Arabia."

"That's women."

"I figure she must love me a lot, bad as she hates me."

Harvey scraped the foam off the beer with a tongue depressor.

"I wish you'd do some of your imitations," Harvey said. "I like the one of Walter Huston singing 'September Song.' That nearly makes me cry. You should of been on the stage, Jason. You got natural talent."

"The catt-le," said Jason. "The catt-le are dyin like flyshe."

"I got it. That was Walter Brennan. Great. Do some more."

"Not tonight."

"You ain't done any in here for a long time. You ain't been in here so much lately."

"I was here this afternoon."

"I didn't come on till six."

"I've been going back to the office and working late."

"I get it," said Harvey, winking.

"Anybody been in?"

"A few guys. Flutebinder and St. Clair and Norman Green are playing the bowling machine. New doll in here I ain't seen before. Setting back there against the wall."

As he turned Jason found himself hoping it would be Willy. But it was a plump blonde woman with a heavy bosom and hair drawn back into a bun so tight that it stretched the skin of her face. She rapped on a glass of orange juice with a swizzle stick as if she were playing drums. A bottle in a sack lay on the table.

"She's drinking screwdrivers," Harvey whispered. "While ago she played both of our Guy Lombardo records three times each. I said give us some Louie and Keely, honey, and she looked at me like I was a nigger. She's an odd one. I don't know if she's waiting for somebody or what. She won't talk to nobody. St. Clair tried to talk to her and she wouldn't even look at him."

"Buncha burglars!" yelled a voice from the bowling machine.

"They've took Green for about fifty bucks," Harvey said.

"He ought to know better," Jason said, and he was glad when Harvey went away to serve another customer.

Jason lit a menthol cigarette and stared at the bubbles in the beer glass. How many nights had he spent exactly like this? How many of these lonely, wasted nights when he couldn't have explained reasonably why he was here and not at home with Willy. Could it be the possibility of adventures that hardly ever happened? Or maybe Willy was right. Maybe he was a scum of the very earth. It used to be better, he remembered. It used to be that it would be Ben, Harry, and Jason, and sometimes Walter Anderson and a few other people. Occasionally they had girls with them, but mostly it was just Jason and his friends sprawled in somebody's car at a drive-in, or drinking beer at a place like the Oui Oui Club. They gambled on the bowling machine or the pinball machine. They sang songs and made big plans. Then later they'd have cheeseburgers and coffee at an all-night cafe, and there would be talks. Ben would get into some kind of serious subject, as Ben always eventually did, and his long face would get very earnest and excited, and he would argue with Harry, red-faced Harry with blond hair that looked as if it had never been combed, and Jason would sink peacefully into the leatherette cushion of the booth and smoke and listen with pleasure to his friends. When they went away to college in Austin, the three of them shared an apartment at the bottom of a hill between a Jewish sorority house and a co-operative dormitory where Jason thought anarchists lived. Across the street was the stone wall of the gardens of Scottish Rite Dormitory, for girls, and Jason recalled how he could sit in the living room of their apartment and look out beyond the wall at crows circling above the trees and know that his friends were close and feel peaceful. In those days Jason had begun going out with Willy, and Ben was seeing Jean, and Harry was dating one girl or another, and everything was fun.

Jason wondered if Ben would share an apartment with him again. He wondered how it would work out. Now that Jean had filed for divorce, and Willy had threatened to do the same, perhaps they could recapture the fun of a decade past. Moving among the same people, except for their Army service, Jason and Ben had each had a wife and two children, but Jason couldn't think of himself as older or different than he had been at nineteen or twenty or twenty-one. Jason did some mental arithmetic. It had been nine years since Ben quit law school to go into the Army. Jason, Ben, and Harry had shared that apartment for three years, until Jason got married. Jason remembered the apartment with more affection than any other home he had ever known.

By God, those had been fine times. Willy used to tell him that he didn't remember them right, that the years had warped his memory, and that he was nostalgic for something that never quite was. But he remembered. He remembered it was only ten feet across from their bedroom windows to the windows of a large sleeping room in the Jewish sorority, and he remembered the wonderful sweet naked girls he had seen. He remembered the night Harry drank a fifth of Jack Daniel's at a party, took a swing at a football player, broke his hand against the cupboard, went to the hospital to have it set and cast, and returned to drink again before the party ended. He remembered their trips to Laredo, and the big football weekends when they would all go to the game to boo Walter Anderson, and the first time he laid Willy on a blanket at a picnic at Barton Springs. He remembered Ben opening a thousand-page government textbook that Ben had never before glanced at. It was two days before the final exam. Ben read the book for thirty consecutive hours, played eighteen holes of golf, and then made an A on the exam. He could still see Ben sitting at the table bent over the book with the light from the gooseneck lamp on Ben's face—a thin face with gaunt cheeks and a straight nose and shaggy pale brown hair—and Ben's shirt hung on the back of the chair, and his wide thin shoulders hunched, and cigarette smoke floating up through the lamplight. That same night, he remembered, Jason had intended to study for a marketing exam but went instead to listen to Dixieland music and came back at six in the morning and found Ben in exactly the same position as if he hadn't moved at all. Cigarette butts had overflowed the ashtray and fallen onto the table; smoke rose from several that smoldered. Jean came in and fixed breakfast. Jean was never very much on cooking, but she could scramble eggs and use a toaster. She was a tall girl and had the reputation of being able to outdrink any man on the campus. Everybody had a good time.

The trouble was, Jason thought, things were always happening that you couldn't do anything about. The Korean War and the draft ruined the life they'd had in the apartment. Jason got scared he was going to be killed, and he rushed out to marry Willy. By the time the three friends returned from the Army they were all married, and things had changed between them just enough for Jason to detect the subtle difference. It was more than a subtle difference with Harry. He was a lot different. He was quieter. He had grown a blond beard while he lived in New York and he came back with a ballet dancer wife and some peculiar ideas. Ben came back married to Jean and started concentrating on law school and finished at the head of his class. Jason went into the construction business and ran into something else he couldn't do anything about: twenty-seven days of rain.

"I don't see why Green bowls with them guys," Harvey said. "They eat him up like pork chops."

"I don't know," said Jason.

"Seen Ben Carpenter lately?"

"Yeah. Some."

"I been reading about him in the papers. About how Ben keeps filing suits and stuff to try to keep that guy Guthrie from taking over that big electronics company in Dallas? I don't understand it all," Harvey said.

"Neither do I."

"But I know one thing. If you're gonna screw with guys like Guthrie you better have a hard pecker. That's big league."

"Ben's working at it."

"Ben's a funny guy," said Harvey. "I seen him come in here and set for hours without speaking to a soul. He'd look like he lost his last friend. Other nights he'll come in here and be the rowdiest sonabitch in town. I guess he's got a lot pressing on him with his old man getting into that trouble and with Ben breaking up with his wife. His wife still in town?"

"She went back to Houston."

"She live there?"

"Her folks live there."

"She's supposed to be rich, ain't she?"

"Her folks have a lot of money. Her daddy owns about nine thousand shoe stores, or something like that."

"Well, it's not so bad then," Harvey said. "What's behind them breaking up? She catch Ben with his head on the wrong pillow? That'd be my guess."

"I don't know."

"Say, remember when you and Ben and Harry Danielsen used to keep them pennies in the beer steins? What was it? You'd each put in one penny for each beer you drank, and then you was gonna take out the pennies at the end of the year and throw a party, wasn't that it?"

"Yeah. That was a long time ago."

"I remember you got about eight hundred and thirty-six pennies in them steins in a month and then you decided you really didn't want to know how many beers you was drinking and you quit. I think the girl that used to work in here took the money."

"We let her have it," said Jason.

"How come you ain't with Ben much any more?"

"We've both been busy. We don't seem to be free at the same times."

"Harry, he's about quit hanging around these places, ain't he?"

"Looks like it."

"He's better off, if you don't mind me saying so," Harvey said. "Damn, that blonde wants some more orange juice. She's gonna have the sorriest case of indigestion anybody ever had."

The truth was, Jason thought, Ben had dropped him because he wouldn't stop meeting Chub Anderson. "Jason," Ben had said, "I just don't believe in screwing the wife of a friend. If there are degrees to adultery, yours is the worst kind. Evertime you mount that girl, you're helping to kill something. You're doing something that can't ever be undone. I think it's wrong." About then, Ben had started having serious trouble with Jean. Fights in public. A lot of bitterness. Ben never told him what it was all about.

There was one thing Jason was sure of. Chub Anderson wasn't worth what she was costing him. He would get so stricken with remorse that he could hardly look at himself when he was shaving. He would stand under hot water in the shower until the steam made the towels sodden and melted the toilet paper and covered the mirror. But he kept getting further involved and more careless, and now Willy and the kids were gone. He'd lose his house and at least one of his cars, and a big piece of his salary would go to child support. He'd miss his little girls, and he felt very sentimental about old Willy even if she did sometimes have a hard tongue. And there was always the chance Walter Anderson would find out and get a gun and come and murder him. You never knew how a man might react. Yet, Jason thought, Chub might be in love with him; he didn't want to hurt her, either.

Maybe the only sensible thing to do was to kill himself. He was tired anyhow and had a headache. Willy was gone, the little girls were gone, Ben wasn't close to him any more, he had difficulty talking to Harry, he was bored with estimating buildings, and Chub couldn't get out of the house until tomorrow afternoon. By then, Jason might not be around. They could read about him in the papers. It would give them something to talk about. Willy would do plenty of crying, probably, and Chub would feel awful about it. But his poor daughters. The other children would kid them.

The damn thing, Jason told himself, was that he either had to kill himself right now, as soon as the Oui Oui Club closed, or else he had to straighten up and quit seeing Chub and quit drinking and staying out late and messing around. If he could prove to Willy that he wasn't a scum of the very earth, maybe she would come back to him. Willy, Willy, the horrible things he'd done. There was the night he was supposed to take her to a big society dance, and she got dressed up and put on her mink stole, and Jason never did get home to pick her up. He got drunk that afternoon in the Oui Oui Club and when he went home at four in the morning with blood on his overcoat Willy was asleep in a chair in the living room. She looked good. Her hair was in some kind of a French cut, and she wore a red evening dress. He woke her and told her he loved her. She hit him with a china figurine, and then she hit him with an ash tray, and then she called him a name he'd never heard her use before, and then she hit him with a Book-of-the-Month Club novel about the French Revolution, and when he finally went to sleep on the couch he could hear her crying in their bedroom. He was crying too. Willy, Willy, such horrible things.

Chub was a hungrily tender girl to make love to, and she had good flesh. Jason was sorry she was dissatisfied with her own husband. Willy was the kind of woman that you could feel her ribs, uncomfortable to caress, but she was an old horse that had pulled with him for a long time. The idea of being without her gave him a view of his own loneliness that was quickly flooded with sentimentality. He remembered the way old Willy used to wake him up at night and tell him he was strangling. He remembered his daughters in their white dresses at Easter, as fragile and lovely as butterflies.

"What say, Jason," said Walter Flutebinder.

"Nothing much. How bout you?"

"Terrible," the butcher said, wiping his hands on the thighs of his white trousers as if he'd just finished cutting a roast. "I got a sinus infection. You know? Ever had sinus? And I get pains in my heart. I don't think my anal canal is in very good shape, either, but the sinus, phoo! It's terrible."

"I don't have sinus at the moment," said Jason.

"Sinus is the worst thing that can happen to a man," Flutebinder said. "You don't know what trouble is if you never had sinus. Yarf! Those terrible pains behind the eyes! Your face swells up, Jason, I mean it. Your teeth hurt. Your head is full of marbles. You hear these little creekling crackling noises inside your face. Wuh! I gag ever morning and think I'm gonna die."

"His nose drips on the meat," said Norman Green.

"Shut up," Flutebinder said. He blew his nose and looked into his handkerchief. "Aw oh. Blood."

"I've got sinus," said Norman Green. "I've got hay fever, asthma, a bad heart, and scars on my lungs. I've got cavities, neuritis, neuralgia, pink eye, dandruff, bronchitis, sick glands, and bad luck. I'm down on my ass. But you don't hear me complaining."

"Give it a rest," St. Clair said. "Let's bowl."

Jason looked at the three men who had come to the bar to get their beer glasses refilled. Flutebinder was fat, Green was dark and Syrian-looking, St. Clair was tall and lean in a tight suit and Tyrolean hat. To sit and talk to men like these, Jason had spent a great many evenings away from Willy.

"Your bunch going to get that new brewery?" asked St. Clair.

"We're trying," Jason said. "Looks like it might not ever be built."

"It'll be built," said St. Clair. "The city fathers want it. Our town is collapsing, old man, going to sleep. We're an old dog lying in the sunshine. We need new business. I landed the brewery today as one of my accounts. They plan quite a lot of advertising."

"Nice going," Jason said.

"I must say my personal business is doing very well," said St. Clair. "I'm the only executive at Ludlow & Mumm that doesn't have ulcers. There's not another one of them who could stand in here and drink beer all night the way I do. Their stomachs are floating in acid."

"Gar! Mine too," Flutebinder said.

"Seriously, Jason, do you know why I don't have ulcers? It's because I don't care about anything," said St. Clair. "A client can take my brilliant campaigns and scrap them for idiocies his son-in-law thought up, and it doesn't bother me. Why should I worry if they ruin the good things I try to do? People are unjust, ignorant, dishonest, and mean. I recognize that, and I laugh about it. I don't expect them to be different. I don't fight it. I don't care."

"He's lying," Green said. "He cares but there's not anybody who cares whether he cares or not."

"I don't believe I could live without caring," said Jason.

"You know what I say to life?" Green said.

"Who cares?" said St. Clair.

"I care," Green said. "I care plenty about everything. But I say life, up yours, boy."

"There's a lady here," said Harvey.

"I say life, you do it to me. You beat the hell out of me. And boy when you're through you take a long running start and jump up my ass. You can't whip me."

"Let's go back and bowl," Flutebinder said. "It makes my head hurt to listen."

As Jason watched them walk toward the rear, he saw the woman again. She reminded him of a blonde, warm, motherly, sensuous, fleshy milkmaid in a Swedish travel poster. There were dark pockets beneath her eyes, but her skin was smooth and clear as vanilla pudding. She smiled at him, very slightly. He smiled at her and then turned to face the unseen shelves of beer steins.

He wondered what Willy was doing at that moment. Most likely watching television with her father and mother and the little girls. Maybe, though, she was getting dressed to go out. Maybe she'd already found that other man she mentioned in the letter. Maybe she'd found him before she wrote the letter. How did he know what Willy had been doing? She could have lied to him about her bridge games, as Chub had lied to Walter. Movies with a girlfriend last week? Shopping all Saturday afternoon? Junior League meetings? A lecture at the Woman's Club? She'd come home from that lecture with liquor on her breath, he thought, although it was hard to tell because he'd had liquor on his breath. One thing Chub had taught him was that you couldn't trust a woman. Maybe this other man already existed. But how could he know? The idea made him nauseous. Willy wasn't the best, and she didn't smell sweet all over as Chub did, but she had been his and he didn't want to share her. He didn't want her saying things into the ear of another man, or being naked with him, or finding out that somebody else could do that physical thing besides Jason and probably better. What flaws in himself that would expose to a woman who'd never known anybody else. Willy, Willy, he thought, you know me with my skin torn off and my sins laid out. Nobody can ever know me as well as you.

Jason got up and went to the telephone in the back, by the men's room. As he walked past the blonde woman's table, she nodded to him. A bob of the yellow hair. Jason went past the bowling machine where St. Clair leaned over the board with his hand on the puck and the other two men watched the lights. Jason put a dime into the phone and dialed Willy's parents.

"Hello," said Willy's mother.

"Hello, Mrs. Poulsen. May I speak to Wilhelmina, please?"

"This is Jason, isn't it?"

"Yes."

"No."

"This is very important, Mrs. Poulsen."

"She's not here."

"Where is she?" Jason said, sinking.

"She told me to tell you she isn't here, Jason. That's all she told me to tell you. She doesn't want to talk to you."

"But I want to talk to her."

"I don't know why you kids can't work it out between you," said Mrs. Poulsen. "All I want is for you both to have good lives, Jason. Good clean lives. All I want is for you to be happy. Think of your little daughters, Jason. They need their father. I want all of you to be happy."

"Yes ma'am. So do I. Now can I talk to Willy?"

"No," Mrs. Poulsen said, and hung up.

Jason listened to the heavy silence for a moment and then put the receiver on the hook. Behind him was the door to the men's room. He pushed it open and went in. As he stood there he remembered the dozens of nights he'd had to brace his hands against the wall to support himself. The dozens of nights he'd tried to see himself in the cracked mirror and had hardly recognized the face. He read the signs scratched on the wall. One said: *for a good deal call*

Gertrude. Another said: *I am a Nazi don't mess with me.* Another said: *Max is a dirty neo-classicist.* The door opened, and Flutebinder came in.

"My head hurts so bad it keeps me awake," said Flutebinder. "My eyes get puffed up, and all the time creekle crackle inside my face it goes. Creekle crackle. Shifting around. Hanging in my throat and making me sick to my stomach." He blew his nose. "Aargh. That's horrible looking."

"How much you got Green down by?" Jason asked, stepping aside to let Flutebinder in position.

"About sixty-seventy. I don't know where he gets the money. Pore bastard oughta quit."

"Scuse me," said Jason. Jason himself was the pore bastard that oughta quit, he thought. Shuffle off the mortal coil, and all like that. He was ruining everybody's life—Willy's, his daughters', his own. Perhaps kissing Jean at the Christmas party, when they kept at it too long, had even contributed to Ben's trouble. He was hurting Chub, and Walter Anderson. If he kept up his work he'd somehow hurt Harry and Doris. He'd bring rain down on the bank job and put his company out of business.

He squeezed past Flutebinder and returned to the main room. The jukebox was playing a song that made him think of Willy: "Be My Love," with poor dead Mario Lanza singing it. The song reminded him of Austin and he could see Willy as she was then—bright and clean, unhurt, dancing above the water on the terrace at the Lake Austin Inn, with a nice breeze coming in and the sound of motorboats, and no stretch scars on her belly and no pain in her eyes.

Jason started toward his seat at the bar. Here he went, a scum of the very earth, carrying agony with him like a Santa Claus bag of gifts he handed out to this one and that. The one fine brave thing he could do would be to erase himself, to cut out his scenes from their flickering lives; it would be a surgical operation to remove a spreading illness. A scum of the very . . .

The blonde woman stopped him with her voice.

"Don' yew git tahd of drankin beah all naht?" she said.

He looked down at her large teeth and at the huge breasts which lay on the table beside the glass of vodka and orange juice.

"Yeah, sure," he said.

"Set dahn heah an tawk tuh me and hev some vodka."

"I . . ." said Jason.

"Yew lonely, ainch-yew, baby?"

"Yeah. Sort of."

"So'm ah. Anythang yew got tuh dew thet cain't wait?"

"Lord, You made us human," Jason said.

In the next two hours Jason did six imitations of movie stars. Everybody was laughing. Even Norman Green pulled out of his wretchedness to laugh at the conversation between Cary Grant and Gunga Din. Flutebinder pressed his hands beneath his eyes as he laughed, worried that his sinuses might blow up, while Jason, as Jimmy Stewart, invented the Winchester Model 73. A soft shoe and James Cagney singing "Yankee Doodle" got Harvey. Lionel Barrymore was St. Clair's favorite. The blonde woman sat and smiled over her giant bosom and eyed Jason voraciously.

When the Oui Oui Club closed, Jason and the blonde woman got into his car. She slid across the seat and kissed him with such passion that he was both intrigued and frightened.

"Ah hevent hed a man in a long tahm," she whispered. "Thuh nex man tuh git me will thank he hez holt of a tigah."

"We could go to my place," said Jason.

"Honey, hurra up. Ah could splode."

He started the engine as the blonde woman chewed on his ear.

Willy, Jason said to himself, Willy I love you I think.

The Land of the Permanent Wave

Harper's, February 1970

This began as a story on the destruction of the Big Thicket for *Sports Illustrated.* My wife Doatsy and I drove from Austin into East Texas in the convertible her grandmother gave her as a wedding present. We did the things described here, but the story I wrote was about the Big Thicket and had nothing to do with permanent waves or Congressman Dowdy and the atomic bomb.

In New York, André Laguerre, the managing editor of *Sports Illustrated,* called me into his office and said he wasn't going to print the story. A lumber company had become a major stockholder in Time Inc., with representation on the board of directors. The climate at *Sports Illustrated* was changing from a writers' and photographers' magazine into a more corporate-influenced shop. André was a great man in my opinion, but the new directors didn't like him much. This story about timber interests destroying the Thicket would help push André out the door. I certainly didn't want that to happen.

I went to Elaine's for a few drinks that night. Old friend Willie Morris, then the editor of *Harper's,* joined me. I told him what had happened. Willie said, "When you get time, rewrite it and tell about the hair and the night at the lodge, and send it to me."

So it became "The Land of the Permanent Wave" on the cover of *Harper's.* André got kicked out anyhow.

For about five hours I had been drinking Scotch whiskey and arguing with a rather nice, sometimes funny old fellow named Arch, who was so offended by my moderately long hair that he had demanded to know if I weren't actually, secretly, a Communist. "Come on now, you can tell me, hell, I won't hate you for it. Wouldn't you really like to see the Communists take over this country?" Arch had said, placing his bare elbows on the table and leaning forward to look trustingly at me, as though he was certain that if I had one virtue it would prove to be that I would not lie to him about such an important matter. Arch was wearing a jump suit; swatches of gray chest hair, the color of his crew cut, stuck out where the zipper had got caught in it when last Arch had excused himself from the table. We were in the guest lodge of a lumber company in a small town in East Texas. Arch is an old friend of the president of the company. Sitting around the table or nearby were my wife, a State Senator in town to crown a beauty queen at a "celebration" the next evening, a U.S. Congressman who had come down from Washington to make a speech between the parade and the barbecue the following noon, a lumber lobbyist who is mayor of still another town owned by this same lumber company, and I think one or two more people but my memory of that evening has a few holes in it.

"I don't mind telling you what I believe, Arch," I said. The Congressman, John Dowdy, was sitting in a chair in his shirtsleeves holding a glass of bourbon and water that had been paid for—as had the Scotch that Arch and I were doggedly pouring down—by the lumber company in whose lodge we were comparing philosophies. Dowdy is a plump man with a pink face and sparse white hair. He sat forward with quite some interest when I spoke. Probably this was the first time he had ever been so close to a person he considered to be a Communist dopefiend hippie terrorist drunk. At first Representative Dowdy had been reluctant to drink in my presence. He knew I was a writer by trade, and thus unreliable, and it is not at all good for the Baptists in East Texas to discover their politicians have any vile habits. Most of East Texas is dry except for moonshiners and those who can afford to join country clubs or the private clubs to be found in motels. Representative Dowdy had no faith that I would not cruise the lonely roads through the pine forests shouting, "Dowdy drinks!" to the farmers on their porch swings and their wives chopping weeds in hollyhock beds in front of their wooden houses. However, a pretense of fellowship had been built up by the State Senator, Charlie Wilson, a tall Annapolis graduate who also works for the lumber company but is one of those curious creatures in Texas politics, a liberal. Wilson is enthusiastically disliked by Dowdy, and returns the feeling, but politicians will smile at and drink with their lowest, sorriest enemies. So Dowdy took a drink of bourbon and then two or three more and got interested in listening to me as he might have got interested in listening even to a nigger cotton chopper after sufficient liquor and with no physical menace.

"Arch, why are you scared of Communists, anyhow?" I said. "Do you think they're going to raid Waco and steal everything you've got?"

"Damn right!" said Arch. "Haven't you read Karl Marx? They're gonna take over our whole country if we let them! And you'd really like to see that happen, wouldn't you now?"

"You know what I think about Communists?" I said.

"You tell me," said Arch, waiting.

"What I'd like to do to Communists, like in North Vietnam for example, is I'd like to blow their ass to yellow powder," I said.

"What?" said Dowdy.

"I mean take that big bomb and blow their dirty ass to yellow powder!" I said.

"The whole country?" said Arch.

"The whole north part. South part, too, if that's what it takes. You can't give a Communist a damn inch, Arch. You know that."

"Well, but the whole country . . ." Arch said.

"Me, too. That's what I'd like to do, too. Use that big bomb over there," said Dowdy.

"That'd get our boys home in a hurry. Just blow their Communist ass to yellow powder. Turn 'em into sulphur," I said.

"You're right!" said Dowdy.

"You know it; I know it, the generals know it, Arch knows it, so what are we waiting for?" I said.

"We ought to do it right now!" said Dowdy. Dowdy's bullshit detector had not been functioning while wet, but now there was a clattering in the machinery inside his head and he cast a suspicious, stricken look at us.

"I need to get some sleep," Dowdy said abruptly and headed off into one of the bedrooms.

I noticed that whoever had made my last drink had done so with too light a hand on the Scotch bottle. Arch and I required a couple more and, with the Communist worry settled (if not to his total satisfaction), we talked about fishing. East Texas has some fine fishing and used to have better before towns, lumber companies, oil companies, paper mills, and real-estate developers began pouring their crap and garbage into the rivers and creeks, and sportsmen's clubs began blocking off the choicer streams from the public. There are two very large lakes in East Texas—Sam Rayburn and Toledo Bend—and several smaller ones, as well as countless bayous and ponds where the water is held by the red clay soil. Four sizable rivers carry crap down through East Texas into the Gulf of Mexico. One of them, the Trinity, flows through both Fort Worth and Dallas in the north and has become the color and consistency of green paint by the time it reaches the Big Thicket, a truly vanishing wilderness.

The Big Thicket has been a hiding place for bears, wild pigs, panthers, ghosts, Civil War deserters, moonshiners, whooping cranes, ivorybill woodpeckers, Texas's only reservation Indians, snakes, magnificent stands of hardwoods and virgin pines, so many rare plants that they have hardly begun to be identified, and some very withdrawn, reclusive people. Biologists view the Big Thicket with profound wonder, and ecologists regard its passing with despair. Roy Harris, the heavyweight fighter, came from the town of Cut and Shoot, which used to be in the Big Thicket before the invention of the power saw. Six Texas governors have sprung from the Big Thicket. For many years its tight-eye forests blocked the westward trek of pioneers and forced them onto the plains to the north. But the Indians hunted in canoes in the Thicket's bayous and knew its few footpaths. Sam Houston intended to hide his Texan army there if he lost the battle that was finally fought at San Jacinto. Not far from what is now the Hoop N' Holler Estates, weekend cottages for people fleeing Houston and Beaumont, the Indians used to bathe in hot mineral springs and drink crude oil as medicine. The springs are dried up now, panthers are seldom seen, bears wander in confusion as far north as Lufkin, where they are shot trying to escape, and the oil of the Indians has been drilled in dozens of pools that bred boomtowns and formed such giants as Texaco. Senator Ralph Yarborough, a Texas Democrat, is trying to save a piece of the Big Thicket as a National Park, but it is perhaps a vain hope. As much as they may feel blood kin to the woods and streams that have nourished them for generations, most of the people who live in the Big Thicket, and in the rest of East Texas, depend for their livelihood on the industries that are destroying them, and so they vote for candidates chosen by the big companies. "I don't see how anything can be done about a park, no matter what the Sahara [*sic*] Club wants," Representative Dowdy had said earlier in the evening. As a lumberman's friend, Arch would prefer to see the Thicket leveled. "It's a hot old swamp, full of bugs and snakes and not fit for man," he said.

After a while, as we were arguing about the Thicket, it occurred to us that all in the house save Arch and me had gone to bed. The two large ponds out front lay silent in the moonlight. The ducks, geese, pigeons, and peacocks that roam the grounds of the guest lodge had ruffled themselves into a great restless quiet for the night. The squirrels had ceased to dart about in the cage that my wife had wanted to release them from, and there was no sound from the sawmill along the railroad tracks beyond the fence. Now it was just Arch and I, keeping up the noise at the table in the living room of the lodge, and we became congenial, no doubt from the liquor as much as from the sensing that someday, disparate though we were, we might be the only two whose asses were not blown to powder, the only two left alive, as we now were alive on this night.

"I'll tell you something," Arch said. "You're not such a bad fellow. I could learn to live around you, and I could even get used to your hair. But there's one thing I've got to admit. I hope you won't get mad at me for saying this."

"Let's hear it," I said, having begun to be fond of the old man and finding it unimaginable that he could anger me.

"Well, like I said. I could get used to your hair. But there's no way in the world I could ever make myself like your wife's hair."

At Preacher Bob's shack on the set of *Kid Blue* in Durango, Mexico, 1973.
Photo by Doatsy Shrake.

My wife's hair! So that was part of it too! I had assumed the hostility we had encountered in the last few days of driving through East Texas in our convertible was directed at me. But my wife had been receiving her share of it, and maybe more, all along. My wife's hair! My wife Doatsy is young and pretty and her hair is the color of caramel; it is soft, it shines, it smells like baby soap, and it is long, hanging to the middle of her back, a glorious drop of hair that my grandmother would have been proud of, that young girls of today strive for, and that Arch could never make himself appreciate!

"I'm amazed there is a man in America who objects to long hair on a woman," I said. I don't know what Arch thought I was calling him, but he got up and went to bed, and I could tell he had been insulted. But as I thought of the way we had been treated for the past week, I understood what Arch was telling me. As the beatniks long ago learned, out there in America hair matters, and here we were in the land of the permanent wave. The shellacked bouffants and beehives, sprayed hard as a real hornets' nest, had become acceptable at last, along with high-heeled shoes, in East Texas, where information does not readily penetrate, but the thing for a real lady still to have was a permanent wave like my mother used to come home with twenty years ago. In East Texas, long-haired women went out of mode with long-haired men, about the time McKinley was shot, and in my big-city naiveté I had thought I was the only one being scorned by the natives for disregard of custom in a place where custom means everything.

My hair was not really all that long; it was just rather shaggy, somewhat in the manner of an old-fashioned country lawyer or editor or judge. If I had worn a white cotton suit and black string tie, we probably would have had no trouble at all. In East Texas, the older ones would recognize that character. I would have smelled of the courthouse to them, and they would have been no more curious about me than about the rows of slave shacks that had stood in the fields all their lives, or about the black people who lived in those shacks and worked in those fields as if there had never been a Civil War, or about the black children who still went to black schools as though there were no Supreme Court in this country. To the younger ones, I could have pointed out that my hair was no longer than, say, Pat Moynihan's in a photograph in the *New York Times*, but then I would have had to explain who Moynihan was, and in the process I would have bored and annoyed them.

We had been at the Indian reservation on the north edge of the Big Thicket in splendid forest and dogwood country and then had visited the Heritage Museum—the only town rebuilt in the manner of a hundred years ago that I know of that is accurate in detail and does not look as if it were put together by Walt Disney's set designers. We drove up Highway 69 through a corner of the Angelina National Forest, and it was growing dark as we approached Lufkin. Billboards for the Shangri-La Motel advertised color TV. We were tired and that attracted us: dinner in the room, color TV, a long sleep, and the next day a drive over to the lumber company guest lodge near Sam Rayburn Lake. It was a good plan. Nothing went wrong with it until I checked in at the Shangri-La and discovered the color TV was in the lobby instead of in the room, where I would have preferred it. I looked in the Yellow Pages and saw that the Holiday Inn also advertised color TV. The girl at the desk in the Shangri-La had been examining me as though I were a maverick bear, and when she figured out my desire she said, "Naw, they don't have no color TV ove-ur."

"It says so in the Yellow Pages."

"Shoot! I don't care whut's in at book. I use to work ove-ur. They don't have no color TV." She phoned the Holiday Inn. "Marge, yew got color TV ove-ur? Naw? I knew it, but they's some guy here says yew do. Yeah, he sure is." She hung up, giggling. I signed the register. The sight of the motel name on the card threw me into a fit of melancholy. "Thet'll be fourteen dollars in advance."

"Why in advance?"

"Why yew *thank?*"

I thought it was because they catered to traveling salesmen and urgent shackups. I paid, and the girl gave me a card that would allow us to buy a drink in the private club that occupied the rear of a restaurant. "We got a good barbershop here," she said as I went out. I stopped and looked around, understanding. The door of the private club looked as if on many occasions someone had tried to propel someone else through without turning the knob. The rooms at the Shangri-La faced directly onto the parking lot, in the middle of which sat a swimming pool with a brick wall around it. My wife and I sat on the bed in our room, listening to car doors slamming, thoroughly despondent, peering wearily at a menu while the black-and-white TV played static and ghastly figures for us. Then I jumped up.

"This place is on fire!" I said.

"A car is burning in the parking lot!" she said.

When I opened the door, a heavy white choking smoke floated into the room. I rushed to the office. "Something's burning!" I cried. The girl at the desk sniffed and said, "Oh, thet smoke? Thet's just the creosote plant. It gits like thet ever nat." I went back to the room, and we hustled our bags out to the car. By now smoke was drifting up from the bedspread and clinging in wisps to the grimy towels on the rack, like swamp mist rising early in the morning. A cop was at the desk talking to the girl when I returned to the office, and in my rapidly expanding, galloping East Texas paranoia, I knew they were talking about me. I said I was leaving because of the smoke and wanted my money back. The cop eyed me as if he expected I would pull a pistol and begin to speak with a foreign accent.

"I *tole* yew it's only the *creosote* plant!" the girl said. "Nobody ever complained about it before. Thet smoke'll be gone by mornin'."

I said my wife had terminal bronchitis and would also be gone by morning if we spent the night there. After protesting that there was no procedure for this, the girl grudgingly gave back the whole fourteen dollars. The cop followed in his car as we drove to the Holiday Inn. He parked near us and sat watching and chewing gum or something. I paid in advance without asking why, we went to our room, locked the door, called room service and requested a menu.

"You got to pay in advance or we won't send you no menu," said the room-service woman. "Pay in advance for food? Is that a general policy, or did they specify this room?" Doatsy asked.

"This is the deal for your room. You send down twenty dollars or we won't send no menu."

A frightened bellhop, an addled white boy who had probably seen *Bonnie and Clyde* at the drive-in and expected to be greeted by a kick in the belly, stood well back from the door as he collected the twenty-dollar bond and handed over the menu.

"Is this, ah, unusual?" I asked.

"I just started work here today, but I ain't done it before," he said. We ordered dinner. The boy brought up the food along with change from the twenty. I asked if the cop was hanging around the lobby. "Y-y-yeah," said the boy, trying to sneak a look at the famous mad dog outlaws without rousing us to violence. I will always wonder what that boy overheard in that lobby.

In the morning I compounded our crime by wearing rubber shower thongs into the coffee shop where I ordered breakfast in a room crowded with red-faced, crop-headed men in short-sleeve shirts. The waitress had but to glance at me to know she did not wish to approach very close, lest Godlessness somehow leap from me to her like a pox. The problem of serving she solved by sailing my plate to the table as if playing Frisbee. Still ignorant of the measure of our offense to society, I thought matters would improve when my wife arrived; at least they would see I wasn't queer. I hadn't reckoned that few people in East Texas believe there is such a thing, anyhow. In vast sections of America, sexual deviation means the woman on top (this of course does not take into account rural love affairs with cows and chickens). My wife caught her breakfast with both hands as it skipped on the table bound for the window.

Then the notion struck that I could quite simply change all this. I went to the parking lot, opened the trunk of the car, and put on a battered, well-crushed cowboy hat that I have owned for years. As I turned back toward the coffee shop, there stood the cop. His mean face slowly resolved into a baffled, respectful expression, like that of a weasel facing a trap.

"Good mornin," he said.

"Hot sumbitch today," I said.

"Yes sir, it is."

In the coffee shop I sat down at the table with my hat on. My wife, her long hair flowing down on either side of her face, whispered, "They'll kill you." But the waitress came right up to the table and called me sir. As we sauntered dramatically out, I paused at the front desk and told the clerk I'd made a local call from my room. "That's all right, sir. No charge," she said, smiling.

On the way out of town we stopped at a drive-in grocery to buy ice for the cooler. I still wore my hat. When I got out of the car I was assailed by another of the noxious stinks that Lufkin is distinguished for. This one came from the huge paper mill across the road. Smoke poured from the stacks and spread across the neighborhood like a fog that smelled of rotten-egg puke. The odor wrenched the stomach and made one hesitant to breathe.

"If I lived around here, I'd blow up that place," I said to the man at the drive-in.

"No sir, you wouldn't," he replied. "If you lived around here, you'd work there."

For the "celebration" the following day I kept on my hat, partly so as not to cost Charlie Wilson any votes. He congratulated me on having lived for a week bareheaded in East Texas without getting beaten with a tire iron. "With that hat on, they can see your hair hanging down, but a long-haired cowboy is likely to be a dangerous man that is best left alone," Charlie said. We leaned against Charlie's car parked on the main street and watched the parade. There were a couple of black children on one of the floats, and a plump black tuba player marched with the high-school band. Charlie, the liberal, said that was progress. To hear the speechmaking we sat on pine logs in a field. Representative Dowdy, the main speaker, fretted about luring the people away from the Ferris wheel that had been set up across the road. The rides were shut down. Dowdy spoke about the ship of state on the river of life. The crowd gazed dully up at the platform where Dowdy's white and pink head bent forward as he read his text through glasses. Three women cantered past on palomino horses, raising dust. "A patriot is a man that don't take orders from Washington," Dowdy said. A fellow in tooled boots hopped up and cheered, and they had to carry off an old man, overcome, in an aluminum chair.

Afterward I told Dowdy I liked that part about the ship of state. He seemed neither to have heard me nor to have ever seen me before. For most of the afternoon we sat and ate—barbecue, fried chicken, venison chili, potato salad, coconut cream pie, chocolate pie—while I kept my hat on and people smiled and inquired politely about news from the other world, as though my wife and I were peculiar but important visitors from the Pampas. Except for my wife's, there was not one skirt much above the knee to be seen in town, not even on the cheerleaders. I searched among the throng for a pair of bellbottom trousers, a moustache, a peace symbol, any small sign that the styles of urban youth had been heard of. But no. They were clear-eyed, homeloving, right-thinking folks here. They would tell the Easy Rider to crawl on his bike and haul his bones out of the county, and if he moved fast enough he might make it.

The final phase of the "celebration" was held that night in the parking lot of the shopping center. Kids in cowboy boots and hats danced with girls in cotton dresses, a scene from years past. A fiddler, imported from Fort Worth, scraped at his fiddle and made scrowling noises; you couldn't tell what tune he was playing but the kids danced the two-step cowboy polka, nevertheless, and what did it matter? Their elders formed a square and clapped hands, waiting for the drawing at which a boat, a shotgun, and a TV set would be given away. Charlie Wilson stood on the truck-trailer platform with the beauty-queen contestants. Charlie had got a haircut for the occasion. The beauty queens were sweet-looking girls, all of them very nervous and shy in their evening gowns, their hair newly done up and crinkly as valentines, reeking of cologne. "Hey, Sen-ter!" someone yelled. "The people back here say that fiddler's got to go!"

Charlie introduced the beauty-queen candidates and from an envelope pulled the name of the winner, who cried as he lowered the crown onto her permanent wave. "Bless your heart," he said and kissed her. Lugging her trophy, the bawling girl wobbled down the ramp into the arms of her beaming family and boyfriend. At the top of the ramp stood Charlie, an enormous bouquet of roses in his arms. "Your flowers! You forgot your flowers!" he called. But the girl was gone. Charlie shrugged and said into the microphone, "That's all. The program's over." The crowd stayed where it was. There was a spreading mutter. A voice shouted, "Sen-ter, who won the damn boat?"

My wife and I went to our car before the drawing. We ran into Arch, still in his jump suit, his eyes showing that his hangover ranked right up there with mine and that he was troubled, besides. "Listen, I hope you're not mad at me," he said. "By God, I can't help how I feel. I'm an old man. It's too late for me to change, but it ain't too late for you."

"Yeah, Arch, it's too late for me," I said.

We shook hands. With an old Southern courtliness, he said goodbye to my wife and wandered into the crowd around the platform. Then we were on the road again, heading out of East Texas, the headlights picking up bits of sparkling water, black patches of thicket, dark houses well back from our passing, and we could smell the pines in the night wind with the car top down. I took off my hat. It was giving me a headache.

John Lee Wallace, Reporting from Dallas

From *Strange Peaches* (1972)

I took a leave of absence from *Sports Illustrated* and went to London to write *Strange Peaches.* Doatsy and I got a flat on Cheyne Place in Chelsea, a couple of blocks from where Mick Jagger lived. We had a nice view of the Thames along the Chelsea embankment from the window seat where I placed my faithful Smith Corona Skywriter—the same machine I had carried around Europe eight years earlier while I was writing *But Not for Love.* And, as art would have it, the events I found myself describing as I wrote *Strange Peaches* took place in my life, more or less, shortly before and after the publication of *But Not for Love* and the murder of President Kennedy soon after I returned to Dallas.

The first half of this chapter is set on an ordinary night in Dallas at Parkland Hospital in the emergency room where Kennedy was pronounced dead. The second half describes the working life of a reporter in those days. It is mostly all true. Reading the novel, a friend asked, "When does the fiction start?"

I went to London to write this book for the same reason I went to Europe to write *But Not for Love*—to protect myself from myself. In London the pubs closed at 11 p.m. In New York or Austin 11 p.m. is the time things would start getting lively. Everyone I knew in England had a job and had to get up early. I would work on the book until about five. Then Doatsy and I would go for a long, ambling, aimless walk and smoke a couple of joints along the way. Nobody seemed to notice. Dick Growald was attached to the London Bureau of UPI at this time, and we knew a few other people quite well, like theater director Michael Rudman. But all of them turned in at a reasonable hour and got a lot of work done, and so did I.

The telephone woke me up. It was Dorothy saying I had to come over there quick, her mother was dead. I didn't know if I had really been asleep, because I was still dressed in my Brooks Brothers suit. My legs ached, and I seemed to be having a speed flash with sweating and palpitations. I said I would be there and hung up and tried to read my watch. It would not make sense. Washing my face I noticed that the top was off the Alka-Seltzer bottle. Every night before going to bed I took two Alka-Seltzers and three aspirins, and in the morning I took three aspirins, two Alka-Seltzers, two multivitamin capsules, a couple of vitamin E tablets, three or four vitamin C tablets. Depending on how I felt and what I had to do, I might also take a Dexamyl or Dexedrine spansule, 15 milligrams. But I made it a point of laying off the amphetamines for days or weeks at a time so my tolerance level wouldn't go out of sight.

However, I had swallowed so much Benzedrine in the past week that I knew I couldn't face Dorothy's dead mother without chemical assistance. So I mashed up a Dexamyl spansule to quicken the timed-release and took it with a cup of hot instant coffee to kick it off faster. Then I took another Dexamyl spansule that would come in later. I found myself idiotically whistling and looking at my teeth in the mirror. Again I remembered Dorothy and her dead mother. I had gotten involved with these medicinal rituals. I looked at my watch and saw that it was one A.M., earlier than I'd thought. I couldn't have been home for more than half an hour before Dorothy phoned me, but I could have believed any amount of time had passed.

I crept into Buster's room to get the keys to his station wagon off the bureau. Groping on the bureau in the dark, my fingers touched nothing. No keys. No billfold. No crumpled money. I turned on the light. Buster's room was in its usual condition. Sheets wadded up, mattress showing, piles of dirty clothes on the floor. It smelled like a locker room. At the foot of the bed lay the tennis shorts that he wore when he had no clean underwear. His jockstrap was hanging on a lamp. I opened the top bureau drawer, pushed aside a pair of pink silk panties and a brassiere, a pair of white athletic socks, a black sock that contained the matchbox of marijuana, a pair of pale blue panties and a pair of black silk panties. Buster was fond of panties.

Dorothy's dead mother. I kept looking in the bureau drawer for the keys to Buster's Morris Minor, but he had put them somewhere else or gotten rid of the car. I phoned a taxi. Thirty or forty minutes after Dorothy's call, I saw her sitting on the hood of her car under a streetlight on the corner by her mother's apartment building. I had expected that the police would be there, and the neighbors would be up, with the lights on. But it was dark and quiet.

"Where'd they take her?" I said.

"She's still inside," said Dorothy.

I looked at the dark brick building.

"Who'd you call?"

"Only you," she said.

"Well, my God, let's go call the police."

"I can't get in. I called you from the Waffle Shop."

"How do you know she's dead?" I said.

"The door is locked from the inside. She won't answer."

"Are you sure she hasn't got somebody in there with her?"

"This is my mother you're talking about," Dorothy said.

"All right. So what am I supposed to do?"

"Break in."

"I'll get shot for a burglar."

"Please, John Lee, just this once don't act like a butt."

The only tool I could find was a beer-can opener in the glove compartment of Dorothy's car. I tore a hole in the screen of a window in Dorothy's mother's bedroom. Threshing in the hedges and waiting for the people upstairs to shout at me or Dorothy's mother to blow my face off with a pistol, I unhooked the screen and took it off and heaved up the unlocked window. Then I got a knee up on the ledge and climbed inside. Crawling through the window, my hands immediately touched the mattress, and I was thinking how this was going to be a French farce with me coming in through the window and a lover hiding under the bed. Carefully I felt around on the bed and touched soft flesh. I shook the flesh gently, thinking to wake her, and realized that I had hold of Dorothy's mother by the breast and she had not moved.

Mumbling an apology, I crawled across her mother's body, got to my feet on the other side of the bed and switched on a lamp. In the pale light, her mother lay with her eyes shut and her mouth open, one shoulder strap of her nightgown pulled down and a breast revealed. She had a waxy look. I picked up an empty prescription bottle off the night table and opened the front door for Dorothy. She gasped when she saw her mother. "Goddamn you, Mother," she said. She went over and covered her mother's breast. I gave Dorothy the prescription bottle.

"This was for a hundred Seconals. It was nearly full," she said.

"I'll call the police," I said.

"Couldn't we just call a funeral home?"

Looking around for the telephone, I was struck by how drab and awful the bedroom was. Dorothy's mother looked like an older sister who'd had some tough times that showed in her face, but this was the room of a lonesome old woman. It had a pungent, sickly stench, as though the air had been all breathed up and only human exhausts were left. It was ridiculous for Doro-thy to live in a place like this.

I saw the telephone on the floor by the bed. I put it on the night table and was starting to dial when it occurred to me to make sure her mother was dead. I couldn't feel a pulse, but I usually can't find my own. I bent down to her mouth and smelled vomit around her lips and discovered that she was breathing.

"Ina Mae," I said, shaking her. "Ina Mae, wake up."

"Are you crazy? Get your hands off her," said Dorothy.

Just then Ina Mae opened her eyes.

"Mother!" said Dorothy.

"We can take her to a hospital faster than we could wait for an ambu-lance," I said.

Dorothy wrapped her mother in a housecoat, and I dragged and car-ried Ina Mae out to the old blue Cadillac. She managed a kind of half-wit smile but could not talk. Dorothy sat in back with her and kept her awake by prodding and slapping and continually asking, "How many pills did you take, Mother? How long ago did you take them?" After several wrong turns, I drove to Parkland Hospital. It's the public hospital in Dallas, and it rises above the surrounding landscape off a broad road. I turned into the emer-gency entrance and parked about twenty yards from the emergency room. They were unloading somebody from an ambulance. Several police cars were parked in spaces allotted for them. Supporting Ina Mae between us, Dorothy and I walked her into the emergency room. By now it was nearly two-thirty. The bars had been closed for more than two hours, and the night's beer-joint casualties had passed through the emergency room into surgery or wards, or out again into jail or onto the street. The nurse at the desk had blood on the breast of her white uniform. We waited while she wrote down information given by a Negro boy who was holding a bloody rag to his forehead. She told him to sit on a bench where a dozen other people were waiting. The nurse looked at my hair and mustache for a long moment and then took in the vest and tie as well as Dorothy's clean young beauty.

"She swallowed a bunch of barbiturates," I said.

"Name?"

"Ina Mae Leclaire," said Dorothy.

"Age?"

"Thirty-eight."

"Address?" Dorothy told her. I looked at Ina Mae, who was gazing at the nurse through half-shut eyes with a tiny smile, like an imbecile watching a kitten. I had spent years around emergency rooms with 16-millimeter movie equipment when I was a TV news reporter and cameraman, but I had never gotten accustomed to the way nurses persisted with their routine in the parade of agony.

"Are you responsible for her expenses?" the nurse asked me.

"She has Blue Cross," said Dorothy. The nurse nodded.

Another nurse appeared with a wheelchair. They put Ina Mae in it and pushed her off down a corridor. Dorothy tried to follow, but the desk nurse stopped her.

"Johnny, we got an attempted suicide here," the nurse said to a cop. The cop looked at the form and began copying the information onto his clipboard. He was wearing a black leather jacket, and his cap was pushed to the back of his head, as if he were playing fighter pilot. A pistol and a flashlight hung off his belt, and the leather handle of a slapjack stuck out of a hip pocket. The cop peered curiously at me.

"You her husband?" he said.

"I'm her daughter," said Dorothy.

"How come'd she do this?"

"I don't know."

The outside doors swung open. An old man was carried on a stretcher into an examining room. His legs looked like sausages that had split open. He was sobbing, and his arms stuck straight up into the air, fingers curled, reaching for something. The desk nurse followed him into the examining room with her papers.

"Not even cold yet and he's caught his robe on fire at the bathroom stove. His plastic pajamas stuck to his legs," the cop said as the old man's ashy face went past. "Be a lot of burns soon as we get a norther."

The cop was making friendly conversation. "You got something against barbers?" he asked me.

"I like barbers," I said.

"Oh. I thought he had something against barbers," the cop said, grinning at Dorothy.

A black man walked in through the swinging doors. His eyes were wild and yellow. Blood covered the front of his shirt and soaked his pants legs, and his shoes squished with it when he walked.

"They shot me," he said to the desk nurse. "I 'bout to die."

An intern urged the man to lie down on a wheeled bed. A nurse unbuttoned his shirt. I saw the look that passed between the nurse and the intern. The man had been hit by a shotgun. His stomach had exploded. A Negro orderly came out with a bucket and began mopping up blood.

"Who shot you, boy?" the cop said.

"Raymond."

"Raymond who?"

"Raymond over at the Polka Dot Club."

"What's your name?" said the desk nurse.

They had wheeled the man into the examining room beside the old man with the burned legs and were sticking tubes and needles into him. I moved over to where I could see in the door, but Dorothy turned away.

"Jesse Lee Jones," the black man said.

"Your address?" said the nurse.

"What you say?"

"Where do you stay at?" the cop said.

"I live with my auntie."

"How come'd Raymond shoot you?" the cop said.

"Doan know."

"You messing with Raymond's girl?"

"Nawsuh."

"Tell the truth, boy."

"I tell de troo."

"Where does your auntie stay?" said the nurse.

"On Evans Street."

"What number on Evans Street?" said the nurse.

"Raymond shot me."

"We'll take care of Raymond," said the cop. "What number on Evans Street do you stay at?"

"Doan know. By the bus stop."

Then he died. The nurses and the intern began unhooking their tubes. They pulled the sheet over the black man's face. The cop phoned headquarters downtown and said, "If you got a car handy go by the Polka Dot Club and see if they can find Raymond with a shotgun."

The cop came back over to us.

"Your mama's gonna be okay," he said to Dorothy.

The telephone rang and the desk nurse beckoned to the cop.

"It's that new kid from the *Herald* that stays up all night," the nurse said.

"Yeah, it's a gunshot," the cop said into the phone. "Deceased name is Jesse Lee Jones. Age unknown. Address unknown. Forget it, kid, it's a nigger deal." He hung up the receiver.

"If they put ever' nigger killing in the paper we wouldn't have room for the comics," the cop said to us.

A Negro woman was standing at the desk. She wore a uniform of some kind, hotel maid's perhaps.

"Talk louder," the desk nurse said.

"'Quire 'bout Jesse Lee Jones," said the woman.

"You his girl friend?" the cop said.

"Yassuh. His wife."

"He's dead," said the cop.

The woman nodded and stared at the wall behind the nurse.

"You know Raymond at the Polka Dot Club?"

"Nawsuh."

"Wouldn't tell me if you did," the cop said.

The woman began to shake and emit squeaking noises. I remembered a night at the police station when Buster and I had walked into an interrogation room where two uniformed cops were whipping an old black man with their belts. He had dropped his pants and the belts would smack against his brown ass. After each blow the cops would ask which of them hit hardest. No matter what the old man answered, he was in for another belting. In high school our two football coaches used to do the same thing to us, except they used boards and did it in the Ping-Pong room and people went home from these sporting occasions with blood seeping down their legs.

"Miss Leclaire?"

A doctor in a white smock had come along the corridor and walked up to Dorothy.

"Your mother says she swallowed about eighty Seconals, but she threw up most of it. We pumped out her stomach, anyway. Now a staff psychiatrist has to talk to her. That's required. It'll be another half hour at the most."

Dorothy and I sat down on a bench. Five car wreck victims were carried in. Three were teen-agers, one a dying girl. A traffic cop who came in with them said they had been driving more than a hundred on the Central Expressway and had hit a truck. Dorothy glanced at me. A pregnant Mexican

woman entered with her husband and five children, a number she was minutes away from increasing to six. A thin white woman, looking demented,
came through the swinging doors with a little boy under her arm. The boy
was about four, and his head dangled like that of a dead chicken.

"My boy's hurt," the woman said.

The desk nurse rushed around and laid the boy on a bed.

"His neck's broke," the cop said.

"He's hurt bad," agreed the woman.

"How'd this happen?" the cop said.

"He got his head caught in the chain on the porch swing. It was wropped
all around his neck," said the woman. The cop looked at his watch.

"What was he doing swinging on the porch in the middle of the night?"
the cop said.

"He got hurt about supper time. I thought he'd be all right. But he never
come to."

As a TV news cameraman I used to shoot film of the relatives of children who were very recently deceased, and sometimes ask for photographs,
old snapshots or studio portraits of the kids smiling and dressed up in their
birthday clothes. I competed with newspaper reporters for these photographs, and more than once I went into somebody's house and stole every
photo of the dead child I could find to prevent other TV or newspapermen
from getting them. This was what we called good journalism of the old Chicago school, and when that stolen photo would appear on the TV screen for a
couple of seconds I was supposed to feel good about it, and sometimes I did.
We were supposed to be proud of being professional, as much as the cop in
the emergency room. One afternoon a little boy had been run over in front of
his house. A reporter from the *Herald* walked through the little boy's blood
without knowing it and tracked the blood onto the front porch, where he
asked the mother: "How old was your son and how do you spell his name?"
The mother collapsed. I told my ex-wife Geraldine about this later and
laughed with the usual lighthearted cynicism I put on in the face of events
that were incomprehensible. I remarked to Geraldine that the reporter was a
real pro. "He's a monster," she said. . . .

I had first encountered Buster when I was a TV news reporter toting a 16-
millimeter movie camera that I had only a dim notion how to operate. In

those days I was responsible for radio news also. I would start a working shift at five-thirty in the morning at the pressroom at police headquarters. I would check the desk sergeant's reports of the night ending and make rounds of various divisions—traffic, homicide, juvenile, vice, the general detective office, the jail sergeant, the radio dispatchers. If anybody interesting was in jail I would look up his record in the ID Bureau and always assume that if a record existed it was correct. Early in the morning I phoned hospitals and questioned emergency rooms about the night's activities and then talked to nursing supervisors about patients who might be good for feature stories—unusually gruesome operations, terrible hard luck, any number of oddities. I phoned the Fire Department every morning. Often the people I knew on my beat would call me if there was a story. Nearly all of them liked seeing themselves on television or hearing their voices on the radio. Sometimes I would rush out to shoot film at a hospital or a fire or a crash site, or at the scene of a murder or holdup. Always I had to phone the news department and tell them what was up and dictate the radio reports either live or into a tape machine. I hated dictating from the pressroom. I put on a dramatic radio voice for these reports, another self. It came across fine on the air, but in the pressroom it sounded as if I were auditioning for announcing class. Other reporters, those from newspapers, would listen and applaud. If they knew my broadcast was live, they would yell "fuck!" We constantly listened to the police radio. In the flow of talk we were alert for the dispatcher's voice cutting in with a Signal 9 (shooting), 8 (fire), 7 (accident), 14 (stabbing), 17 (gang fight), 20 (robbery), 20a (robbery in progress), and 27 (dead person), and we listened for him to say Code 3, which meant it was a top emergency. Upon hearing one of these signals we would phone the dispatcher for more information and then we'd run for our cars and race each other to the scene. Many stories washed out when we recognized the address as being in a black neighborhood, or if the dispatcher or detectives involved brushed it off by saying, "Nigger deal," just as the cop at Parkland had done on the night of Ina Mae Leclaire's stomach-pumping. Maybe the blacks were on municipal golf courses and in hotel lobbies now, but some things hadn't changed. Newspapers, radio and television did not report violence involving blacks unless it was against whites. They did not report much of anything at all involving blacks, with the exception of professional sporting events, unless it was humorous, like watermelon stealing. But if a black man killed a white man or raped a white woman, you would see detectives in the hall with shotguns, and you had a story.

One of the last stories I ever shot film on—this was after I had moved from police reporting into general assignments and was working out of the TV station—was a civil rights sit-in at a drugstore near the SMU campus. Twenty young Negroes and whites sat at the soda counter waiting to be served. The drugstore doors were locked and a fumigating company was called to spray the inside of the building with insecticide. The demonstrators withstood the white smoke for fifteen minutes or so. Then they came to the glass doors and begged to be let out. Police and firemen dragged out several who were unconscious. The drugstore owner shook his fist at the demonstrators and told them they had ruined the goods on his shelves. Some of the demonstrators were theological students. I interviewed the owner, the police, the demonstrators and the crowd and went back to the station with my film and tapes. The film was not used. The incident was never mentioned on the air or in the newspapers. If such a thing should be reported, I was told, it would encourage other radicals to cause trouble in a peaceful city.

In the pressroom, many days were tedious. I read paperbacks and played cards. There were only two narcotics officers on the force then. They had little to do. One of them sat on my desk almost every day and talked. Several times he gave me bags of marijuana he had taken away from people.

"This is low-class dope. Only people use it are niggers, Meskins, musicians and white trash," he used to say. I kept the marijuana in a desk drawer. I didn't bother to tell him that I sometimes smoked it. He didn't tell me that he was a morphine addict. Several years later he got busted by a state agent.

One morning Buster E. Gregory walked into the pressroom carrying a Speed Graphic camera and wearing a shoulder bag full of plates. He was in his early twenties, about my age. He was much thinner then, the way I still remember him, and very brown with thick black hair. Neither of us had been out of the Army for long. This was Buster's first job in journalism, as it was mine. We got coffee from a machine in the hall. He told me he had gone to photography school in the Army and then had been assigned as a lifeguard and swimming instructor in Honolulu, where he became serious about photography as a potential hustle once he got out. He admitted that he was a great photographer and would prefer shooting 35-millimeter natural light with his Rolleiflex, but the *Dallas Morning News* insisted on Speed Graphic shots with flash, for fast news. Buster had come to police headquarters with a reporter who was also a rookie. They were supposed to do a feature on the radio dispatchers, a story that was done every eighteen months.

While we were drinking coffee, the police radio announced a Signal 27 in Oak Cliff. At that moment a homicide detective named Brady, a white-haired fellow who wore a snap-brim hat and flicked cigar ashes onto his tie and vest, hurried past on the way to his car. "Don't know, boys. Can't tell yet. White woman dead in her bathroom. Probably had cancer," he said. Buster and I and the rookie reporter rode with Brady, who was working alone because his partner had the mumps. It was a two-story white frame house with another family living upstairs. A junked washing machine lay in the front yard. The houses on either side were very close. The dead woman, who was in her sixties, had lived downstairs with her fifty-year-old nephew and his wife. We stepped around sticky patches of blood in the hall. The woman lay back on the bathroom floor with her arms spread and one foot up on the toilet. But her head was turned so that her eyes looked at us in the hall. The cut went clear through her neck to the spinal cord. "This is a terrible thing, boys, terrible," Brady said. The Justice of the Peace arrived and looked at the body. Brady and the JP talked to the nephew and wife, who said the woman had been depressed. The nephew wore work khakis and had an Adam's apple the size of a lemon. Brady showed a double-edged razor blade he'd found on the sink. The JP pronounced the death suicide. Buster had taken a hundred pictures by then, three or four with the Speed Graphic. We pointed out that the woman's fingertips had not been damaged as she sawed through her throat. "Poor woman must of been desperate," Brady said.

The photos that Buster took and the film I shot did not appear in the newspaper or on television. Suicides ordinarily rated about a paragraph of newspaper space and no television time unless there was an angle more interesting than the distasteful death of a poor woman in a low-rent neighborhood. Buster brought back prints for the pressroom bulletin board. We thumbtacked them up with the caption SUICIDE OF THE WEEK. We had no sooner put up the photos than there was another dead person call, and we found ourselves in Brady's car again. He complained about having to work too hard with his partner loafing at home. Buster gave him a print of the dead woman, and Brady said he'd keep it for his scrapbook. When we arrived at the scene of the call, a swollen bundle was draining on the shore of White Rock Lake. A fisherman thought he'd hooked a record catfish. Instead, he had snagged the body of a young prostitute and narcotics informer, whose skull was crushed and whose hands and feet were bound with chains. Brady looked at the body for a long time, very annoyed, showering his vest with cigar ashes. Finally he said, "Boys, I sure do hate to say this, but I'm afraid it looks like foul play to me." That became a slogan around police headquarters and the bars where we hung out—*it looks like foul play to me*—and I suppose Buster and I were both struck by the fact that our first two experiences together had been on the piquant side, and if we kept at it we might remain entertained.

Buster's full name was Buster Elam Gregory. He came from Grand Prairie, a small town between Dallas and Fort Worth. His father worked in a bank. Buster had played halfback on the high school football team and had belonged to the DeMolay and 4-H clubs. He had raised swine and calves and had been on the Grand Prairie shrub-judging team. He had boxed in the Golden Gloves, winning his first match by a knockout and losing his second the same way. He went to Arlington State College for a year and transferred to TCU, in Fort Worth, to get further from home. Buster married Alma while on leave after photography school and took her to Honolulu with him. She talked about Honolulu incessantly. Alma had a tremendous memory for detail. In the next five or six years I learned Honolulu street names, gasoline prices, distances from one point to another, shop-window decor and much more. In a lengthy, nasal description of sights along a Honolulu thoroughfare, Alma would drop in *you know's* after nearly every phrase and before proper nouns. We introduced Geraldine and Alma to each other while drinking beer and eating pizza at Gordo's about two nights after I'd first met Buster. The two women didn't like each other much, but they had a common dissatisfaction leading to disgust with most of the things Buster and I did. Alma endured her life more stoically than Geraldine. That first night, while Buster was at the jukebox, she told us with a mild frown that Buster forced her "to play wheelbarrow." The worst thing, she said, was when they played wheelbarrow up and down the stairs. Afterward I was never able to get entirely out of mind the picture of Alma being wheeled around the apartment, up and down stairs, while she presented Buster a lecture on a scenic tour of *you know* Honolulu.

Shortly after we met, Buster and Geraldine had a romance that lasted for a week or two before they both, separately, told me about it. But I didn't care. I trusted Buster not to do me harm. Geraldine was in one of her spells when she thought I was getting along too well and needed humbling. One of her methods of moving in to break up a friendship of mine or otherwise cause me trouble was to use her considerable sexual powers in some devious manner. At times she set out to block me off from everybody else. Or she would encourage me to rush out and be free. I took some hard falls at the end of Geraldine's rope. Anyhow, I knew Geraldine didn't want Buster, and he wouldn't want her when he got to know her better.

A year or so after we met we all moved into the same apartment building. It was U-shaped, with grass in the center and the open end facing the street. Buster and Alma, who'd just had twins, lived in the front of the building. Geraldine, Caroline and I were in the rear. The apartments had a living room, dining room and kitchen downstairs, two bedrooms and two baths up. The apartments were owned by SMU, and the rent was one hundred thirty-five a month, unfurnished, utilities included. Buster and I were both making about a hundred dollars a week. Some months, Geraldine would make five hundred doing TV commercials, some months nothing. Alma got a job as reception-ist and secretary at a furniture store for sixty a week. Alma and Geraldine each hired a Negro woman at twenty-five dollars a week to clean the apart-ments, do the laundry and look after the kids from about eight till five or six, five days a week. The maids would baby-sit for fifty cents an hour. That left the four of us relatively loose to roam. Buster was fooling with some girl from the circulation department he persisted in screwing on a bamboo mat on her bedroom floor. For two months his knees and elbows bled. He told Alma he kept falling into a rose bush. Then one evening Alma came to see Geraldine and me, weeping, and said she'd been carrying on with a guy at the furniture store. Buster had found a rubber in the car. I would have been nearly as surprised if my own mother had confessed to an affair with Mickey Mantle. Now that all four of us were known to have moral failings, Buster and I began to devise elaborate schemes for wife-swapping. But Geraldine said it was wicked and corrupt to think of such a thing, and Alma said we ought to get right down on our knees and tell God we were sorry for our dirty minds. Since we knew that Alma had fooled around and Geraldine had even screwed Buster in the car parked by the tennis courts, it didn't make sense that we couldn't get it going among the tight little family we had become. One midnight at Gordo's, Buster and I thought up an idea that seemed so simple and beautiful that it could not fail: when we returned home, I would get into his bed and he would get into mine. In the dark the two women would be relieved of whatever they considered their moral responsibilities. I crept up Buster's stairs and saw Alma lying in the moonlight in her short chiffon nightie. Knowing from her own complaints that she was accustomed to being mounted at any hour, I crawled into bed with her and went straight to work. Somehow, Alma planted a bare foot against my forehead and thrust me onto the floor. "John Lee Wallace, if you don't get out of here I'm going to call your wife!" she said. I went back to my own apartment and sat on the porch to drink a can of Falstaff while Buster explored Geraldine upstairs. I heard Geraldine yell from the window, "You wretched ass, you're worse than a goat!" Buster came down and sat on the porch with me, and we drank and talked until the Venezuelan woman law student across the way stepped out in a nightgown for her morning paper.

One summer Buster and I went to the landlord, a dean, to complain about the condition of the paint and the landscaping. We were evicted. I bought the gray-brick house in North Dallas. Buster and Alma bought a red-brick house, nearly identical to ours, with a GI mortgage, a few miles to the west. Discounting separations, when Geraldine would flee with Caroline to Houston or I would find a room someplace, we lived in that house for three years before Geraldine packed me that final bag. We had a fight, I don't remember how it started, that had lasted too long and gone too far, and there was no way to come back from it. I brought home a Chevrolet convertible and two bottles of champagne as birthday gifts for Geraldine, but she pointed out that she'd already packed the bag and I may as well pick it up and keep moving. Geraldine kept the car, but I took the champagne.

There Will Be Chickens

Dallas Morning News, November 4, 1962

The *Dallas Morning News* was the biggest, richest paper in the South, and everybody read the newspapers back then. There was no cable television or Internet, and sports news on television newscasts was brief. The sports section was the most popular and best-read part of the paper. My column ran six mornings a week on the front page of the sports section beneath my photograph, the closest I ever came to being a celebrity.

I always grin when I picture the scene if the chicken trick described in this column had actually worked. I imagine the dogs going crazy chasing the chickens and dragging Santa's careening sleigh into the horde of marchers, scattering them on the field in the driving snow on national television in our capital.

Some rich guys never lose their inner kid. Clint Murchison Jr., who created and owned the Dallas Cowboys, was that way. Clint was the one who would leave a bag of manure on your porch, or tie a nervous, fainting goat to your doorknob, or pull any number of other pranks—all for a laugh.

Clint Jr. and his friends or associates played Animal Wars. Discover a white turkey in your bathtub? Find out who did it and put a brown bear in his hotel suite. Buy a funeral home and put a slobbering, angry lion in a hearse in place of the departed. Clint Jr. laughed a lot, spent generously, and appeared to enjoy life a great deal. But a crippling disease slowly and painfully killed him and depleted his fortune and power. In the end he watched his personal possessions going away cheap in a yard sale like you would see in a working-class neighborhood—except this sale was at the Murchison mansion, which in its time was just about the classiest house you could find in Dallas. A photograph of Roger Staubach personally signed to Clint went for a couple of dollars. The lesson is clear. Laugh while you can.

Washington—The biggest crowd to ever see a football game in this city will bundle into the new stadium Sunday to watch the Redskins play the Cowboys, and George Preston Marshall is very nervous about it. Somebody keeps telephoning Marshall at his secret number and clucking like a chicken.

To understand the significance of that, and the reason for Marshall's anguish, you must remember what happened here last year. The night before the game, agents of the Cowboys Chicken Club crept into the stadium and sowed the field with chicken feed. The next morning a panel truck loaded with chickens was parked in front of a hotel, and up in a suite a man was walking back and forth saying, "I did not. I did not."

"I'm practicing," he explained.

Marshall, owner of the Redskins, is proud of his halftime shows. The halftime show for that game was to have a Christmas theme, with Santa Claus on a dogsled. Marshall had worked hard at it. The Cowboy Chicken Club had schemed at least as hard to spoil it.

The panel truck was driven into the stadium, and the chickens were hidden in a dugout. They were to be released at the half. The idea was that the chickens would quickly locate the chicken feed, and that Marshall's halftime show would become chaos on CBS television.

But the basic flaw in the plot is that it is impossible to keep 50 chickens quiet.

A few minutes before time for the deed, a man wandered past the dugout and noticed a couple of crates covered with canvas. He stopped and listened. He heard chickens. The noise of a chicken cannot be mistaken for any other noise.

"What's in there?" the man asked the Chicken Club agent who was guarding the crates.

"Ice cream," said the agent.

"Ice cream doesn't sound like that," the man said.

The Chicken Club agent looked at the man and figured him for an usher. "Here, buddy," said the Chicken Club agent, taking out a $100 bill and pushing it into the man's hand. "Get lost and forget what you saw here."

The Cowboy Club agent had badly misfigured. The man was not an usher; he was Dick McCann, who was then general manager of the Redskins.

Police were called. The chickens and the Chicken Club agent, who began yelling "I did not," went to jail. Marshall complained to NFL commissioner Pete Rozelle. The Cowboys officially disclaimed any knowledge of the chickens. But Marshall was angry. He named Bob Thompson of Dallas as one of the plotters, and he made threats. Rozelle told the Cowboys to cut it out. Everybody was saying, "I did not." Everybody except the chickens, which were dressed and given to Redskins halfback Dick James as a reward for scoring four touchdowns against the Cowboys.

This year, as the Cowboy game approached, Marshall began making plans for security. The stadium entrances will be closely watched. Chickens will not be allowed inside.

To protect himself from bother, Marshall had his phone number changed in the middle of the week. He got the most very private of unlisted numbers. It was so secret it took the Chicken Club nearly half a day to learn it.

Now they call him at odd hours and cluck.

"And there will be chickens in the stadium," a Chicken Club agent confided on Saturday. "I'm not saying how many, but there will be chickens. George knows it, and he can't sleep. Not only chickens, we've got some other stuff planned, too. They can't stop us."

The moment nears. Suspense clutches the city. Somewhere at this very hour a man is saying, "I did not."

The Hunts of Dallas

Sports Illustrated, September 7, 1970

When I got word from Lamar Hunt that his father wanted me to come to lunch at his mansion on White Rock Lake, I was both excited and curious. Billionaires were rare birds in those days. H. L. Hunt had rarely been seen, photographed, or interviewed. Why had he chosen me to unload on? I'm still not sure, but he was a self-proclaimed psychic and he knew I would be an enthralled audience as he warbled his favorite songs from *No, No, Nanette* in his parlor.

I was pretty friendly with Lamar by then, had spent a lot of time with him in various football-related places as the American Football League came into being. I was sociable with Lamar's brother Bunker—who had leased about half of Libya for the oil—and knew brother Herbert a little, but I had never dreamed that I would get to meet their oldest brother, Haroldson Lafayette Hunt Jr., who was the fabulously wealthy mirror image of his father. Except that Junior—called "Hassie"—had lost touch with what we call reality. He spent his days sitting in a lawn chair in front of his own replica of Mount Vernon next door to Daddy, watching the boats on the lake and trying not to stare at the sun.

One of the most remarkable parties ever held for the autographing of books took place 10 years ago at the Cokesbury bookstore in Dallas. At most of these affairs the author is a rumpled, lonesome figure, more than a touch embarrassed, sitting at a table beside a placard announcing his noble work, miserably wondering whether anyone further is going to stop by and speak to him now that his mother, cousin, former roommate and publisher's representative have left and the clerks have ceased to pretend they are expecting to cope with a crowd.

For this Cokesbury party, however, several hundred people lined up on the sidewalk along the block among the downtown stores and office buildings. They waited with great patience, as if there were football tickets for sale inside. It was said then that only in Dallas would such a crowd have turned out for this particular event, but no doubt that was a prejudiced judgment.

Lamar Hunt and Bud Shrake on opening night of a Dallas bar called Bud
Shrake West, 1965.

The author of the novel called *Alpaca* would have attracted a crowd in any city in the world where they use money as a reckoning of position.

Inside Cokesbury's, as the line approached the table where the author was smilingly signing his name on flyleafs of paperback copies of *Alpaca,* a sound could be heard. At first you thought it was . . . no, no, it couldn't be . . . yes, yes, it was . . . singing! Those two little girls, plump and sweet-faced, with ribbons in their hair, holding hands behind the author's chair, were singing:

How much is that book in the
window,
The one my daddy wrote?

Although the tune was nipped from a sweetly sentimental song popular at the time, *That Doggie in the Window,* the author would beam and bob his head to the music and turn ghostly blue eyes toward the people who filed past to buy his book for 50 cents. The author liked the way the little girls sang. They were his stepdaughters and the family would sing often in the evenings around the piano in the parlor—and, besides, the author himself had written these lyrics.

Alpaca is set in a romantically imagined country of the same name and is the story of a confusion of the hearts of Juan Achala and an opera star named Mara Hani. But it was not for its literary merit alone that people lined up to purchase the book and to have the author autograph their copies. For one thing, in Dallas they liked the ideas expressed in *Alpaca*—that matters of government could not be discussed on radio or television or at meetings of more than a few hundred, that extra votes should be awarded to citizens who built up fortunes, scored at the top of their class or declined to take money from the government. Perhaps most important to the book's appeal, the author of *Alpaca* was either the richest man in the world or was so close to it that nobody could say for sure.

Sitting there that day in Cokesbury's signing autographs, Haroldson Lafayette Hunt looked like, if not a deity, then at least a ranking angel, and, in any case, altogether unlike a beginning novelist at his first autographing party. At 71 he had the face of a cherub, with fine white hair and smooth, pink-baby skin. Only recently people had begun to hear about Hunt's youngest son, Lamar, then 27, who had thought up the American Football League and had got it moving against obstructions that maybe only a prince of an international financial kingdom would have dared oppose. But the old man had not previously offered a look at himself to crowds in his home town.

Until 1948 few people in Texas or anywhere else knew about H. L. Hunt. That year *Life* magazine published a rather fuzzy photograph of Hunt on a sidewalk in Dallas, looking like an annoyed chiropractor on his way to the clinic, and in the caption proposed he might be the richest man in the world. The day the photo was taken Hunt thought the photographer was a street operator who was going to hand him a ticket offering six prints for a dollar. When Hunt didn't receive a ticket he figured the photographer was shooting the buildings in the background. Lamar saw the magazine and was startled—he hadn't realized his father was near to such a title. As a kid Lamar had thought a regular Saturday morning was to get a dollar from his mother and go stand in line at the Lakewood Theatre to see the *Perils of Nyoka* and later have a hamburger and milk shake. Though the old man didn't mention it to them, that photo caused considerable consternation to Lamar and his two closer brothers, Bunker and Herbert. They'd never paid much attention to money; no more would they be able to ignore it.

So is H. L. Hunt really the richest man in the world? J. Paul Getty, who is often said to be, says he would probably be richer than Hunt if position in wealthy corporations were the only consideration, but most of Getty's corporations are publicly owned, whereas Hunt and his large family own practically every piece of their businesses, and thus Hunt is the richer. And, of course, nobody knows where Howard Hughes ranks. All Hunt will say about it is, "If you know how rich you are, you aren't very rich."

After publication of the photograph in *Life* Hunt slowly emerged as a public person. He became known as a patron of *Facts Forum* and, later, *Life Line*—two means of presenting Hunt's fundamentalist, anti-Communist views to the people—and he began to write letters to the editor and to phone newspaper writers to issue lengthy warnings about the enemies of America. His appearance at Cokesbury's was somewhat of a coming out. By that time Lamar was already in the newspapers daily with his new football league. Not that the father and the youngest son were in any sort of competition for publicity, of course; the old man had done very well without it.

H. L. Hunt had known nothing of Lamar's plans to form the AFL and did not approve once he found out. He thought pro football would be a flop in Texas and if Lamar felt he had to have a team, one could have been obtained a bit cheaper. Hunt's secretary, Juanita Edwards, recalls his reaction when newspapers called to tell him about the AFL: "He'd just discovered it a little while earlier and said he was a typical parent, never knowing what his kids were up to." There was a story that someone told H. L. Hunt that Lamar would lose a million dollars a year and the old man replied that if this were true, Lamar would go broke in 150 years. Both H. L. Hunt and Lamar deny such a thing was ever said. "The story is so good it ought to be true," says Lamar. "But I do know my dad thought I'd gotten a little silly."

H. L. Hunt's grandfather, Waddy Thorpe Hunt, was a Confederate cavalry leader who was called to the door of his farmhouse toward the end of the Civil War and shot to death by Quantrill's Raiders, according to a family history Hunt has had compiled. Hunt's father, after serving in the family cavalry, settled on a farm in Vandalia, Illinois, where H. L. Jr. was born in 1889. Youngest of eight children, little Haroldson could read by age 3 and could beat the entire household at checkers by the time he was 5. He quit school in the fifth grade and later wandered down to Arkansas, where as a young man he made a fortune in cotton and timber and began to deal in oil leases. In 1930 a famous wildcatter, Dad Joiner, hit a discovery well, Daisy Bradford No. 3, in what became the East Texas field. Hunt had a hundred wells of his own by then, and he put all his money into buying leases to the east of the Daisy Bradford wells. That was the wrong side. The pool lay to the west.

"I went into the oil business without knowing what I was doing, but pretty soon I recognized the structure of that East Texas field, and the big companies didn't," Hunt recalled recently. As he spoke, the old man was sitting in a wicker rocker on the front porch of his mansion in Dallas on a hot Sunday afternoon, wearing a gray plaid suit and a clip-on bow tie. Out before him the lawn sloped down to White Rock Lake, where sails of a regatta boomed across the water. Like Trimalchio, Hunt has a favorite dog, a little poodle named Muffin, which tiptoed up and down the porch giving out tiny yaps. "This was around Thanksgiving in 1930, not long after the stock-market crash, and there was no money available. But a clothing-store owner in Arkansas just loved to lend me money. I got $30,000 from him, $45,000 from some banks, and I bought out Dad Joiner as well as all the land I could get west of Daisy Bradford. I gave Joiner $1.26 million in future production payments, first time anybody'd ever thought up a plan like that." Hunt used to be a shrewd and heavy gambler and a noted poker player, and for years it has been said around Dallas that he played poker for three days with Joiner in a locked hotel room before walking out with the leases. "Nonsense!" said Hunt.

"I quit playing poker in 1921. Only played twice since. Never played any cards with Joiner. People claim I kept him in a room by duress, but he had a suite in the Baker Hotel and so did I. He could come and go as he pleased." The East Texas field, the largest in the world until the Middle East discoveries, was the springboard to Hunt's extraordinary fortune.

Chuckling at the mechanical-doll prancing of Muffin, the old man heaved himself out of his wicker rocker to lead a visitor on a tour of the grounds of his 10-acre estate, Mount Vernon, an outsize replica of George Washington's home. Always alert for a bargain, Hunt bought the house for $69,000 in 1937 from an engineer who could no longer afford it. The whole place would fit in the flower garden of some of the estates of the wealthy on Long Island, but it must be remembered that Hunt is within sight of downtown Dallas and that he does own a few million acres elsewhere.

Behind the house, Hunt pointed to the seven deer he keeps in a wire pen and then, moving slowly, he gestured toward the path that leads between the trees to the red-brick home next door where his oldest son, Haroldson Lafayette Hunt III, now lives. Hassie, as the old man calls him, is 52 and looks eerily like his father. At the age of 3 he accompanied the old man into the oil fields and by the time he was 20 he was a legend in the oil business. It was said that Hassie had a divining rod inside his head, that he could drive down a country road and smell oil where no one had ever dreamed of looking. One Hunt employee recalls overhearing the old man angrily lecturing to his assembled geophysicists one afternoon, "My son Hassie can find more oil with a road map than you so-called educated fellows can find with millions of dollars worth of equipment!"

"Hassie was the smartest thing ever to hit the oil business," Hunt said. "When he was 19 he emancipated himself from me and took a stake of $181 and headed for Mississippi. He made a lot of money for himself, an awful lot. Hassie just knew things that there's no way anybody could know. I've got extrasensory perception myself, but Hassie had it stronger than anybody. He was such a brilliant boy that he scared people." Hunt looked toward Hassie's house and shook his head. "I made a terrible mistake with Hassie. He was a rugged boy and wanted to play football. But I wouldn't let him. Football players get kidney damage, and I didn't want Hassie hurt. As a boy I was a baseball fan, could recite hundreds of batting and pitching averages, knew 'em all. Hassie could have played baseball, but he didn't care for that. He went off to Culver Military Academy, where the discipline was too strict for a sensitive boy like him, and one day I found him boxing with Culver's best pugilist and giving that fellow all he could handle. Hassie needed a lot of action."

Hassie entered the Army in 1943, during a period when the Hunts were producing more oil than Germany and Japan combined. While going through officers' training at Fort Knox he had what the family calls "a nervous break-down." Since that time he has been under almost constant medical care. Some say that Hassie is, ironically, still the richest of the Hunt sons. Leading his visitor into the dining room for lunch, the old man kept talking about Hassie. "With my other boys," he said, "I never was so strict as with Hassie. They could do what they wanted."

On Hunt's dining table were two telephones, a portable radio and a box of Kleenex. He began his meal by drinking a glass of carrot juice, a glass of grape juice and a glass of papaya-cranberry juice. Then he nibbled from a plate of mixed nuts and apricot seeds. "I intend to live to be 140, like the people in a certain tribe in the Himalayas, and one of their secrets is if you eat enough nuts you'll never get cancer," he said. Now 81, Hunt is unwrin-kled as a peach—which he attributes in part to the daily use of a body lotion cosmetic sold by one of his firms, but he is somewhat concerned that he is shrinking from his former six-foot height. "My grandmother lived to be 97 and kept getting smaller. When she died she was no higher than this table," he said. The asparagus soup was set out—to be followed by roast beef, green beans, brown bread milled from uncracked wheat grown only in Deaf Smith County, Texas ("Never had a dentist in Deaf Smith County until an old den-tist retired and moved there"), fruit salad, apricot cake and carrot cake.

"In 1925 I had $600,000 cash and decided to go to the Florida land boom," he said. His first wife, Lyda Bunker Hunt, who died in 1955, went with him on the trip and they detoured for their first visit to New York City. While there the Hunts saw No, No, Nanette and Rose Marie on Broadway. Inspired by the works of Youmans and Friml, Hunt wrote an operetta in Florida between land deals. "It's never been published," he said. "Never had the time. But I've published nine books of my own in the last few years, and now I think I'll have my light opera produced. It's a sentimental thing, I admit, but it's right pleasant. Listen." And in a small, quavery old voice he began to sing the ma-jor ballad of the piece: Wherever Dreams Come True I'll Be with You:

Up to the time I met you,
Life was as drab as can be . . .

Something was missing for me . . .
You are my love now forever,
If only in sweet reverie . . .

Growing up at the Dallas Mount Vernon was, Lamar remembers, a fairly relaxed and uneventful experience, at least until the world discovered H. L. Hunt. When Lamar entered Southern Methodist University in Dallas it was no longer a secret that he might have the richest father in the world. Some of his football teammates called him Poor Boy, an unimaginative nickname that Lamar endured with good humor. In one way the nickname was appropriate. Lamar seldom has any cash in his pocket.

Not long after graduating from SMU, where his athletic labors had lifted him to the position of third-string end, Lamar tried to buy the Chicago Cardinals, a pro football team, at a time when pro football was as foreign to Texas as downhill ski racing. Curiously, Clint Murchison Jr., son of probably the second-richest man in Dallas, tried to buy the same team at about the same time.

Lamar and Clint did not know each other, had never even met, but within a few years each had a pro football team in Dallas—the Cowboys of the NFL for Clint and the Texans of the new American Football League for Lamar. For three seasons Dallas saw a sort of civil war, and a lot of businessmen didn't know which way to jump. The Murchisons were a more social family and had a more diverse empire. But it was very dangerous to underestimate the Hunts. One result was that a great many Dallas business firms declared themselves neutral and deprived themselves of football altogether, refusing to buy blocks of tickets to the games of either team.

In the three seasons that Lamar's Texans competed with the NFL Cowboys for the Dallas audience, attendance at the Cotton Bowl was announced as "estimated" rather than by turnstile count. The announced attendance had very little to do with the number of people in the stands. Lamar gave away tickets with groceries and inside bags of potato chips. He sponsored a Friend of the Barber Day, which allowed any barber in a white jacket to enter the Cotton Bowl free, and it wound up with anybody in a white shirt being admitted. Once Lamar hired a number of girls and put them into a fleet of foreign cars to cruise the city selling tickets. One of these girls was a pretty schoolteacher, Norma Knobel, who later became Lamar's second wife. Lamar says now that in 1962, his team's last year in Dallas before moving to Kansas

City, the genuine attendance average was 10,000 per game. "The Cowboys drew only 9,800," he says, "but we had a championship team and they were losing, so beating them was nothing to be proud of."

Lamar is a somewhat unprepossessing man, quite modest, even naive. Like his father, he does not drink liquor or coffee and has never smoked (H. L. Hunt quit smoking cigars when he figured out that he had used up $300,000 worth of his time tearing off the wrappers). Though he has now moved into an elegant section of Dallas and lives in a large home that resembles his father's version of Mount Vernon, Lamar still dresses like a preacher and cannot bring himself to use the power of the Hunt name in a public place. He has been seen at league meetings with holes in his shoes and he has frequently borrowed small sums from acquaintances. His wife has tried to modify his manner of dress. "I stay after him, but he never changes," she says. However, he did approve of flaming red as the color for the official blazers of his football team. In a Dallas nightclub one evening two men who identified themselves as a famous acrobatic team called The Flying Punzars borrowed the red blazers off the backs of Lamar and Jack Steadman. The Flying Punzars went into the spotlight, requested a fanfare and a drum roll and then did an involved trick that landed one of them in the drums and the other dazed and flattened on the floor. "These red jackets are just the thing we need to attract attention," Lamar said.

Lamar and Clint Murchison Jr. have offices in the same building and occasionally encounter each other in the elevator, although they rarely meet socially. An exception was in 1960 when, on Clint's birthday, a large package was carried into a party and Murchison was asked to unwrap his present. Out of the box leaped Lamar. "They really howled," he says.

Lamar decided to move his football team to Kansas City in 1963 for what he admits were in the beginning purely financial reasons. "Clint was determined to stay in Dallas and originally so were we. But we both couldn't survive there, and an economic decision had to be made. Now a lot of people in Dallas are saying the wrong team left town, but it's worked out great for both teams." The Kansas City Chiefs have sold 70,000 season tickets for their new stadium. "It's phenomenal," Lamar says. "Not long ago a lady saw the big Super Bowl world championship ring I was wearing and said, 'Oh, I didn't realize football was lucrative.' Well, it certainly can be."

Lamar considers that he spends his working time 80% in the "entertainment business" and the rest in oil and real-estate ventures. At one point he was the principal backer of a professional bowling league. He is part owner of the Chicago Bulls basketball team. With his nephew, Al Hill Jr., he owns a professional enterprise called World Championship Tennis, which now has such stars as Rod Laver, Pancho Gonzales, Don Newcombe and Tony Roche under contract. He co-owns a minor league baseball as well as the Dallas Tornado, a team in the North American Soccer League. Despite mountains of evidence to the contrary, Lamar believes soccer will flourish in the United States within 10 years.

All these athletic interests have given Lamar probably the most varied assortment of investments in professional sport. "I guess I'm the biggest sports investor in terms of projects but not in terms of dollars," he says. "I always go in on the ground floor. The Chiefs, for example, cost me $25,000 for the franchise. Then I had to pay the losses for a few years. But what are the Chiefs worth now? Leonard Tose paid $16 million for the Philadelphia Eagles, and that's far more money than I've put into all my sports endeavors combined."

"Lamar is something like me," says H. L. Hunt. "He's stubborn and knows how to fight." The old man, who is liable to fly off alone tourist class with a suitcase bound up by leather straps to visit a sheik and try to beat a 20-man delegation from another country out of an oil concession, is an authority on determination. Once he crashed a party given by a foreign potentate at the Plaza Hotel in Manhattan for Russian Premier Khrushchev ("the old rascal grinned and shook my hand on his way out"), and there are many tales of financial enemies overcome, of deals made and games won. Although he insists he had no part in Lamar's effort to put the AFL across, H. L. Hunt clearly enjoys watching it. "Lamar's turning out to be a pretty good trader," the old man says.

Visit to Big Earl's

From *Strange Peaches* (1972)

This comes about as close to being a verbatim transcript of my lunch visit
with H. L. Hunt as I could write and still call it fiction.

What Big Earl says about taking Little Earl with him into the oil fields
as a child is what the old man told me about his oldest son, Hassie. He said
Hassie had enormous psychic powers and could find more oil by looking at
a Texaco road map than geophysicists could find with million-dollar equipment. Bunker Hunt—who has been compared, somewhat unfairly, to the
character of Little Earl in *Strange Peaches*—told me Hassie was the richest
of the Hunt brothers. "He pokes his finger at a spot on the map, and we find
oil there."

The green liquid Big Earl rubs on his skin is made of aloe vera, which is
very popular now but was largely unknown in this country until H. L. Hunt
rediscovered the ancient plant by reading about it in the Bible. Hunt set
his agronomists to growing the plant and made it a favorite among health
enthusiasts.

I drove to Big Earl's house in Jingo's bronze Cadillac convertible with JINGO
on the driver's door in gold letters an inch high. Big Earl lived in an unlikely
location for one of the world's richest men. Rounding a curve in the midst
of a worn-out neighborhood of small red-brick and white-frame houses with
bicycles and junked red wagons lying among cedar trees in front, and two or
three old cars parked in nearly every driveway, you suddenly came upon a
big Tudor house on a hill surrounded by a high cyclone fence. Timbers crisscrossed through cream plaster and disappeared into brick walls. Above the
bay windows and high gables, dozens of chimney pots of various sizes rose up
like organ pipes. The flag of the United States and the Lone Star flag of Texas
flew from twin poles in the yard, beside a brass cannon aiming out across the
neighborhood. I stopped at the gate. From a speaker, a quavery voice said:
"Who are you and what do you want?"

"John Lee Wallace. I want to see Big Earl."

"What for?"

"I don't know. He sent for me."

The wire gate unlatched itself and swung open. I drove slowly up the long semicircle of gravel, being careful not to collide with the deer, goats, peacocks and squirrels that roamed beneath oaks on acres of grass. An old Hudson, an old Buick and a shiny new black Chevrolet stood beside the house in the driveway and on the grass. As I got out of the car, Mr. Clwyd, Big Earl's secretary, came down from a side porch. He was tall and gray and wore a black suit and black tie. "We're so pleased you could come," said Mr. Clwyd.

"I admit your call was a surprise," I said.

"He's waiting for you on the veranda, other side of the house," said Mr. Clwyd, glancing inside Jingo's car to be sure I had come alone.

I walked across in front of the house past the tall, scroll-carved double doors of the main entrance. On the west side of the house, a long veranda had been tucked in. The old man was sitting in a rocking chair looking out at his animals and at the rooftops among the trees below his hill. A tiny white poodle with a blue and pink collar started yapping. Big Earl paid no attention to the poodle or to me. He picked up a pair of binoculars and peered in the direction of the front gate. I could see a car down there. Then he lifted a hand mike from beside his chair and said, "Who are you and what do you want?"

"Who said that?" said a voice from a speaker in the wall.

"Who are you and what do you want?" Big Earl repeated.

"I come to see Big Earl."

"For what purpose?"

"It's about a fund for sending missionaries to Red China."

"Big Earl is out of the country," Big Earl said.

"I seen him this morning."

"He left since then. Go away."

"This is something Big Earl would like to help on," the voice said.

Big Earl turned a switch on the microphone and said, "Mr. Clood, there's a man down at the gate bothering me." Big Earl put down the microphone and smiled gently.

"Hush, little Ginger Pops, this nice fellow won't hurt us," he said to the yapping poodle.

"Is that what you call him—Mr. Clood?" I said.

"That's his name," said Big Earl.

"Francis Franklin calls him Mr. Clyde."

"Now then, Francis Franklin is an excellent person, but he doesn't know everything in the world, does he?" said Big Earl. He smiled again, most gently, almost like a dear contented baby. His skin was pink and smooth as a baby's, and his hair was silvery white and so fine that it moved in a breeze I could scarcely feel. I found myself thinking that he looked like God.

"There's a wonderful view from up here. I watch the sunsets. All the colors laid out there along the roofs. It gives me the greatest pleasure in the world. Ginger Pops and I watch the sunsets together. Young man, why aren't you sitting?" He saw the reason and picked up the mike. "Mr. Clood, can't I have a chair out here for my guest?

"Look at this," Big Earl said. He pointed to a large leather-bound book on the floor beside his chair. I lifted the book and saw written in gold *The Family Chronicle*. "It's a history of my family. There are nine volumes. I had a fellow do the research for me and write it up. This volume deals with the Spanish-American War. My youngest brother fought in the Philippines, you know. I'm sure you'll want to read these volumes."

A maid with hairy legs dragged a rocking chair onto the porch, and I sat with the book in my lap. Big Earl began rocking with his eyes shut. I opened the book and saw an old photograph of Big Earl's youngest brother in a campaign hat. The first sentence started: "In the glorious tradition passed down from their ancestral kings . . ."

"I was a very good poker player when I was a young man. You'll want to know about that," said Big Earl. "There were a lot of good gamblers in those days. We went all over East Texas and Arkansas and Louisiana playing poker and gambling with leases. I made a million dollars before I was twenty-five, was dead broke at twenty-six, a millionaire again at thirty and before I was thirty-two I had holes in my shoes and not a crumb of bread to eat. No matter what you might think, there is no security in this world. Everything can be gone in a wink. If they can't rob your money, they'll steal your life. I used to be afraid of them, but not any more. I went to a wonderful doctor in St. Louis, Missouri. He taught me how to crawl. Do you know how?"

"I suppose so," I said.

"You think you do, but I doubt if you really do," Big Earl smiled.

He deposited the poodle on the floor, where it began to prance in circles, yapping, like a toy. Then Big Earl himself slid forward out of his rocking chair, went to his knees on the porch and slowly crumpled onto his face. Thinking he'd had a heart attack, I jumped up.

"Sit down, sit down," he said. "Look here, now, I'm showing you how to crawl."

His face flat on the floor, his arms stretched out, Big Earl began to wriggle forward, with the poodle yapping at his ears.

"Most people think crawling is on your hands and knees. That's creeping! You must learn to crawl before you learn to creep. If you don't learn to crawl, you can never be healthy as God intended. Right from babyhood, your system will be all out of sequence."

Big Earl dragged himself to the wall and lay gasping. At last he rose to one knee, grabbed the door handle and trembling with a desperate effort pulled himself upright. He dusted his palms, straightened his bow tie and inspected the buttons on his double-breasted suit.

"How tall do you think I am?" he said.

"About five feet ten," I said.

His small mouth screwed up in displeasure, and his small blue eyes peeped suspiciously at me.

"I used to be six feet one, but now I'm only five-nine," he said. "Before she died at ninety-six, my grandmother had gotten so short she could walk under the dinner table." He placed one hand against the wall to prop himself up and looked down at a couple of deer that had come to the porch. "What do you think of chemistry? Do you think it can affect the mind?"

"I certainly do," I said.

This was the correct answer. Big Earl grinned. "I have a wonderful chemical that a doctor in Little Rock, Arkansas, gave me," he said. "When I used to be nervous and uneasy, I went to this man and he told me chemistry could bring marvelous cures. Have you ever heard of chlorpromazine?"

"How much of it do you take?" I said.

"Not so much now. But I used to take fifteen hundred milligrams a day. It made me feel pleasant."

"Good Lord! What did you do after you took it?" I asked.

"Oh, I sat in the yard with my animals, and sometimes the nurse would come and move my chair and remind me not to stare at the sun. Do you think psychiatrists are crazy?"

"I'd hate to say that. There's a lot of them I don't know."

"I think they're full of shit!" Big Earl said. He smiled and patted his lips. "I don't use that word ordinarily. But psychiatrists are the crazy people. They should be locked up and made to prove they can cure themselves before they are allowed to work on others. Ho Chi Minh says when the jail doors are opened, the real dragon will fly out. Have you heard of Ho Chi Minh? A little bit? Well, I prefer him to that Madame Nhu, to tell the truth. I don't like any of them in fact. Madame Nhu wants to come see me. When she speaks here in Texas next month. I won't let her in. She says they're going to kill her husband and her brother. Shoot them and beat them and stab them! Good riddance! Let the yellow people worry about the yellow people. I don't fear them half so much as I fear the worms in our own foundations. There's a Communist empire building up ninety miles from our shores. Kennedy thinks he can fool us by doing things the wrong way around. Did you know President Kennedy is coming to Dallas?"

"I read it in the paper," I said.

"Yes, Caesar is coming to the provinces to see how us Gauls govern ourselves," said Big Earl. "Caesar should stay in Rome where he belongs! Let's have our lunch. Don't forget to bring the book with you."

I picked up *The Family Chronicle* and followed Big Earl and Ginger Pops into a large parlor with a beamed ceiling. The furniture was fat with stuffing and looked comfortable, and there were colored photographs in gold or silver frames on the mantel and on several small tables. I saw a number of photos of Little Earl and his wife and family. Above the mantel was a portrait of a handsome woman with a regal pioneer strength in her face.

"My wife has been dead for seventeen years," Big Earl said, noticing me looking at the portrait. "It took me six years to pay off her inheritance tax."

"Why don't you have a portrait of yourself in here?" I said.

"I don't have so much vanity that I would wish to look at a portrait of myself when I can look at my loved ones instead," he said.

Scooping Ginger Pops into his arms, Big Earl tottered across a foyer and into a dining room where yellow sunlight shone on a long table that had been set for two. Big Earl took a chair at the end of the table. Beside his plate were a portable radio, a microphone, two telephones, a notebook and a fountain pen. Platters of nuts, radishes, celery, butter and brown bread had been placed around three pitchers containing different colored liquids.

Big Earl started munching nuts by the handful. There were half a dozen kinds. He offered me a silver dish of large rusty nuts I had never seen before.

"These are the hearts of apricot seeds," he said. "It is well known, even though the medical bureaucracy denies it, that apricot seeds cure and prevent cancer. Certain tribes who eat apricot seeds as a staple never had a case of cancer in their history. Years ago I had cancer, but now I am cured. I like you, young man. You pay attention to me. Eat apricot seeds, so you won't have to die so soon."

Big Earl flicked on the radio. The squawk of music brought the hairy-legged maid out of a swinging door. He turned off the radio, and she left, to reappear again with bowls of steaming soup. Meanwhile, Big Earl had poured each of us three different glasses of liquid.

"Fruit juices. I mix them myself. Haven't settled on the true elixir of perpetual health yet," he said, "but grapes are quite important. Whoever said wine is the water of life was on the right track. Do you believe in ESP?"

"Yes," I said.

"Do you have it?"

"I think with me it comes and goes."

"I have it more than anyone I have ever known. I know things there is no way I could know. I know where pools of oil are hiding under the ground. I know what people will do before they even think of doing it. I know everything that's going through your mind, and I'm impressed with you. I know that when I tell you there is a very real possibility that unscrupulous Communists have invaded John F. Kennedy's brain with radio waves and are influencing his decisions even though they don't yet control his mind, you will accept this as a legitimate possibility. Eat that soup. It's made out of uncracked wheat, like the bread. It's grown for me in Oklahoma in a little town that's never had a dentist or a cavity."

The yellow telephone rang. Big Earl held the earpiece to his ear for a full two minutes while I ate the soup. It tasted sort of like hot chicken feed, but not bad. Each glass of fruit juice tasted like a different punch, one with an orange flavor, one grape and one that could have been papaya. The hairy-legged maid took away the soup bowls—Big Earl's had hardly been touched—and laid out a platter of dry brown roast beef. Big Earl put down the phone.

"It wasn't for me," he said.

"Can you communicate with ESP?" I asked.

"With certain people I can. There is a lady whose name I won't mention. I talk back and forth with her from all over the world. Sometimes I see the future. I get flashes of it very clearly."

He snatched up the microphone and yelled: "Mr. Clood!"

Mr. Clwyd immediately stuck his head in through the swinging door. "Did you get rid of that fellow?" said Big Earl.

"Yes sir," Mr. Clwyd said.

"He's still in the neighborhood someplace. Keep a watch for him," said Big Earl.

Without expression, Mr. Clwyd vanished. Big Earl turned to me. He was eating slices of roast beef like potato chips.

"I want to thank you for living the way you do," he said.

"The way I do?"

"Yes, young man, you are an embodiment of what all young Americans should be. I only wish Little Earl was a bit more like you. Strong as a good Christian soldier should be strong! Clean of mouth and mind. Fearless. It's a pleasure for me, an honor, to have you at my table."

Letter: August 7, 1969, on Dallas

This letter is an answer to Larry L. King's request to tell what living in Dallas was like at the time of the JFK assassination. Larry was intending to write about the city for *Harper's* magazine. His story never appeared, but by the time of this letter I had begun thinking about writing a novel set in Dallas in 1963. Two years later I went to London and wrote *Strange Peaches.*

Dear Dr. King:

I don't really know how I feel about Dallas. I lived there for six years and six months, got married and divorced there, bought two houses and had eight different apartments that I can recall offhand, and I never could make up my mind how I felt about it. Even when the Prez was shot and killed there and most of my friends were blaming the city for it, I thought their reaction had more emotion than reason. I had watched the Kennedy motorcade come down Lemmon Ave near the bar we used to hang out in—and had marveled at how he looked like a movie star and how I simply stepped up to the curb and looked at his smiling face a few feet away and could have knocked out his white teeth with a golf club had I the notion to—and was driving to the SMU Drug to meet Jap [Gary Cartwright] when I heard on the radio what happened. My first inclination was to drive to Turtle Creek, where [General Edwin] Walker lives, and beat the shit out of the first person I could find. That is how sure I was a Dallas fascist had killed the Prez, and so I guess that is one indication of how I felt about the city on one level at least. On Sunday the NFL played as usual and I went to Cleveland and Chuck Howley, Dallas linebacker, mailed a package from the Post Office and a postal clerk in Cleveland told him: "Don't count on this package getting there. When people see the Dallas address, they're liable to rip it up." But none of that makes sense. Dallas cops are notoriously mean, but Highland Park and University Park cops are notedly nice (to residents of those two incorporated towns inside city limits, tho woe to intruding spades, longhairs, or poor folks). But what's different? That's America.

Oligarchy likes to keep things quiet, smooth, gray, lifeless. It is not uncommon to read about 10 or 20 year sentences for having in your possession a cigaret rolled of weeds. Protests are not allowed. I remember when I was living near SMU there was a civil rights protest—a sit-in at the counter—at the SMU Drug (Mustang Pharmacy I think it was called, on the drag) where a few blacks and some white kids demanded equal service. Owner closed the drug store and called for exterminators who came out and sprayed inside the store with noxious gases until kids had to be dragged out sick. That was about 1959–1960, and the newspapers wouldn't touch the story. Typical Dallas explanation: don't want to cause no more trouble by giving them bad guys publicity. Drugstore owner complained about damaged goods. . . .

One more thought: Dallas is what Nixon would like all of America to be . . .

Further thought or two on Dallas . . .

Dallas has a lot of crackpots and unfortunately that number includes many of the town's more substantial citizens. Even LBJ, who cannot be accused of having very liberal or humanitarian impulses, was jostled there and his wife spat upon, Adlai Stevenson was insulted and threatened, red-white-and-blue clad folks waited at the Trade Mart to bait John Kennedy on the fatal day. But the hope and love in the faces of the crowds who watched the motorcade was genuine, and who knows what decency (and even goodness) is untapped in the silent people who are buried alive there. . . .

The Kennedy Motorcade

From *Strange Peaches* (1972)

I did have the terrible thought as the motorcade went past that I could lean out and hit the president if I wished him harm. His eyes caught mine at that instant. Some communication passed between us. I tried to explain it in the novel but wound up writing what I thought JFK was saying to John Lee Wallace, not exactly what the message was to me. I believe now that what the president was saying to me—in those few minutes before his brains were blown out—was that life had never been sweeter than it was at that moment.

I had trouble starting the Morris Minor and feared I might miss the motor-cade, but the engine finally caught and the radio came on. Because of the cleared weather that caused me to stop and roll up my sleeves, the bubble-top had been removed from the President's black Lincoln, the radio said. Plenty of Dallas cops had been at the airport, where the President had touched hands with admirers, and hundreds more were spotted along the route—a map of which had been printed in the newspapers—where three hundred thousand people were waiting to see the Kennedys ride past in the open car with Governor Connally and his wife, and Lyndon Johnson riding a few cars behind. I drove fast and parked the Morris Minor by the Texas & Pacific Railroad tracks on Pacific Street in a brown-brick warren of warehouses. As I stepped over railroad tracks and around boxcars, I saw a few people sitting on loading platforms eating sandwiches out of paper bags, but most of the workers had gone over a couple of blocks to Dealey Plaza to watch the President. The sidewalks at Elm and Houston beside the School Book Depository Building were crowded, and I didn't immediately see an opening in the crowd across Elm in Dealey Plaza, so I trotted on along Houston to Main Street, going past the Criminal Courts Building, looking for a view for the Bolex. At the corner where the cars were to turn north off Main onto Houston, I squeezed among people at the curb as I heard cheering and the motorcycles coming amid a roar that boomed toward me along Main like the roar of a football crowd. People flinched back from me, but it didn't matter. I leaned out and saw the motorcade approaching very close, first the motorcycles and then a pilot car of cops, then six more motorcycles and the white lead car with the Sheriff and the Police Chief and the Secret Service boss, and finally four or five lengths back came the black Lincoln. Through the viewfinder I saw Connally's wavy blue-silver hair. Mrs. Connally was in the other jump seat, hidden from me. Now I found John F. Kennedy. He was on the side of the car nearest the curb, his eyes crinkled and puffy underneath, an arm on the rim of the open car, shirt cuff showing, wearing a dotted necktie, looking at the people along the curb as they applauded and called out to him. Kennedy was smiling a very good smile with very white teeth, and his wife was smiling almost the same way but without as much heart in it. His hair looked thick and healthy, and his face was tanned, and his eyes were clear and seemed to be enjoying what they saw. I was struck by how much like a movie star he looked, what an air of ultimate celebrity there was about him, everything put together exactly right and a good heart showing from that smile and the eyes, with his wife sitting there beside him trying to smile in the same manner. She had the look of celebrity, too, but more distant from the people and from life, a movie star's smile that was like a fence between her and the crowd; where her smile said *keep away I'm doing all right,* his said *we've got it going and I love it all.* They both looked as if they had been made up for the cameras, whites of the eyes sparkling, teeth polished, skin tinted copper, grander than the rest of us, but his face shone with intelligence and humor that broke through the celebrity mask without apology for the mask itself.

As the car pulled abreast, I didn't want to see him through the viewfinder, but the movie might require this vision. I lifted the camera and the President's gray eyes looked directly at me leaning out from the curb, took me all in with an instant's deep gaze, and looked squarely into my lens, and his lips moved a bit, the smile broadening, and he raised a finger and pointed at me, and I took my eye away from the viewfinder and looked straight into his eyes, and a communication flashed from him to me that said *there you are you freak what a time you must have among these people I like you for it don't give up.* At the same second he was sending me that message I was receiving it and thinking as well, with surprise and embarrassment that I would have such a thought, that if I'd wanted to hurt the man, I was so close I could crack his skull with a five-iron or couldn't conceivably miss with a pistol. But I could tell this perverted thought never reached him. He had trained himself to tune out small paranoias. I smiled at him as he looked at me, and his right eye squinted very slightly as if it occurred to him that he had seen me before but could not recall where. Then his eyes left me and held their place in the crowd that was moving past the car, and he said something to his wife, and she looked back, smiling with the flowers in her arms, but our eyes never met, and then the black limousine was going on down the road and I was looking at the back of the President's head.

I didn't wait to film Lyndon Johnson or any of the others. To me they were just politicians, not great men, just part of the crowd the same as me, and I still didn't care for all this big-ass politics, but I knew a great man when I saw one. Reflecting on the sensation of having connected in a mental relay with the President, and repeating to myself *there you are you freak,* I ran and caught up with the car as it turned onto Houston Street. I flipped on the long lens and got the Lincoln in my magnified sight again as the motorcade turned once more onto Elm at the red-brick Depository Building and started down toward the triple underpass and the railroad trestle.

POP

I knew it was a rifle shot. The sound is so common as to be quite distinctive. Later, many said they thought it was a firecracker, or the popping of a paper bag, or a backfire, but I knew at once that it was a rifle shot and I heard myself moan as I looked through the viewfinder and saw Kennedy raise his hands toward his throat and Connally starting to turn back toward him.

Pigeons flew up from the Depository Building. The car kept moving slowly. I was expecting the car to leap ahead and disappear through the underpass, but it moved so very slowly.

POP

The car had passed an oak tree, and now people were screaming and had begun running around in Dealey Plaza, and the pigeons were circling in the sky, and cops in helmets on motorcycles were looking back and forth, wondering where the shots were coming from. Through the viewfinder I saw Connally sliding down, and Kennedy leaning to the left toward his wife, and the black Lincoln almost seemed to be stopping, edging down from slow motion into stopframe.

"Go on!" I cried. "Goddamn you, go on before they kill him!"

Someone shouted into my ear. I kept my finger on the button. I was waiting for another shot. The first two shots echoed through the Plaza, bounced off the county jail and the Depository, caroming around the Plaza, and people were running, falling, dodging, throwing themselves onto the ground as in war movies. On the grassy knoll I saw figures scattering, and Kennedy continued to lean in the creeping Lincoln.

POP

Pieces of skull sailed out of Kennedy's head. A red spray flew out, as if a stone had been thrown into a pot of tomato soup.

"No! They've got him now!" I yelled.

At last the car moved. As the President's wife began scrambling out the back of the car, out of this blood and madness, at last the car moved forward, carrying its passengers too late down into the underpass.

I knew he was dead.

No Day for Games

Dallas Morning News, November 25, 1963

I can't imagine why in this column I mentioned people gathering in Cleveland Browns owner Art Modell's office to watch television before the game—but I didn't mention that was where I saw Jack Ruby murder Lee Harvey Oswald. It must have been cut out of my column by an editorial decision made at a higher pay grade than mine.

I do recall that I rushed out of Modell's office and saw Gary Cartwright walking across the stadium parking lot.

"Hey, guess who just shot Oswald?" I shouted.

"Jack Ruby," he yelled back.

The thing was, he was just guessing.

Cleveland, Ohio—This was a game that nobody was interested in playing, coaching, watching or writing about. National Football League Commissioner Pete Rozelle, using as an excuse the irrelevant fact that the late President Kennedy was a football fan and a sportsman, refused to cancel or postpone the Sunday schedule.

As a result, the Cowboys and the Browns ran through their routines on a bright, cold afternoon while people sat in Municipal Stadium with portable radios mashed against their ears.

To keep the Cowboys from being booed by those in the crowd who might resent the city as well as the deed, the usual introductions were not held. Instead there was a moment of prayer for the slain President, the National Anthem was played while people stood and looked at the big flag on the scoreboard against the dull water of Lake Erie, and the colors were trooped.

An extra company of reserve police had been called out to guard against incidents. There were no incidents of importance although there was of course a lot of overheard conversation about Dallas. When you were identified as being from Dallas you were looked at with curiosity and were always asked the same question, "Where were you Friday?" As if you should have prevented it, which is how you already felt about it.

While the Cowboys were dressing for the game, the word went through the locker room that Lee Harvey Oswald had been shot in Dallas. The players talked about it quietly and Tom Landry walked around the room with his head down, as if his thoughts were elsewhere.

"I'm still not sure if we're doing the right thing by playing this game," said general manager Tex Schramm.

One Cleveland columnist wrote, "I have no heart for this game." Neither, really, did anyone else.

The CBS television network had wisely and respectfully called off television NFL games, both out of deference to the late President and to cover the biggest story in years.

The American Football League had delayed its Sunday schedule. Most college games were wiped out or postponed Saturday. Even the radio broadcast Sunday back to Dallas was disrupted by the shooting of Oswald.

"This seems useless," one player said. "Who cares?"

Members of the visiting party—except naturally the players and coaches —gathered in the Browns' executive offices inside the stadium to watch television until game time.

Browns owner Art Modell was unenthusiastic about the prospect of playing on such a day.

Advance ticket sales had dropped off quickly on Friday. But this was a game the Browns absolutely had to win to have a chance in the Eastern Division, and 55,096 people wandered into the huge closed horseshoe of Municipal Stadium, which seats 83,000. It was, at least, a commercial success.

Sunday's game seemed silly and frivolous and was very poorly played, and it was no indication one way or the other of the ability of the two teams. Football players are aware of events, too. Playing a game while the nation is mourning did not seem to them of the highest importance, either.

PART 2

From New York to Chihuahua

Letter: February 12, 1966, to NFL Commissioner Pete Rozelle

I must have had a few cocktails before I wrote this letter, which I thought was very funny at the time. I had a good relationship with Pete Rozelle, as did most sportswriters. Pete had a great sense of humor and was good company on a fishing boat or at the bar at Toots Shor's. He acted as if he thought this Santa Fe letter was as funny as I did, which proved his political skills.

I represented the Houston Oilers at the first player draft after the NFL and AFL merged. It was a very long day in a hotel ballroom in New York, but the league ran an open bar for participants. With the 25th pick that year the Oilers (me) chose my boss, *Sports Illustrated* editor André Laguerre. Once again it seemed funny to me at the time. Pete Rozelle held up the selection for further study. Don Klosterman was general manager of Bud Adams's Oilers and had asked me to represent him at the draft. What I didn't realize was that Klosterman had put me on the speaker and all my opinions as I got drunker during the day were broadcast to the whole Oilers office in Houston.

Mr. Pete Rozelle
Commissioner
National Football League

Feb 12, 1966

Dear Sir:

Please accept this as my formal application for a National Football League franchise to be placed in the city of Santa Fe, New Mexico. Enclosed is a dollar ($1.00) to show my good faith in this matter, and don't you worry, buddy, there's plenty more where that came from.

I have been hearing much talk about Houston, Seattle or Cincinnati getting the 16th NFL team. I wish to express to you my opinion of those cities, which is that not a one of them has to offer what we can offer in Santa Fe. Besides our excellent transportation facilities (there is an important rail hub up in Lamy, DC-3 service to Albuquerque and more horses and donkeys in the area than you would ever need to look at), we have a tremendous output of Navajo blankets, beads, silverwork, green chile omlettes and other readily marketable items that can be tied in with our team in a merchandising package.

I propose to call our team the Santa Fe Nuclear Holycosts. Our colors will be ash-gray and yellow, and we will have mushroom clouds as our helmet decals. Through marketing, we plan to have mushroom cloud decals on every auto windshield in the country, inspiring terrible fear in our opponents that may even match that felt by our players. I pledge to you that we will build an underground stadium, camouflaged on top to look like a buffalo wallow. Thus we will be the only team in the league that can play a regularly sched-uled NFL game right through the middle of an all-out atomic attack. Could Cincinnati do that, Mr. Rozelle?

. . . In the matter of television, I envision for us a vast network covering the rich and populous territories of Nevada, Wyoming, Colorado, Utah, the Dakotas, Montana and New Mexico. We do not want Arizona. Don't even ask . . .

While in Florida last month for my health, I encountered a great number of people who had in their pockets checks for eight million dollars ($8,000,000) and like amounts and who wanted franchises but could not seem to attract your attention. As you will notice, I have put up our down-payment, or ear-nest money, in cash. Shortly you will receive a visitor bearing an antelope kidney stuffed full of cash in the sum of at least eight million dollars. Do not insult him by counting it. His name is Nachise, which means Willow Stick, and his grandfather was named Hickory Stick, or Chochise, and he is a very nasty customer when insulted and often when not. His Spanish name, when translated, is Mean Rascal. He is also our Director of Player Personnel and Chief Scout and has been known to track a potential player for a month over rocky ground before finally denting the fellow's skull with the store-bought hatchet you will notice in his belt.

In regards to our stadium, I have arranged with friends at nearby Los Ala-mos to do the excavating. They assure me they can cause a sizeable crater with a single afternoon's work . . . I am considering hiring John Ford as coach if Tex Maule is unavailable or too expensive. But I must have confirmation from you at once, since I have told my Los Alamos friends to proceed with the excavation next week and the people out there are liable to get very aroused if we do not have a team to put in that hole.

Yours sincerely,
Edwin Shrake

NFL Draft Day in New York, 1970. Shrake (at left) confers with NFL commissioner Pete Rozelle (standing). Shrake represented the Houston Oilers and chose his boss, *Sports Illustrated* editor André Laguerre, with the 25th pick. Photo by Tony Triolo.

Letters from New York, 1964–1966

May 15, 1964

We had a lot of meetings over long, loud, liquid lunches at *Sports Illustrated.* This description of planning the college football issue is typical of a meeting presided over by Andy Crichton. The Crichtons are a family of writers—bright, energetic, and combative. I was very fond of Andy. He was a runner long before it was popular. Often Andy would sleep through his stop on the commuter train, wake up at some village ten miles past his home late at night—and run back.

Fellow deviates, wing & masquers, club managers, orgyists, faddists, scholars and sex magicians, as well as pork chop devourers and cream gravy makers, plus anyone out there who happens to love me or vice-versa:

Several of us have just come back from a very important editorial conference in which we planned the contents of the college football issue. We went to a place on 48th street called "the absinthe house," which I suppose is meant to be like the place in New Orleans but isn't. Crichton is the editor of that particular issue and he began the meeting properly by ordering three rounds of martinis and putting his elbow in the pate, de fois, of course. They talk here about hard sports, which I gather means where guys knock down other guys and like that, and about soft sports, which is anything that is really interesting. Andy started about hard sports but after a few more rounds of martinis and an accident with the eggs benedict we got around to soft sports. More particularly, to girls. The theme, now, of the college football issue is to be girls. I am going to write the story—about majorettes, cheerleaders, dates, marching squads, and such things—and am going to go to the cheerleader school (for observation only) at SMU, the very place I used to have to drive through, with severe psychic damage, when I was married and lived near SMU. By the end of the lunch Andy was shouting "check, check" in a loud and demanding voice and was talking incoherently and was trying to pay with a travelers check that he signed in the wrong place. On the way back to the office he berated me for giving a quarter to a beggar who was "only half your size," but I pointed out if he had been bigger I might have had to give him a dollar. That sort of reasoning appeals to Andy. The girls story ought to be easy enough, but before that I have to do a golf instructional, on how to hit fairway woods or whatever they call them, under the name of Betsy Rawls. That means I have to go see Betsy Rawls, and, by god what coincidence, she will be playing in Dallas week after next, so that is where I will catch her. By even more coincidence there is a possibility she may go to Austin for a couple of days, and it would be most necessary for me to follow her. That is pretty goddamn tough luck for some of us, most of all for Betsy Rawls. I will bring news of Willie Morris, and anyone who sees Billy Lee might tell him that *Harper's* wants desperately to publish a section of his Lyndon B. Johnson book if he ever finishes it or perhaps even if he doesn't.

I have moved into another hotel while waiting for my apartment house to be readied for occupancy. This hotel is called hotel 14 and is at 14 east 60th, next door to the copa and around the corner from the sherry netherland. It is a theatrical hotel, when I went in yesterday the lobby was full of copa girls in tight pants and with poodles. It, I am told by Maggie Cousins, is also the place where William March had his final nervous breakdown, which figures. But the good thing about it is you go out in the morning and walk around the corner onto Fifth Avenue at the park and walk down past the plaza and Bergorf's and Tiffany and the places like that, and it is very pleasant. At 53rd Street the bells of St. Thomas Church are clanging and the saints are blackening in their niches and it has the look of Paris. It makes a very nice walk, the nine blocks down and one block over (I always turn at 52nd so I can go past 21 and Shors) to the office, especially if carrying an umbrella to swing or poke with. I made it leisurely this morning since my head and feet hurt, result of important discussion with Willie last night at Chumleys, and came into the office at 11, and talked to Doubleday about the new contract I am signing and found a letter from Rex Stout inviting me to join the authors league (which I did on Maggie's advice), and then [George] Plimpton called and invited me to a party in two weeks for "Candy," which is the old-new Terry Southern and Mason Hoffenberg book. He promised it will be an outstanding party. After that I had to put together my incoming-outgoing box, which took an hour. Then I had to put together my desk calendar, which took an hour. Then I had to cuss the coffee machine for 18 minutes, and by that time Dan [Jenkins] came around and fetched me for the college football issue luncheon. We are just back from the luncheon. . . .

(No date)

When I went to New York in 1964 to work for *Sports Illustrated,* the first place I lived was the Hotel Fourteen, which had a door at the rear of the lobby that led to backstage at the Copacabana nightclub. Then I moved down to the Chelsea Hotel on 23rd Street. The poets Brendan Behan and Dylan Thomas both lived at the Chelsea while drinking themselves to death at the White Horse Saloon in the Village. It was a ratty hotel, dirty and loud, with tattered bedspreads, but it was cheap and appealed to writers, actors, and musicians. Eventually I rented an apartment at Fifth Avenue and 15th Street and settled there until I married Doatsy and we bought a house in Austin and did several years of commuting. During those first years in New York, I was constantly charged up. This letter says what the city was like, and I loved it.

. . . This is a beautiful city. True it may be filthy, noisy, expensive and over-crowded, but there is such sport to be seen in the streets. Queers, pimps, cops, thieves, whores, toe-freaks, blackjacketed motorcycle faggots, behind every lamp post a guy with his dingus out. Everything is torn up. Great rips in the pavement, machines hammering and drilling, open manholes, smash, bang, honk honk, everybody cussing and screaming, black muck all over faces and collars, pushing, shoving, hitting, rudeness, stupidity, sewers gurgling, dogs crapping where you walk, big deals, big decisions made by drunks at executive lunches, clawing, stealing, Bobby Kennedy making sure the TV cameras see him take John-John to the old mansion in Riverdale, wires down, doormen drunk, suspicious instruments poking against your leg in subways, Chinamen underfoot, the laundries taking a week with shirts and returning them with buttons ripped off and soot on the cuffs, hamburgers for $1.75, mobs, riots, stabbings. I believe that is what they call the hustle and bustle of a great city. . . .

June 18, 1964

While living in the Chelsea Hotel I developed a strangely intense friendship with the great dancer and Haitian folk hero Katherine Dunham. The intensity was soul-deep and no doubt helped along by chewing the exotic green mushrooms a Haitian medicine priest was handing out in Katherine's suite the night we met. Influenced by her, one morning I went to the bus station and got on a Freedom Riders bus bound for Mississippi. Before the bus could pull out, I came to and remembered the magazine expected me to be in Buffalo to go clubbing with Cookie Gilchrist, the fabled fullback who had starred for many years in Canada before moving to the AFL, and I jumped up and got off the bus and went to the airport. Cookie weighed about 260 pounds. We were in a bar one night in Toronto and a guy started giving Cookie some lip. Cookie said to him at last, "Pal, the way you're talking, you either have a gun or you are insane. Either way, good night." And we left the bar. Outside Cookie said, "I wouldn't be alive today if I stood up to every drunken lunatic who gasses off at me. Sooner or later some fool would get me. Look at what happened to Wild Bill Hickok."

Fellow deviationists, performers, underground fighters and unspeakables.

Sadly, my lovely walk down Fifth Avenue is no more. When I got back the other day from a trip to Chicago and Boston, the bastards at Hotel 14 had raised my rent $120 per month, and so I made a dispute of it and huffily moved out and moved into the old Chelsea Hotel down on 23rd Street. . . . The Chelsea is a very old place with a lot of black iron grillwork and a stairwell with iron grillwork, and the door to my room is exactly the right height that I have scalped myself on it twice. Thomas Wolfe, Dylan Thomas and Brendan Behan each lived the last year of his life at the Chelsea. Arthur Miller lives there now, as does me, or as do I, for a while, and so does the painter Larry Rivers, and lots of other swell people. The hotel is across the street from the 23rd Street YMCA and you can see all the naked men you ever care to see. I myself have already seen quite a few more than I wished. For my bargain price there is no TV included. Yesterday I bought a TV but I cleverly left it at a girl's apartment. I would not risk being seen in the streets with a TV set. Not after some of the things that have been happening lately. I was at Vic's a couple of times watching TV and helping to get rid of the birthday present his brother sent him, and one night we ate half-dozen ham and cheese sandwiches each, about a case of beer, and a lemon pie and an apple pie, and watched a movie that we could not even understand the dialogue much less the plot . . .

I have been dating a girl . . . who is one of New York's highest paid fashion models and is a German and is 26 and is very pretty, but she says Americans are not sophisticated, and I said, "Shit, baby, I'm as sophisticated a sumbitch as you'll ever see," and have proved it repeatedly by falling over garbage cans and other endearing things, like also sitting on her cat. She thinks I am funny. I think I must be. Night before last after spending about $70 on a date with her (and she had to be in at 11:30, which is one very bad thing about models who can't afford to look dissipated) I went down to Chumleys feeling how goddamn funny I was to be that stupid, and I saw a girl at the bar there. Now that is the kind of girl I really like, I thought, very attractive and sensual-seeming and pleasant and with a nice laugh. She was with a couple of guys with beards and another guy who looked like a leather freak and a girl with long red hair, but I got to talking to her at the bar and we got along well. Then one of the beard guys told her it was time to go, and I found out who she was: Gina Lollobrigida. Well, crap, another one gone. Where does it end?

Sept. 1, 1966   ·

The producer I am writing about here is not named Bob. I guess I changed his name because his behavior was so outrageous at times that I was trying to protect him—from what, I don't know. He went on to become very wealthy and successful.

Dear Lady Luv:
. . . We had another of those Ginger Man nights Monday. Started at Shor's, then went to a place named Moriarty's on 3rd Ave and hollered a lot. One guy with us was Bob, a CBS producer, who danced with a little wino sailor named Vinnie who hugged Bob's shoulders with two feet off the ground and then yelled: "He bit me on the neck!" I am afraid that later Bob and I had our pants off in P. J. Clarke's, an event I can hardly believe. Well, though, you may

recall Bob. He was at our table in the hotel in Kentucky and I think he may have also gone out to the party at your friend's house. He was one of the two guys who left early from the saloon where we had our pictures taken. He is if anything even wilder and more unpredictable than Jap [Gary Cartwright] and I at our worst. We last heard from him at 8 a.m. as he was on his way to the airport shouting things like Ejacorama! And Suckathon! And "You do it to me TWA baby you . . . put me in your big silver carriage and . . . fly me in the goddam sky and. . . ." He had to fly to St. Louis, rent a car, drive two and a half hours to a little town in Illinois and go immediately into a production meeting with his camera crew and directors on the Hamiltonian race about which he knew nothing. It should have been a considerable telecast but I forgot to watch it. During the evening he also ran off his girl, Karen, whom he told: "You don't understand anything. Go fuck somebody." She came over to me and said, "I think I'm a little too young for this group" and left. I am waiting to see how he straightens this one out. . . .

March 6, 1965

The first few years at *Sports Illustrated,* I was constantly on the move. They gave me an all-airlines credit card good for first-class flight on any airline in the world to any place in the world. I still have the card. It doesn't work anymore, of course, but it is proof of a way of life journalists today can hardly believe.

In those days you parked right in front of the airport and just ran up to the counter—or even the gate—at the last minute and showed the card and got on the plane, where you sat in a big, sweet-smelling leather chair and had a martini and a dish of caviar with chopped egg and toast before take-off—and once in the air two or three lovely, friendly stewardesses served a stream of martinis, wine, shrimp cocktail, filet mignon, salad, baked potato, and ice cream, followed by coffee and brandy.

No, really.

Dear Miss Fiance:

. . . The last couple of months have been interesting. Since I saw you I have been in Miami, Austin, Dallas, Fort Worth, Ding Dong, Comfort, Dripping

Springs, Wimberley, Acapulco, Mexico City, Mazatlan, Guadalajara, Durango, Torreon, Monterrey and Johnson City, among other places. . . . I dragged back in here yesterday, weary and broke, and immediately they assigned me to cover the lightheavyweight championship fight. Which means I have to leave at once for the Catskills and the training camps. But that should not take very long. . . .

April 10, 1964

And I did become a partner in an art gallery in Austin. It was called the Gallery Goo. It was supposed to be Gallery 600, but the lettering on the sign was a little off. Fletcher Boone was the proprietor and resident artist. Financially it was a flop, but that was to be expected. Another partner in the gallery was Ann Richards, who eventually became governor of Texas. Reading this letter, I have to laugh at the date. I had only been in New York for a month. Already I was looking in other directions.

Poolzy Paulzy:
A serious suggestion—
   We have reached the place in our lives when we have to decide what is important to us, what we truly want to do and what we do not want to do, what matters essentially and what is essentially crap. Not only because we are getting older. But also because the world is getting older. The Chinese are making a bomb. The blacks and yellows are in revolt in Africa and Asia. God is stirring. All that. Everything. But mainly we are getting older and why use up our lives in futile grabbing for status and money that neither of us really wants. Why follow the pattern they lay down for us? Why bust your ass in something you do not really feel worthwhile merely so your child or children can grow up exactly as you did and get into the same chase and feel the same discontent? We have both been moderately successful in what we do. We are making pretty good money and have pretty good jobs. In my practical field I have one of the very few very top jobs in the country. But it's not satisfying. Of course I work on novels and that can be, and I hope it will be, the ultimate satisfaction. And I hope to wrangle around with a couple of deals and escape New York. But if I can't get those deals and can't make enough money by

writing novels, then what am I going to do with the last 30 (luckily) years of my life? Among money earning possibilities, the only things I care about are bars, books and paintings. So why not open a book shop–art gallery–coffee house? It would of course have to be in a place we like. I would say either Austin or Santa Fe. . . .

. . . In favor of Austin . . . Austin is close to Mexico. Austin has the lakes. And I would like to keep roots in Texas since if I am ever any kind of writer at all it will be as a Texas writer, I think. . . .

The Once-Forbidding Land

Sports Illustrated, May 10, 1965

I was always watching for an opportunity to go to Austin. At the bar on the ground floor next door to the Time-Life Building in New York one evening, I suggested a story on the Texas Hill Country to André Laguerre. There was no direct connection to sports, but a mention of fishing or rodeo would make it close enough to get in our magazine. Lyndon Johnson had been president for nearly two years. He was making the Hill Country famous. André agreed to the idea, and I took off for Austin. Two years later I would buy a house in Austin and split time between there and New York until finally I quit *Sports Illustrated* and moved back to Texas for good.

I can see now that pieces of this story showed up later in *Blessed McGill*. No experience ever goes to waste.

The dust came up from the wheels of the car and settled like talcum powder on the leaves of the live oak trees. There was dust on the trunks of the trees, too, and on the cedar fence posts. But back in the meadow, where the sheep were, the winter rye was green. As the car approached on a farm road near the Pedernales River, Hondo Crouch saw the white of the New Jersey license plate. He squinted, pulled down the brim of his straw hat to shade his eyes, stuck a piece of grass between his lips and did not look up again until the car stopped and the driver leaned out the window.

"Hey, sport," the driver said, "where's the LBJ Ranch?"

"The whut?" said Hondo.

"The LBJ Ranch," the driver said.

Hondo chewed on the grass and looked dubious.

"Lyndon B. Johnson, the President of the United States," the driver said.

"Oh, yeah, the Presydint," said Hondo.

"Well, where's his ranch?" the driver said.

"Don't know's I can say whur it's at," said Hondo. "I don't live around here mahself."

"Where *do* you live?" the driver said.

"Down the road about a mile," said Hondo.

The car disappeared in a furious fog of caliche dust. Hondo tossed away the piece of grass and pushed back his hat with a thumb. "A man cain't go telling these foreigners everthang he knows," Hondo said. "First thang, you'd wake up one morning and they'd of carried off ever stump and loop of bob-wahr on the whole ranch for souvenirs."

Hondo Crouch, a former All-American swimmer at the University of Texas, whacked the dust from his Levi's and wandered off to look at the Comfort Wool & Mohair Co., which he owns, and at *The Comfort News,* where he writes a column under the name of Peter Cedarstacker. Until Lyndon B. Johnson became President and moved The Other White House to his ranch outside of Stonewall on the north bank of the Pedernales, few people other than Texans had ever heard of the Hill Country and most Texans had only the scantest idea of where and what it is.

Texas is a number of contradictory territories bound together roughly inside the Red River to the north, the Rio Grande River to the west, the Sabine River to the east, and the Gulf of Mexico to the south. The territories are like, say, seven frequently quarrelsome brothers living in the same house. There are the pine forests and the cotton culture of east Texas, the black farmlands of north Texas, the prairies and cattle country of the West, the lonely and stunning mountains of the Big Bend, the orchards and truck gardens of the Rio Grande Valley and the shipping, sugar, petrochemicals and sand dunes along the Gulf Coast. But the part of the state that Lyndon Johnson most often talks about, that inspires the protection of a native like Hondo Crouch, is a hunk of kneaded ground covering about 14,000 square miles.

The Hill Country begins around Killeen in the north, runs south to Austin, curves southwest to San Antonio and goes west to the far side of Kerrville. The Colorado River comes down from the northwest with its six Highland Lakes for fishing, boating, water skiing and flood control. The Colorado twists through Austin and heads southeast to empty into the Gulf. To the west and southwest of Austin are other rivers—the Guadalupe, the Pedernales, the Blanco, the Llano—that cut through the hills and can boil into flash floods that tear away bridges, houses and herds of livestock. The thick soil and the overgrazing that destroyed much of the grass and allowed scrubby cedar and mesquite to stubble miles of hills have not made it an easy country in which to live. There is no oil in the Hill Country, no simple path to wealth.

It is the sort of country where one is on the earth under a big sky and there is no way to fake it. The false skills of the cities—the huckstering, the maneuvering at multi-martini lunches, the high-camp cultism, the slippery small talk of the cocktail parties, the frantic grabbing for status, all the fustian time-destroying word games and social ploys that give life in the cities a sense of temporariness and uselessness—these count for nothing in the Hill Country. What matters is that one is honest in what he does and that he has a certain largeness of spirit. The late Stanley Walker, former city editor of the *New York Herald Tribune*, wrote in a book called *Home to Texas*: "The kindliness of the citizens, their calm but friendly interest in the well-being of their neighbors, is apparent enough, but there are exceptions. The man who exhibits a small, mean side is not exactly ostracized, but his mangy little acts are remembered. He may not be censured, but he is avoided."

The Friendly Bar is in Johnson City, 44 miles west of Austin on the highway that goes through Dripping Springs—a town that looks like the place where the first *High Noon* hero ambled down that wide, dusty street. The Friendly Bar is the refuge of James Ealy Johnson, cousin of the President. A cowboy and occasional dealer in real estate, James Ealy is a tall, brawny man with the famous nose, ears and chin of the Johnson family and a face that is creased and browned by the sun and wind of the Hill Country. At 55 James Ealy goes nearly every day to play dominoes with his pals at the Friendly. He wears a straw hat and the boots of a working cowboy, with walking heels, and a few buttons have popped off his green corduroy shirt. His long johns show at the cuff and neck. He rolls his own cigarettes and can do it one-handed if the other hand happens to be occupied with holding a beer bottle. Like his cousin, James Ealy has a ranging mind. But, unlike his cousin, James Ealy never cared to be anything much but a cowboy in the Hill Country.

"What most folks go their whole lives without realizing is that everthang comes from the earth," James Ealy said one afternoon in the Friendly. "All money comes from the ground—this bar stool, this cigarette, these boots, the fancy cars the tourists drive through town, it all comes out of this earth. When you forget how you stand with the land you have forgot the most important thang about being a man. It used to be, back in 1929 or so, you could hardly get into Johnson City for all the people. I had 94 Mexicans working for me. Then the ground wore out and everybody moved off. If LBJ hadn't of got to be President, we might of all starved to death around here. But now we're building dams, building the country back up, replenishing the earth, remembering where we come from."

Bud Shrake and James Ealy Johnson, cousin of President Lyndon Johnson, exit the Friendly Bar in Johnson City, 1965. Photo by Shel Hershorn.

A few minutes earlier on Highway 290—the Austin-to-Fredericksburg road —a new purple Cadillac had been creeping along at 30 mph. Texans are restless and mobile people. They leap into their cars and drive 300 miles to see a football game or to whoop at a party with hardly more hesitation than a New Yorker would feel in venturing from midtown Manhattan to Brooklyn Heights. Ordinarily they push the 70-mph speed limit, roaring along with their radios playing loud and the air conditioners blowing and a can of beer open on the seat. But this purple Cadillac was barely making it at 30. At the wheel was a grim old woman, hunched forward, steering with both claws, fierce old eyes peering straight ahead as if to be sure the road was clear of Apaches. On the rear window was a sticker: He's Not MY Kind of Texan.

"I remember," James Ealy said, laughing about the old woman, "when Lyndon used to shine shoes here in town. Everybody was against us. Whenever we walked out the door we knew we might have to fight. Now most of 'em got these LBJ ALL THE WAY stickers on their cars. But you know that's a lot of bull. Plenty of people right here in town didn't vote for him."

James Ealy got up from the domino table. A visitor was playing *Everything's O.K. on the LBJ* on the jukebox, which gives six records for a quarter. Pushing open the screen door, James Ealy stepped onto the sidewalk. Half a block away, on the square, was the Pedernales Hotel, which was being remodeled into a drive-in bank. Out at the southwest edge of town were several stone barns, farm buildings and a smokehouse that were built by the President's grandfather, Sam Ealy Johnson, and an uncle.

"Lyndon and I used to have a bike," James Ealy said, looking off toward the highway. "We had only one bike. Couldn't afford two. If we rode it 100 yards a chain fell off or something. So we worked on that bike all the time. We left it in a building right here in town. One night the building burned down. 'Whut happened to our bike?' Lyndon asked me. I told him it was gone. An awful thang. An awful thang to happen to kids."

James Ealy rolled another cigarette, expertly furrowing the paper and then pulling the string on the tobacco pouch with his teeth. "The big problem today, here or anywhurs else, is education," he said. "We got to educate the people. They got to learn this is one world, and we all got to trade and deal and get along with one another or we're gonna have turmoil. People right here in this town don't realize that. They read about a longshoreman's strike, and they say, 'Whut is a longshoreman?' They never saw no water deeper than whut's in a cow track."

But the Hill Country is the nation's top producer of mohair and figures in a great amount of international trading. It is difficult to drive a few miles through the hills without coming across herds of goats or sheep in the green, slanting meadows. Down the road from the Friendly Bar that afternoon the Future Farmers of America—a young people's organization—were bringing their sheep, goats and pigs to the Blanco County Fair Grounds for a stock show. Around the pens, where boys wrestled fat complaining sheep in for shearing, the air was thick with the stinging smell of hay and manure and with the rackety cries of the sheep and the buzzing of electric shears. Girls in cowboy hats and long pigtails walked arm in arm. Pickup trucks hauled trailers of livestock. Boys in wide hats, jeans, boots and high school letter jackets glanced sideways at visitors from the outlands—including a Dallas model who wore high black boots, pink stretch pants, a pink-and-orange sweater and wrap-around sunglasses. A few years ago such a costume at the Blanco County Fair would have meant instant gawking. But even the Future Farmers of America are jaded now with creatures from other worlds. The LBJ

Ranch has been host to former German Chancellor Konrad Adenauer, the late John F. Kennedy, López Mateos, Hubert Humphrey, Van Cliburn, Milton Berle, a varied lot of others. After a Johnson City citizen sees Dean Rusk and Pierre Salinger walk into a store and buy jeans and then sees members of the Washington press corps strolling the streets with barbecue sauce on their lapels and with Stetson hats set squarely on their heads, like reservation Indians, then there is very little left in this life for a Johnson City citizen to be startled at.

In an arena next to the FFA exhibit pens that afternoon the Hill Country cowboys were having a rodeo. They ride their own circuit—Marble Falls, Lampasas, Fredericksburg, Johnson City, other towns 100 miles around. The riders, ropers and bulldoggers pay entry fees. The winners collect the money and the losers the splints. The dirt floor of the Blanco County Fair Grounds arena that afternoon had been trampled into a moonscape by hooves and fallen cowboys. Cars and pickups were parked around the wire fence of the arena, and people sat on hoods or stood in truck beds to watch. The grandstand was in shade and the concrete was cold. People came down to stand next to the fence to be in the sun.

While the cowboys, riding six or eight abreast, chased the bawling, round-eyed calves back up to the west chutes for another go-round, the loudspeaker on top of the wooden judging stand crackled with country music: *I'm Just an Amateur at Love* and *There'll Be Some Sad Sangin' and Some Slow Ridin' Next Time You Come Staggerin' in.*

The announcer told jokes and talked to people in the crowd and consoled the losing riders and called out the cowboys' names—names that sounded like Jim McCorkledale, Smokey Kuykendall, Johnny Bearsfoot, Bean Crosby, names that one does not hear outside of rodeo arenas or working ranches. Cowboys are perhaps the only people in this country so tough that a male child can be named June or Jane and survive. It is a handy thing to remember that if one meets a cowboy named June or Jane one should talk softly and smile quite a bit.

Leaning against the arena fence, their fingers clutching the wire and their eyes studying the horses, were two old men. One wore overalls and a baseball cap and the other gray work clothes and a cowboy hat.

"Look thur at Ole Gray," said the one in the cowboy hat.

"Does his job. Lookit him keep that rope tight for that cowboy," said the baseball cap.

"Yew cain't beat Ole Gray for a ropin' horse," said the cowboy hat.

Had they ever seen Lyndon Johnson on horseback?

"Used to see him ridin' a jackass to school," said the cowboy hat.

How is the President's horsemanship?

"Waal, Lyndon can ride a horse somewhat," said the cowboy hat. "But you got to remember he's been on a horse a whole lot more in the last two years than he ever was the rest of his life put together."

The location where the photographs are taken of the President on horseback is a handsome spread 12 miles west of Johnson City on the blue stream of the Pedernales River. The LBJ Ranch itself has about 450 acres, minuscule by Texas standards. "You can't call 400 acres a ranch," the late J. Frank Dobie, teacher and writer, once said. "That's just a place." But the President owns or leases more than 7,000 acres in all, and that does narrowly qualify him as a rancher. Mr. Johnson was baptized at the age of 14 in the Pedernales—which he and other Hill Country people call the "Per-de-nal-is"—during a summer revival meeting of the First Christian Church of Johnson City. Once there were 200 pecan trees in front of the Johnson home on the bank of the Pedernales. But the river came up violently in 1952, as Hill Country rivers and creeks do after one of the hammering rains Texans refer to as gully-washers, and thundered over the bridge and ripped away the pecan trees. ("I'll see you soon," Mrs. Johnson frequently says, "if the Lord be willing and the creeks don't rise.") Mr. Johnson arrived in a helicopter, in the style of the Nouveau West, to rescue his wife and mother from that 1952 flood.

The terraced front lawn, where the pecan trees were, is now a lovely patch of greenery—kept green by a sprinkler system—on which the President's blue-blooded Hereford cattle sometimes stand as if posing for a postcard. To the east of the ranch are two stone forts with thick walls and rifle slits, built a century ago for protection against Indian raids. The original stonework of the LBJ Ranch house was built about the same time. But the house has been modified and added to, and the old gingerbread wood sculpt has been removed from the edge of the roof. It is a plain white stone-and-frame farmhouse now, with a large, curving, heated swimming pool and a landing strip. The President bought the ranch, which is not far from the cabin in which he was born, from an aunt.

Ranch Road 1 cuts north from Highway 290 just west of Stonewall and runs beside the Pedernales before turning south to rejoin the highway at Hye. From the ranch road it is an easy golf shot across the river and the sloping lawn to the Johnson house. When the President is in residence, Ranch Road 1 is closed. The road is guarded at all times. If a car slows on Ranch Road 1 opposite the Johnson house, a security agent goes dashing across the lawn on some urgent mission, and two or three others peer at the car through binoculars. There is the feeling of machine-gun muzzles poking out of the brush and of unseen eyes staring from secret warrens. It is similar to the feeling one gets approaching the Brandenburg Gate on the border of East Berlin.

Geologically, the President's country is where the West truly begins. Coming in from the east across the Texas Gulf Coastal Plain the flatland suddenly breaks at Austin and rises into wooded hills. Along that hill line, known as the Balcones Escarpment, the earth's crust fractured millions of years ago and the Hill Country thrust up. The blacklands of cotton and grain sorghum end at Austin, where the Edwards Plateau emerges. Rocky ledges of Cretaceous limestones and clays rear up from what once was the floor of a warm, shallow sea. Fossil oysters, sea urchins, clams and snails lie among the rocks of the Hill Country with arrowheads and ax blades of the Comanches, Apaches and Tonkawas. Along the Pedernales Valley granite knobs jut out, but on the low slopes in the valley the soil is a sandy loam in which flourish the peach orchards of Stonewall and Fredericksburg. There is little use trying to farm the thin soil of the upper hills, although men have died in the attempt. Cedars, mesquite, and cactus have taken over much of the high country. An almost mythical, gypsylike people called Cedar Choppers roam the great cedar brakes and cut fence posts when they are inclined to work. But the ranchers have begun removing the cedars by knocking them down with a heavy chain dragged between two tractors and then burning them to give the grass a chance to grow again. Acorns from the live oaks and oily beans from the mesquite trees are fattening feed for goats and sheep, although the abrupt variety of the landscape can make goat catching much more difficult than goat raising.

The people out in that expanded country, where from a hilltop one can look for miles across progressions of hills and deep valleys, ridge after ridge, and see nothing moving but a vulture above a sun-splotched peak, have had to learn to laugh at themselves. On their radios they hear music like Cousin Fuzzy playing the *Peppy Pepper Polka*. And they listen to evangelists like Rev. J. C. Bishop of Dallas, who recently urged his audience: "They's lots of you folks out there got barns and farmlands standing idle, and you ain't do-ing nothing but paying taxes on them. What the Lord wants you to do is sell those barns and farmlands and send the money to me." Rev. Bishop fasts for 40 days and nights and, during that mystic period, offers to cure anything from eczema to heartache. For the proper donation.

"My own notion," wrote Stanley Walker after he had renounced his New York newspaper career and returned to his farm outside Lampasas, on the northern rim of the Hill Country, "is that many parts of the Southwest, par-ticularly central Texas, are almost ideal for horses, not bad for dogs, excellent for men who are innocent of Napoleonic aspirations, and just about as good for a woman as the woman wants to make it." In a letter to J. Frank Dobie, Walker wrote: "I love Texas. I returned to the state 16 years ago and never regretted the move. I expect to die out in the hills and to be buried there. But I am not blind. There is much about Texas that is depressing, ugly, disgusting. Why lie about it? Why, indeed, lie about anything?"

The usual grave in the Hill Country is 54 inches deep. The pioneers chose their graveyard sites on loamy or gravelly land with a gentle slope. In the late summer, after farm harvests are done, communities still turn out to work in the cemetery. They clean out the weeds and brush and plant flowers. When someone dies the men from nearby areas grab shovels and volunteer as grave-diggers. That manifestation of human interdependence carries over from the days when each man in the hills needed his neighbor for reasons more vital than borrowing a pound of coffee. It was less than 100 years ago—on July 21, 1869—that the last scalping occurred in Blanco County.

On Cypress Creek, a short ride north of Johnson City, a raiding party of Comanches rushed out of the trees and attacked the cabin of Thomas C. Felps. The Indians stripped Felp's 19-year-old wife, Eliza, beat her with a war club, speared her through the breast, cut a circle on the crown of her head, and yanked off her hair. Tom Felps was killed but not scalped, possibly be-cause of his red hair. Neighbor Sam Ealy Johnson Sr., the President's grand-father, who had been raising cattle in the Hill Country with his brother, Tom, and driving herds up the trail to Kansas markets since the 1850s, organized the pursuit. He left his own wife, Eliza Bunton Johnson, alone with their baby at their log cabin. Returning from the spring with a bucket of water, she saw some of her cows gallop past with Comanche arrows sticking out of their hides. She realized the Indians had doubled back. Eliza Johnson took her baby down into a basement storage shelter. She inched a braided rug over the trap door and tied a diaper over the baby's mouth to hush its cries. She heard the Comanches stomping about in the cabin above. They destroyed the Johnsons' wedding gifts, stole the horses and rode away before Sam Ealy Johnson returned.

Some of the Hill Country's early settlers were Germans. After the French revolution of July 1830, the German princes ruled their provinces with vigorous military discipline and forced out thousands of students, professors, craftsmen and farmers. Many of the exiles came to Texas through the influence of travel books that, unfortunately, were more romantic than true. A group of noblemen, the Mainzer Adelsverein, met various disasters as a result of the naiveté of their ideas of colonization before Prince Carl of Solms-Braunfels bought 1,300 acres on the Comal and Guadalupe rivers and founded New Braunfels, 50 miles southwest of Austin. Baren Ottfried Hans von Meusebach led an exploring party into the hills 75 miles northwest of New Braunfels, bought 10,000 acres and distributed the land in 10-acre plots. There, in 1846, the town Fredericksburg began. The first community dinner was a roasted bear.

One year later Mormon Leader Lyman Wight, who had got himself excommunicated by feuding with Brigham Young for control of the Mormons after Joseph Smith was killed by a mob, brought his followers down from Illinois into the Hill Country and founded the town of Zodiac, five miles east of Fredericksburg. Wight and his people supplied the Germans with meal and lumber and taught them to farm the Texas soil. A flash flood of the Pedernales washed away the mills of Zodiac in 1851. Wight and his faithful abandoned Zodiac and wandered Texas searching for the new Zion. He died near San Antonio, with Zion unlocated.

But by then the Hill Country was becoming sophisticated. In the valley town of Sisterdale weekly meetings of the German scientific and philosophical society were conducted in Latin. Joseph Brodbeck, a Württemberg scholar, taught school in Fredericksburg and built a flying machine that was powered up to the treetops by its coiled spring engine in 1865—less than 30 years after the Battle of the Alamo and more than 40 years before the Wright brothers exhibited their machine. Count Jean Peter Isidore Alphonse de Saligny, French chargé d'affaires to the Texas Republic, was living in Austin, giving fancy parties and cursing the hogs that rooted up his gardens. Square dances at the Bismarck Garten in Fredericksburg were called in French. Sir Svante Palm, a Swede, gave his book collection to the University of Texas in

1897 as a foundation for what became one of the world's finest libraries. Emir Hamvasy, exiled former Lord Mayor of Budapest, was professor of music at Swancoat's Academy in Austin in the 1860s. Long before that the Spanish had built El Camino Real, a highway with fords that could be used in all but the foulest weather. The highway passed through San Antonio en route to Natchitoches to connect to Mexico with French Louisiana. Franciscan Fathers in the 18th century built three missions on the present site of Austin before the Indians drove them out and forced them to relocate in San Antonio. The Villa de San Marcos de Neve was built on a bluff above the Guadalupe River near the El Camino Real crossing in 1807 by Don Felipe Roque de la Portilla. More than a century later, Lyndon B. Johnson was graduated from Southwest Texas State Teachers College in the town of San Marcos.

The settling of Austin by buffalo hunters—one of whom was Mirabeau Buonaparte Lamar, President-elect of the Republic of Texas—in the mid 1830s pushed the Indians into the hills of the south and west and up the river valleys to the north. The Indians retaliated by raiding the outlying communities until Baron von Meusebach made peace for the German villages. Baron von Meusebach, known as El Sol Colorado (The Red Sun) by the Indians because of his fiery beard, guided a party of Germans into Comanche country on the San Saba River to meet with Comanche chiefs in 1847. Indian scouts along the path of march lit signal fires on the hilltop to let the chiefs know where the Germans were and how many men they had. The children in an unprotected cabin near Fredericksburg saw the fires and asked their mother what they meant. To keep from frightening them, she explained that the rabbits in the hills had gathered wildflowers for the Easter rabbit, and the fires were flaming under great cauldrons in which Easter eggs were boiling and being colored by the wildflowers. When the men came back from Comanche territory the children told them the story. It was decided that as long as the treaty held, fires would be built on the hills around Fredericksburg at Easter. The ceremony, with the retelling of the story, has been an annual affair ever since.

But the German settlers did not get on so well with their fellow Texans. When the Civil War came, the Hill Country voted against secession. Most of the Texans had come from southern states and were not only accustomed to slavery but were sentimentally bound to the Confederacy. The Germans had never owned slaves and had no use for them. A party of more than 70 German men tried to march from the Hill Country to Mexico and planned to sail from there to join the Union Army. They were ambushed and killed. Today there is a monument to them in Comfort—the only monument in the South dedicated to Union sympathizers. Groups of outlaws, the *Haengerbande,* rode the mountains hanging Germans and stealing their property in the name of the Confederacy. Bitterness lived for years in the hills and broke out again, though not so violently, during the two World Wars.

The Hill Country is one of seven distinct biotic areas of Texas. But it is the only one that is uniquely Texan, located completely within the boundaries of the state. The plants and animals on the Edwards Plateau are western in nature. Forests of stumpy evergreens—which the cowboys call shinnery because they scrape the legs of a man on horseback—grow in the scant upland soil. In places the shinnery gives way to heavy stands of cedar. Hill Country valleys are thick with post oak, pecans, bald cypress, cottonwood, hackberry, elm, sycamores, the live oaks that the President often mentions and plum and peach orchards. Sugar maples stand along the Sabinal River Valley and give the country in autumn the look of New England.

Wildflowers, one of which, the bluebonnet, is the state flower, carpet the Hill Country. In the spring the roadsides are a crazy palette of buttercups, phlox, verbenas, daisies, black-eyed Susans, fire wheels, ground cherries, prickly poppies, tomatillos, nettles and sunflowers. The blue-green of the mountain laurel and the yellow flowers of the chaparral lure swarms of bees and butterflies. Through that busy garden step an overabundance of deer. Hunting is a major occupation of the Hill Country. With the larger predators—the gray wolf, the red wolf, the black bear and the ocelot—mostly eliminated by ranchers trying to protect their stock, deer are multiplying at an astonishing rate. More deer are killed in Llano County each year than in any other area of comparable size in the nation.

The roadrunner, often seen hurtling through the mesquite in pursuit of a snake, is the celebrity of Hill Country birddom. J. Frank Dobie wanted the roadrunner rather than the mockingbird to be adopted as the state's official bird. Until his recent death Professor Dobie was the leading nonpolitical citizen of the Hill Country. Dobie had a ranch just outside of Austin and a house in town and he taught at the University of Texas.

Austin is the city that most Hill Country people think of as their own. People who are viewed with suspicion and fear in the conforming, image-coveting, salesmanship city of Dallas, 200 miles to the northeast, feel free in Austin. Home to Austin is where John Henry Faulk went when he was blacklisted by the networks. Since then he has won a $3.5 million libel suit over the blacklisting and is working again in radio, TV and motion pictures, but Faulk still maintains his Austin home in addition to his West Side apartment in Manhattan.

Historian Walter Prescott Webb lived in Austin for many years, as did naturalist Roy Bedichek. Poet and self-styled pataphysician Roger Shattuck and prize-winning novelist William Brammer are in residence there now, along with classical scholars William Arrowsmith and John Sullivan. Harvey Schmidt and Tom Jones, who wrote the hit musicals *The Fantasticks* and *110 in the Shade,* do much of their composing at Wimberley, a dude-ranch town west of Austin.

Austin is built on seven hills at a place where the Colorado River Valley is six miles wide. It is a clean and comfortable city of twisting streets that lift and fall among shaded lawns. Many of Austin's old stone buildings and Victorian mansions are still in decent repair, which gives the city a grace that comes with the awareness of the past; however there is a disturbing move toward the new high-rise glass-and-steel apartments that stand on blocks of terraced land like upturned fish tanks. The Colorado River flows through the city and catches its lights in dark water. To the west in the hills above Lake Austin, it is possible to live in splendid isolation in homes that cling to the cliffs like those of Sausalito or the French Riviera, and yet be able to drive downtown in 15 minutes.

Fittingly, the two structures that dominate the city are the University Tower, which lights up orange after a University of Texas victory in a major sport, and the capitol, next largest after the Capitol of the U.S. When the state legislature is in session every other spring, the politicians and the university people and some of the businessmen mix with descendants of the German settlers at the Scholz Garten, an old wooden building with tables out back under the oak trees. The outdoor beer garden is enclosed to the south by a meeting and singing hall (Wilkommen *Saenger,* says the sign above the back door of Scholz's), to the east by a small bowling alley where the pins are set by hand and to the west by the Scholz building. It is at the outdoor tables on spring nights while loudspeakers bellow music from the branches of the oaks—*One Life for Ten Is the Diesel Driver's Code, He's the Widow-maker of the Road* and *Why Do I Do the Bad Things That I Do*?—that the liberals and conservatives of the legislature argue their tedious points and the students observe their professors in the act of being human.

Around a single table at the Scholz Garten one may find a bewildering assortment of people: an Englishman who runs a book store that specializes in 18th-century literature, the editor of *Texas Observer* (an independent liberal newspaper that is one of Texas' clearest, though not loudest, voices), a Dallas newspaper columnist, a physicist called Dirty Tom ("All I want to do is build them bombs," he says), a cowboy, a state senator, a painter, a writer, a fellow with a guitar and sandals and Buffalo Bill haircut, a football coach, a labor lawyer, a classicist, a millionaire. And innumerable girls. The prettiest girls on earth. One of them rides to work on her motorcycle wearing jeans, sweater and headband. "When I get to the office," she says, "off come the headband and the jeans. I'm wearing a skirt underneath. I take my high-heeled shoes out of my purse, and I'm a square's supersecretary. I don't know what my boss would do if he saw me on my motorcycle and found out I'm a beatnik." At the Scholz Garten are students playing chess, Germans shouting songs, politicians scuttling around in the power game, a professor scratching notes for a book on Ezra Pound, some young men putting together a scrapingly funny satiric magazine called *The Austin Iconoclast*—an incredibly mingled group, somewhat like a displaced-persons camp, some of them hating the place and some of them loving it but all of them addicted to it. Folk Musicologist Alan Lomax and Poet Randall Jarrell are Scholz Garten veterans, as is Congressman and Historian Maury Maverick Jr. Novelist Larry McMurtry, author of the novel that was made into the movie *Hud*, comes sliding into the Scholz Garten, grinning, wary, with his small son by the hand. Photographer Russell Lee lives in Austin and recently shared his Scholz Garten table with writers Aubrey Goodman and Jay Milner. Sam Houston Johnson, brother of the President, is an Austin resident. So is a man who breaks wild buffalo for saddle riding.

Owner Bob Bales has provided nourishment for numerous indigent writers. "I'm a businessman, but I'm also a citizen," he says. "What kind of citizen would I be if I helped to make the writers shut up?" His attitude is in contrast to that of an Austin banker who was asked to contribute money toward restoring O. Henry's old house on East Fifth Street in Austin. "I can't help," the banker replied. "In fact, I do not understand this sudden excitement. I knew the man called O. Henry—Will Porter, that is—very well indeed. Worked with him, in fact. He was a very indifferent bookkeeper."

The Hill Country—from the tables at the Scholz Garten to the mountains of Kerrville, from the country store that sells jawbreakers in Ding Dong to the red-tile roofs of the Spanish *haciendas* in San Antonio—is a country where it is still a virtue to own a piece of land and to work it, where there is dancing room for the spirit. The puritans and the thought controllers, who rule much of the state and deny Texans such freedoms as the right to drink, bet on a horse or read an uncensored book, do not have much power in the Hill Country. The wide polished sky and the awesome land reduce their hysterias to absurdities.

But like most of the places in the U.S. that are wild and free, the Hill Country in its present form may be disappearing. Because of the popularity of Lyndon Johnson, tourists are entering the Hill Country, though as yet somewhat timidly. There are picnic-lunch sacks crumpled on the banks of the Blanco River where it rushes, clear over the limestone and blue in the channels, near the high blue ridges of the Devil's Backbone. More dude ranches are opening. Some of the working ranchers are selling out to syndicates from Dallas and Houston. There are grand plans for resorts—hunting and fishing and horseback-riding motels with neon signs and leatherette couches and mustard and catsup in little plastic boxes, which may become known as the last defeat of civilized man. But the Hill Country has one weapon, perhaps an ultimate one, against encroachment, and that is the stubbornness and loneliness of the land itself. It is not the place for everybody.

Gerhardt's Farm

From *Blessed McGill* (1968)

... as I was saying, here is some of that Hill Country research turning up later as fiction. Doubleday was expecting this novel to be the further adventures of the disillusioned, drunken young romantics and oil millionaires that had frolicked in *But Not for Love.* Instead I wrote about the first American saint, and even worse it was set in the Old West, not in modern Dallas.

One way to build a career as a novelist is to write the same book over and over with different titles. I didn't realize that at the time I wrote *Blessed McGill*, but I wouldn't have done it differently.

I hitched up the mules again and we resumed our drive to Gerhardt's farm. I had seen Gerhardt once before, when he came into my father's shop to order the wagon. My father had been dubious about Gerhardt's ability to pay, as the farmers in the hills were having lean times and high taxes. But Gerhardt was a tidy, thrifty fellow, like most Dutchmen, and soon he returned with the entire sum—part in gold, part in wool, and the rest in various produce that was worth more to us than money. Gerhardt was a short, round-headed man with pink skin and blond side whiskers. My father learned Gerhardt had come to Texas some fifteen years earlier along with a number of other Dutchmen who settled in the hills between San Antonio de Bexar and Fredericksburg. The Dutchmen managed to live in fair safety as the result of one of their leaders, a Baron von Meusebach, who was called El Sol Colorado by the Indians because of his red beard, making peace with several bands of Comanches at a meeting on the San Saba River. There were Dutchmen scattered here and there over millions of acres between the Colorado and Llano rivers, but they were good workers and did not try to bully or pester the Indians, nor did they slaughter the buffalo. Generally the Indians were content to accept gifts of coffee and sugar and cloth and occasional livestock and leave the Dutchmen to their labors.

This Gerhardt, my father told me as we drove along, had an unusual wife. She was a Lipan woman who had been captured by the Mexicans in a raid on an Apache *ranchería* near the old town of Zodiac, which is near to Fredericksburg, which is about a hundred miles west of Austin. In the fight her husband, a Lipan war chief called Bear That Walks, was killed. The Mexicans were scalp hunters, an unwholesome profession, as I can attest, but the woman being comely for a Lipan, was spared for other uses until the Mexicans wearied of her or could sell her as a slave. Gerhardt, whose own wife had died on the trip from their German state to Galveston, came across the Mexicans and observed their vile treatment of the woman and also overheard their plans for her. He persuaded the Mexicans to sell her to him for twice the price of her scalp, which in those days would have brought about twenty-five dollars.

The woman worked very hard for Gerhardt, as was her habit. He was not disappointed to learn she had been pregnant when captured. Two hard-working Indians were better than one, according to the Dutchman's reasoning. The woman bore a son. Together, Gerhardt and the woman built his farm. You might suppose the woman would have run off to join her own people. But hard as she worked for Gerhardt, it was nothing to how hard she had worked for Bear That Walks. With Gerhardt she was never hungry, never had to walk long distances with heavy loads, was seldom beaten and had a warm, dry place to sleep. Evidently she became fond of the little Dutchman, who called her Hilda, after his dead wife, and who eventually married her—which act required courage—and had the son baptized Jacob Charles Gerhardt. The boy's mother, the Lipan Hilda, named him Bear That Sings, for he was husky, like his father, and demonstrated a sweet singing voice as a child. It was not until later that he acquired his other names, Octavio being his favorite.

The Gerhardt farm was in a small valley below a humpbacked ridge. Through the valley ran a stream that had recently gone down after spring flooding, leaving bits of driftwood and other debris clinging to the cedars and littering the grazing land of Gerhardt's sheep. Behind the house, as we approached, was a peach orchard. The house was built of stone and we could see the sun striking the tin roof while we were still far off. The corral and outbuildings were of wood, though neatly put together. It was an industrious-looking place and very comfortable. The first we knew something was wrong was when we found a spotted cur laying dead near the barn. The cur's throat had been cut so that the poor beast's head was turned around backward.

"Indins," my father said, taking up his Henry rifle from the seat.

With a feeling of excitement and some apprehension, I produced my Dance Brothers & Park revolver and we drove in the wagon around to the front of the house where we beheld the source of the disturbance.

Half a dozen ruffians were getting ready to hang Mr. Gerhardt.

They had heard us coming. Before we could react, a couple more of them stepped out from the side of the house with handguns aimed at us and ordered us to throw down our weapons. We had no choice but to oblige. I was so surprised that I sat and gaped. My father began cursing in his eloquent fashion and the ruffians laughed.

"In God's name, save me, Mr. McGill!" cried the Dutchman.

His hands were tied behind his back and the noose was around his neck. The maguey rope had been tossed over a limb of a pecan tree. Gerhardt was very pale and wet looking. His wife was trussed up with peales and was lying in the dirt with a hunk of her deerskin skirt torn off and stuffed into her mouth as a gag. Her eyes were big as gold pieces. The boy was standing beside the porch while one of the ruffians held a shotgun at his back. The boy was a healthy specimen about my age, dark and muscular with his black hair loose in Dutchman style.

"What is it you're aiming to do?" my father said.

"Why, we are aiming to hang this feller, as you should be able to see," said one of the ruffians who seemed to be the leader. He was tall and skinny and had a bandanna handkerchief over his face, as did the others, and was wearing a pair of good black Mexican boots with silver buckles on the sides.

"Save me!" the Dutchman cried.

"What harm has he did you?" inquired my father.

"What harm he has did to us is no concern of yours," the skinny ruffian said. "If you choose to make it so, we might have to hang you, too. We got no need to explain the reasons for hanging a Yankee-loving Dutch booger and Jew."

"I'm not a Jew. I'm a Lutheran," said Gerhardt.

"You look like a Jew to me. And it is well known that I hate Jews," the leader said.

The others nodded and said they felt likewise.

I did not know for sure what a Jew was or why it should be bad to be one, but I could tell it did not look good for the Dutchman. His wife had begun to moan and thresh about. One of the ruffians prodded her with his toe and made a remark I will not repeat, and the others laughed. The boy, Jacob, had not moved even his eyes except to glance at us when we appeared but was gazing steadfastly at the tall, skinny man in the Mexican boots.

"As loyal citizens of the Confederate States of America, we are going to confiscate your cattle, sheep, and other possessions, you Jew booger, and we sentence you to death for being a Yankee spy," said the leader.

"They are the Haengebund," the little Dutchman said to my father.

That was what the Dutchmen farmers called them. Under guise of being Confederate patriots, groups of ruffians roamed the hills creating trouble for the Dutchmen, most of whom were Union sympathizers and had no use for slavery, never having been raised on the notion. My father had told me about the Haengebund, but I had not paid it much attention as it had been no menace to me personally. Looking at the trembling little Dutchman with the rope around his neck, however, I made up my mind that the Haengebund were patriots we could do without.

"You are no better than thieves and murderers," said my father.

The leader cocked his pistol and pointed it at my father's head.

"What did you say?" the leader said.

"I said you are a goat-breathed skunk," replied my father, "and also a yellow snake with a peanut for a heart."

The leader thought that over for a moment.

"You got the warter and I got the duck's back. I will attend to you some other time, gimp," the leader said.

"I swear you will get your chance, for I will recognize your ugly face no matter how many bandannas you cover it up with," said my father.

"Shoot him," a ruffian said.

"Hang the Jew," said another.

"Yes, hang the Christ killer," said another.

"Even if this man is a Jew, which he ain't, he don't deserve hanging. And besides Christ was killed two thousand years ago," my father said.

"Well, I ain't my own self got around to doing anything about it till now," said the leader. "Haul him up, boys."

"Oh Lord God in heaven deliver me," the Dutchman said. "Oh sweet Jesus Christ save me for I have done nothing to these men that they should want to kill me." His face looked pitiable, solemn, and frightened, with his eyes rolled up toward the skies as though he really hoped God might elect to come down and save him but could not see his way to believing it entirely.

"God!" said the boy Jacob in a loud voice. "You save this man, God!"

The ruffians laughed again, though somewhat nervously. "Listen to me, God! You save this man!" said Jacob.

"God don't listen to a filthy Indin," one of the ruffians said.

"Nor does He save a Yankee Jew," said another.

"Not especially a Yankee Jew that don't speak good English and consorts with Indins," said another.

"Haul him up!" the leader said.

Gerhardt began singing "Lead, Kindly Light." The boy Jacob joined in. He did in fact have a strong clear singing voice, and I have never heard a hymn sound more sincere or prayerful than what that boy sang that day. Two men grabbed the rope and started hauling on it. The rope squeaked and scraped on the limb and the men cursed and pulled, digging their heels into the ground, as Gerhardt rose up on his toes and kept singing until the maguey cut into his neck and even then his voice came out in little squeals like a rat's.

Gerhardt was not a heavy man, not more than a hundred and fifty pounds at most. But that is a considerable weight to haul up on a rope that is merely tossed over a tree limb. Another of the ruffians ran to help the first two. Jacob kept on singing. Gerhardt's neck was stretching and his eyes bugging out. Then several things happened at once.

My father jumped off the wagon seat, landed on his bad leg, fell to the ground, and the leader kicked him in the head, knocking him up against the hub of a wheel and rendering him dizzy. I jumped, too, and was thrown down and sat on by the biggest of the ruffians. And the tree limb broke with a crack, dumping Gerhardt in a heap and sending the three ruffians who had been hauling on the rope tumbling over backward.

"Thank you, God," said Jacob.

"Shut up, you dirty Indin," said the leader. "God didn't bust that limb and if you think this Jew booger is saved you are dumber than most coons."

By then the other ruffians had got up and were dusting off their pants and cursing. The leader went to his horse and got a rawhide peal about four feet long. It was the sort of cord that cowherders use for tying the legs of a calf. Proceeding to where Gerhardt lay, the leader cut the rope from the Dutchman's neck and yanked him to his feet, whereupon Gerhardt fell promptly back down again. This action was repeated three or four times before Gerhardt found the strength to stand. Naturally, he was a bit short on wind.

"I am saved," the Dutchman croaked when he regained his voice.

"No chanct of that, Jew," said the leader, looping the peal around the Dutchman's neck and grasping each end of it in his hands like a garrote.

"Rotten pig-hearted such-and-such," my father said, approximately, sitting up and touching the back of his head where it was bursted open and bloody.

The leader, who was in quite a rage by now, started pulling on the peal in such a manner as to throttle the Dutchman.

"God! You save this man!" said Jacob, who began singing again.

The leader's bandanna dropped down and his face twisted up with effort and sweat poured off his long nose as he pulled on the peal. The Dutchman's eyes bugged out again. He kicked and squirmed. The leader pulled and sawed on the peal until it cut his hands and they began to bleed. Disgusted, he dropped the peal and looked at his hands. "Look what you have did to me!" the leader said. Gerhardt fell down. There was blood on his neck and on his cotton shirt, but he was still alive.

"Thank you, God," said Jacob.

The leader wrapped his bandanna around his right hand, which was cut the worst.

"I'll be danged if I ever knowed it was so hard to kill a Jew," said the leader.

"Let's leave him be," said another ruffian.

"Yeah, we punished him for sure," another said.

"We've showed him what happens to Yankee spies."

"Boys, I come here to kill a Yankee-loving Jew booger and I ain't leaving till I have killed one," said the leader.

Gerhardt, lying on the ground, sounded like he was gargling. But he was trying to talk. What he was saying was that he was not a Jew and moreover that he did not care for Jews himself and that he was certainly not a Yankee and that there was a terrible mistake being made and if they would only leave him alone they could have all his cattle and sheep. A few of the ruffians listened as if they were impressed by what he was saying, but the rest were in a state of agitation and began arguing among themselves about whether to ride off in a hurry, shoot us all and then ride off, or go ahead and hang the Dutchman before riding off. The big fellow who was sitting on me was the only one who seemed undisturbed. "This is some chicken scratch," he kept saying. "This here is some chicken scratch indeed, my boy." I thought less of Gerhardt for his carrying-on, but I suppose it was reasonable of him to protest even if it was useless. After all he had been hanged and choked and that can tangle a man's thinking. It was a little surprising he hadn't tried that dodge earlier. But in a minute or two Gerhardt quit saying how he didn't like Jews and took to praying again. It was sort of gargle gargle gargle gargle but you could get the drift of it—God save me, I didn't kill Christ, I'm no Yankee-lover, I'm a simple farmer, I'm a decent Christian, I tithe for a regular ten per-cent, I say my prayers every day, I never saw these men before, and so forth. Quite a number of words gargled out of those poor bloody swollen lips.

"They's a bigger tree yander," said one of the ruffians, pointing toward a large oak tree beside the stream.

"Stand up, Jew," the leader said to Gerhardt. That command wasn't worth the breath it took to utter it. Even if he could have stood up, which was un-likely, the Dutchman wasn't about to march down to that other tree so they could hang him again. "Stand up or I will put a bullet in you." That command likewise did not make much impression. "These here Jews is sure stubborn and unfriendly," said the leader, kicking Gerhardt in the ribs.

"All of you must go now," said Jacob.

"Haw, listen at that crazy Indin," the leader said.

"God, I am telling You to make them go now," said Jacob.

"Indin thinks he can boss God," one ruffian said.

"That's a crime against religion," said another.

"I am telling You!" Jacob said and resumed his sweet singing.

The Lipan woman, Hilda, was no longer struggling but lay quiet watching the scene as I have since seen Indians do when they know death is certain and fighting is aimless. I saw my father tense himself as though about to spring up, but a handgun poked against his ear made him sit back again.

"Boy," said the fellow on top of me, "I am willing to let you up so's you can watch this here fine chicken scratching from a better vantage if you will promise not to make me no woes."

"Don't promise him nothing," my father said.

"Let's get on with this," said a ruffian. "I got chores to do at home."

"I need to be getting back, too," another said, looking at his pocket watch and glancing at the sun.

"Stand up, Jew," said the leader.

When Gerhardt did not move, but kept on gargling, the leader bent over and tried to lift him. But the leader's hands were too tender and he was some-what tired by now.

"All right you hard-necked old cow fleck of a Jew, I'll show you a trick or two about killing," the leader said.

He went over and got the maguey rope he had cut off the Dutchman's neck. Fashioning a slipknot, he lifted up the Dutchman's head by the hair and replaced the rope around his neck. He tied the other end of the rope to the horn of his saddle.

Jacob was singing very loud.

"Git!" the leader yelled and slapped his horse on the flank.

The horse slowly backed off until the rope was tight and then stopped. Clearly that was a horse trained for cow work, where the practice is to keep the rope taut on a downed beast while the cowherder rushes to it and binds its feet. The rope had tightened up so that Gerhardt's face turned a blotchy blue, but if Gerhardt didn't move any more the horse wouldn't either. That put the leader out of his head with fury. He grabbed a Mexican quirt from his saddle and raised it to strike the horse.

Jacob's song changed to a scream. He leaped at the leader of the ruffians. The fellow with the shotgun fired at him, missed and hit one of his own companions in the leg, shattering the kneecap and blowing out bits of bone, flesh and denim trouser. The man howled, sat down and looked at the meat of his knee. Jacob was to the leader in two bounds. The leader swung his quirt and slashed it across the boy's left eye. Jacob fell yelping and crying and trying to get up again. The quirt had cut through his eyebrow and eyelid and on down his left cheek for two or three inches. I saw his eyeball come out in a gush of soppy matter. The eyeball was sliced almost in half and lay on his cheek like an onion. Everybody was yelling all at once save for Hilda, who had not moved.

Of course the commotion and racket scared the horse who bolted.

And there went Gerhardt, the little Dutchman, bouncing and banging and skidding across the grass at the end of the rope as the horse galloped toward the creek.

That deed used up the remainder of the ruffians' nerve. Loading their wounded man into the new wagon, they then fetched the leader's horse and cut Gerhardt loose. In their hurry, they did not take the sheep or cattle nor any other plunder and did not even pause long enough to steal our guns which still lay where we had thrown them. They rattled off with our mules pulling the new wagon and with horsemen all around. My father shot three times at them with his Henry before it jammed from the dirt, and they fired three or four shots back as they rode into the woods. I heard a bullet pop as it went past my head.

Hilda put Jacob's ruined eyeball back in its socket and tied a bandage around his face. I hitched a team to the Dutchman's old wagon and my father and I lifted the body into the bed. Gerhardt's head was the size of a pumpkin. His broken neck was twice as long as it was supposed to be.

Coming around to the back of the wagon, Hilda looked at the bottoms of the Dutchman's shoes.

"I command you to leave us now," she said, talking to his spirit. "I command you not to bother us while we live, for we loved you and did the best we could."

"We will get a doctor for the boy and you will stay with us until we are sure the danger is over," my father said.

Hilda nodded. Like all Lipans, she was afraid of ghosts and eager to be gone, for the Lipans believe the dead want their relatives to join them. When there is a death, the Lipans move away quickly and never mention the dead person's name again. Hilda was barely Christianized enough to allow the corpse to ride in the wagon with us, and we could tell she was uneasy about it. After a bit she began to sway from side to side and croon.

We drove back the way we had come, past the orchard and around the ridge. It was still a lovely day, with the light the color of ripe peaches. In the fields were large patches of red and yellow wildflowers called Indian blankets, and we passed a hillside of bluebonnets. We could see gray sheep moving in a meadow with no cur sheepdog to keep them from straying. The cows raised their heads to watch us go by. A mockingbird dived from the branches of a cottonwood, nearly hit my father's hat, then flashed back up to the branches and twittered at us for coming too close to his nest. Jacob spoke once on the way back to Austin.

"That God up there is useless," is all he said.

Matthew Caldwell in Houston City

From *The Borderland: A Novel of Texas* (2000)

This book started with a conversation over drinks in the bar of a Chinese restaurant in Manhattan. I was talking to Ellis Amburn, editor at a major publishing house. I had known Ellis well in Fort Worth. We had many of the same friends at TCU. Not only was he an editor, but he wrote best-selling biographies of movie stars.

I began telling Ellis that I wanted to write a novel about the great Co-manche raid that reached the Gulf of Mexico and then turned north to attack the new capital city of Austin but was stopped at the Battle of Plum Creek. I talked about white women being taken prisoner and made into wives or slaves by warriors. He got interested. He asked questions.

At the end of the lunch Ellis said he wanted to publish the novel. We shook hands. He wrote two words on a napkin that he stuck in his pocket: COMANCHE SEX.

I was paid the first half of a large advance. I began researching and writing bits of the book. Then life got in the way. I got a divorce. I quit *Sports Illustrated.* I wrote a movie about vampire bats. But finally I was ready to concentrate on the novel.

I left my house and cat and dog in Austin in the care of friends and leased an apartment for a year in the Royalty Coin Company building in San Antonio. It is the cylindrical stone building on the River Walk at the Commerce Street Bridge. Margaret Cousins, who had been my editor at Doubleday, had retired to her hometown of San Antonio, where she owned an apartment in the same building. Her friend Billy Baldwin, the New York interior decorator, was there also. My apartment on the third floor had bay windows that opened onto the river. I could practically see the Alamo. There were bars and restaurants up and down the sidewalk directly below me. Boats cruised the narrow river with Mexican bands playing aboard. Surely this was the perfect place to write "Plum Creek."

Pete Gent was helping me move in. The phone began ringing as we stood in the hall with armloads of boxes. I didn't think anyone knew my new number. I unlocked the door and answered the phone and it was Jim Wiatt telling me I was to have breakfast tomorrow at the Beverly Wilshire with Steve McQueen, who had just finished reading *Blessed McGill* and wanted me to work on the screenplay "Tom Horn" that had been written by Tom McGuane.

Pete took me to the airport in San Antonio that night and I didn't come back to the apartment for three months.

Eventually I set up my portable typewriter—the faithful little Skywriter had been retired by the movie business, which requires a lot of spacing—on the kitchen table of the apartment and got back to work on "Plum Creek." I discovered there is a drawback to living on the River Walk. It is a loud party all night long. Bongo Joe thumps his oil drums in the middle of the night. Drunk soldiers are shouting at hookers. There are noisy fistfights. It is sort of like living on Sheridan Square in Greenwich Village.

By this time Ellis Amburn had left his editing job and moved to Key West to write movie star biographies full-time. At about page 300 of "Plum Creek" I sent the manuscript off to the new editor in New York, hoping to collect another piece of the advance. She said, in effect, what the hell is this? Is this Giles Goat Boy Goes West? She said nobody wants to read a novel about Texas. She said forget about the rest of the advance.

I went back to Los Angeles to write a script about Belle Starr. I stopped by Bill Wittliff's office at the old Encino Press building in Austin and gave him a cardboard box that contained the "Plum Creek" manuscript. He had encouraged me to write it in the beginning, so I wound up giving it to him. I told Bill to dispose of it as he wished, I was finished with it.

For the next 15 years Bill would now and then say, "I've still got the 'Plum Creek' manuscript. You should finish it." I always said this was as far as I could take it.

In 1996, Dan and June Jenkins took a house for the summer on a beautiful golf course in the mountains of North Carolina. I went up and spent a couple of weeks with them. Dan and I played golf most days. It was a magical place. A river flowed past our door between our screened-in porch and the thirteenth green. There was a Cherokee museum with a rebuilt village a few miles away. As I was walking through the Cherokee village one day, something hit me.

I rushed back to the house and opened my laptop and started writing "Plum Creek" all over again.

This occupied me for the next two years. Under the title *The Borderland*, the book was published in 2000, roughly 20 years after Ellis Amburn wrote those two words on a napkin.

The portrait of Sam Houston in this chapter may be a little overwrought, but it is the great man the way I saw him from reading his speeches and letters and many books about him. As a character in a novel, old Sam cannot help outshining everyone around him.

Caldwell folded the letter and replaced it in an oilcloth packet that he had bought for the purpose.

"You say this woman is beautiful?" he asked.

Herr Growald, the marriage agent, leaned his elbows on the table he was using as a desk and pinched his plump cheeks with thumbs and forefingers, making a kissing hiss, his black mustache wiggling like a caterpillar. The toes of Growald's brogans dug into the mud and straw that made up the floor of his office, which was roofed by a tent, its canvas speckled with mildew. A sign above the door said: WEDDED BLISS GUARANTEED. The side panels of the tent were rolled up and tied in the hope of a breath of wet breeze in the suffocating heat of Houston City.

"She is so beautiful that it tore my heart just to gaze upon her," said Growald.

"When did you see her?"

"A few months ago while I was traveling through the German states, seeking clients. Her father approached me. I went to their home and observed her in the kitchen and listened to her play the piano. What a marvelous young woman. Delightful in conversation. And she can cook."

"Is her father in real danger?"

"I should think so, yes. Oh, but his daughter, Hannah Dahlman, such radiance glows from her like a charge of electrical sparks. She will furnish you fifteen years of delightful appearance before her beauty fades. She is diligent and industrious, rare qualities in any person. There may never come along another for you so perfect as she is."

Matthew still owned the 640 acres that had once been a cotton farm near Gonzalez, but he had let the land go wild. When he and Nancy and their sons had moved into what was still the Mexican state of Coahuila, the government had given him the cotton land, plus a headright of 4,400 acres and one labor of 170 acres southeast of Gonzalez. After the revolution, Caldwell could have chosen as a reward from the Congress of the Republic of Texas another headright of 4,400 acres of rich soil, timbered, with flowing springs south of Gonzalez. Instead, he asked the Congress for a double headright and two labors of land in the hills and valleys west of the Colorado, in Comancheria, where no other veterans of the revolution were clamoring to settle. He sold his original headright for $2,400 in gold notes, deposited in New Orleans. That was plenty enough to live on while he was ranging. Caldwell wasn't interested in making money or in dying rich. But he did desire a large spread of land to be the lord of and to bequeath to his children. It was in his blood to resume the tradition of the Caldwells.

Since Cristolphe Rublo and Mexican cavalry had burned the cotton farm, Caldwell had lived at Ranger stations or under the stars or in a room at the Fincus Hotel in San Antonio. The farmhouse near Gonzalez stood as a few silent black timbers. The cotton fields were overgrown with grass and wildflowers.

He had no home. But a young bride was on her way.

"Do you accept her?" asked Herr Growald.

"Yes. I think she will do fine," Caldwell said.

"You don't mind that she is Jewish?"

"What?"

"Professor Dahlman is a prominent Jewish intellectual in Hannover. His daughter, Hannah, is a Jew. Do you object?"

Matthew's father had hated Catholics and Puritans but had never mentioned Jews. The Ranger held no bias about Jews. Matthew hardly knew what they were.

"Will she require special treatment? There are no Jewish temples in Austin. There are no churches of any kind."

"No, no ceremonies or rituals, I assure you," Growald chuckled. "The young woman is a strong-minded freethinker, like her father. She will flourish in a frontier like this. But I want to be sure you know she is a Jew before you sign the contract of acceptance. I have had clients object and force me to send the Jews away. It is very unpleasant."

Growald unrolled a paper document, unstopped an inkwell and dipped his pen, fashioned from a turkey feather, into the ink. He held out the dripping pen toward Caldwell.

"I guess I can marry a Jew, all right, but why would a Jew want to marry me?" Caldwell said.

"My dear captain, you are quite a catch," said Growald.

"Besides which, she is desperate," Caldwell said.

"Well, yes, but what she really wants is to make you happy."

"Good. It's going to take a desperate woman to make me happy. Give me that pen," Caldwell said.

After he signed the agreement, he ducked through the door of Growald's tent and stepped into the smothering steam of Houston City. The air was alive with heat and the tiny insects that swam in it. Caldwell had paid $250 of Growald's $1,000 fee—the remainder due upon the bride arriving in good health in San Antonio. Professor Dahlman had refused to accept money from Caldwell for Hannah's passage to America. The professor sent apologies that he was not able to pay a dowry, a notion that had never occurred to Caldwell. Matthew was too proud to marry a woman he was paid to take.

With Hannah Dahlman's letter secure inside his belt, his fringed doeskin jacket hung across his back from a thumb, Sweet Lips cradled in an elbow and his two Paterson pistols swinging from the scabbards on his suspenders, Matthew Caldwell sloshed along the muddy main street in his moccasin boots, heading toward the saloon at the Palace Hotel, where General Sam Houston was holed up on a long drunk that Caldwell had heard about from Rangers at the station at Boca Chica Crossing.

The moisture in the air caused tricks with Caldwell's vision. The tents and shacks that made up the greater part of Houston City around the bayous rippled before his eyes. On a cold winter day in Houston City, the chill soaked straight to the skin. Caldwell preferred Missouri blizzards to a clammy winter in Houston City. But when it was hot, which was most of the year, the city lying on the same latitude as Calcutta, mosquitoes and flies rose out of the bayous in black curtains, and dogs rolled over, their tongues hanging out, and died in the sun.

Three years ago this place along Buffalo Bayou had been called Harrisburg, but Santa Anna's army had burned it to the ground. Two land speculators bought the ruins of Harrisburg the moment news came that Santa Anna had been defeated nearby at the Battle of San Jacinto. The Allen brothers named their new enterprise Houston City in honor of the victorious General Sam Houston.

Houston City boasted the capitol building of the Republic of Texas, built of pine logs and needing paint, three hotels, a theater for musical performances and stage plays and a racetrack. On either side of the main street Caldwell could see saloons in tents, saloons in shacks, saloons in buildings of some presumption. There were thirty-six saloons in Houston City—Caldwell and the Old Chief, General Sam Houston, had hoisted a whiskey in every one of them, so people later reported, during an epic drunk six months ago, during which Caldwell had decided to hire Herr Growald to find him a German bride. There was not one bank or church in the town.

The Palace Hotel was a two-story structure of whitewashed pine with touches of New Orleans style in tall green shutters on either side of each window, and on the second floor French doors opened onto a wrought iron balcony. Caldwell walked past the lobby entrance and went around the corner to the saloon door, which stood open to let out tobacco smoke and entice whispers of fetid air.

"By God, it's Matthew Caldwell! Come and give me a hug, my darling boy!"

The Old Chief, General Sam Houston, the first elected president of the Republic of Texas, slammed a crooked, ivory-knobbed mahogany cane onto the plank floor of the Palace saloon and rose as close to full height as he could manage, with arthritis clutching his lower spine and a load of whiskey affecting his balance. At six feet six, General Sam Houston was nearly half a head taller than Caldwell, and when they embraced, Matthew felt against his chin the wet purple indentation of the general's old broken collarbone wound. Caldwell's arms went beneath the Old Chief's armpits in a Mexican *abrazo* and clasped the backs of his shoulders, feeling the muscles in the wide, powerful torso that had absorbed so many stabs, slashes and lead balls that the scars were thought of as Sam Houston's medals of valor, a true copy of his deeds compared to the ribbons and medallions he was authorized to wear on his tunic. Now forty-eight years old and no longer with official powers, General Sam Houston was regarded by Caldwell and many other fighters in the revolution as the Old Chief, their leader.

"It's wonderful to see you, Matthew, my good friend," said the Old Chief, stepping back and gazing into Caldwell's face as if admiring a painting. "Let me gaze at you for a moment. So colorful you are."

"Compared to you, I'm a dullard, Chief," Caldwell said, thinking the general looked older than he remembered from their recent drinking bout. Wrinkles creased the Old Chief's eyes and forehead. Tangled gray hair curled around his ears. Of course, Matthew thought, he had to consider that probably the Old Chief had not slept last night, possibly had not eaten, and the perspiration on his skin tasted like brandy. The Old Chief winked elaborately and held a finger up to his lips.

"Quiet, Matthew. We must speak softly. I am in hiding. Please sit with me a spell." The Old Chief waved a long arm at the fat man behind the bar, whose apron was dark with sweat. "A jug of rare French brandy for Captain Caldwell!" Sam Houston shouted. "By God, it is a good thing to have friends!"

Leaning on the cane, the Old Chief lowered himself into the hardwood and rawhide chair, allowing a grunt of pain to escape. Caldwell pulled up another chair and sat down. He laid Sweet Lips in a third chair at the table.

"Is this an old wound that's bothering you, or have you been in another scrape?" Caldwell asked.

"This is not a wound. It's a mere injury. You might say it is because of this injury that I am in hiding."

"If somebody is pestering you, Chief, all you need to do is give me their name," Caldwell said.

The Old Chief laughed and began to wheeze. His face turned red and his eyes bulged. His big right hand with the sharp knuckles scooped up his crystal snifter, and his Adam's apple bobbed as he swigged brandy. Caldwell accepted his own clay jug from the fat man, bit into the cork and pulled out the stopper. The first rush of brandy down his throat burned his stomach and chased a shudder up his spine.

"General Savariego is in the field a few miles west of the Warloop," Matthew said.

"Not so loud," said the Old Chief.

"What?"

"Lower your voice, please."

Caldwell leaned both elbows on the table and bent forward and spoke barely above a whisper.

"General Savariego is in the field east of San Antonio. I caught some of his scouts. They say Savariego is hunting Comanches, but he may raid Austin. What do you think?"

"I wouldn't be surprised, or especially disappointed, if Savariego plunders Austin," said the Old Chief. "Austin is a troublemaking place that should not exist."

Caldwell whispered, "Why are we being so quiet?"

"I am hiding from my future mother-in-law," the Old Chief said. "She is a ferocious old bitch. A dragon."

"With all respect, Chief, how can you be getting married again?"

"Oh, I've so much news for you, my brave Captain Caldwell. First, the sad news, the very sad news. Diana Gentry, my wonderful Cherokee wife, who saved my life more than once when rum and the devil threatened to do me in, well, poor Diana has died of a fever as she was being removed from Tennessee to the western territories. Ah, if only she had let me know she was being moved, I could have saved her. I would have grabbed Andy Jackson's throat if that's what it took. But Diana was too proud to ask me for help, and, damn me, I was too vain and self-involved to inquire after the well-being of this noble woman. May she rest in peace in heaven, for she was ill treated as an angel on this earth."

"I'm sorry, Chief. I know you loved her," said Caldwell, waving to the fat man to bring him a cheroot. Caldwell had swiftly examined the saloon for indications of danger to the Old Chief but had found none. Two drunks lay asleep and snoring at a table in the corner, their heads on maps of plats of land in Houston City. Caldwell guessed these were land speculators who had tried to drink with the Old Chief in hope of winning a favor from him but had overloaded themselves, and now would be forever weaklings in his eyes. One sad-looking drummer, his suit sweated through, his satchel of samples on the floor beside his muddy shoes, stood and drank at the bar. Usually wherever Sam Houston was, a crowd gathered. This was a mid-morning lull.

"But now two pieces of excellent news," said the Old Chief. "The first is that my divorce decree from the once precious but no longer desired Eliza Allen, the belle of Gallatin, has at last been granted in the state of Tennessee, and I walk this earth today a free man, without any wife to criticize me."

"Then why are you in hiding?" Caldwell asked.

"The second piece of excellent news is I am about to become engaged to be married. A wee tiny wifey. Every man needs a wee tiny wifey if he is to find peace and happiness and fulfillment on this earth. You must find yourself one, Matthew. You have grieved long and devoutly over the loss of your family, but now you must move toward the rest of your life."

Sam Houston swirled his brandy and smiled at Matthew's expression of curiosity.

"I arrived in Mobile on a commercial venture, looking for investors in a land speculation," the Old Chief said, tapping his game leg with his cane. "This was only two months ago, mind you. I was still a married man, though

I had no wife at hand, In fact, I was still married to two different women at once, but had not a hint of the comfort a woman's touch brings to my oh so human skin."

The Old Chief hunched forward at the table, leaning on his elbows. His cotton shirt was open at the neck. A red scar ran up his breastbone, the testimony, Caldwell knew, of the Old Chief's fight at Horseshoe Bend, Alabama, against the Creek Indians twenty-five years ago while he was serving in the United States army as a lieutenant under General Andrew Jackson. The Old Chief's right forearm and shoulder had been shattered by musket balls in that fight, and an arrow had pierced his groin, leaving a wound that Caldwell heard had never ceased to ooze. The Old Chief accepted a cheroot from the bartender but declined to have it lit. He chewed on the cigar, rolling it in his lips as if it were nourishment. The Old Chief said he had arrived in Mobile two months ago to cast his net for investors in Texas land. As he was walking off the ship on the gangplank, his right heel caught in a piece of rope and he twisted his right knee and fell heavily, rendered unconscious by the sudden pain. His enemies, the Old Chief said, spread the slander that he had toppled over in a drunken swoon, but he swore to Caldwell that he was sober as a Puritan, and was eagerly looking forward to checking in at La Grande Hotel and hurrying to the hotel bar to remedy his condition.

"At the very center of my soul as I lay unconscious, a poem sprang forth: 'Oh, love, thou hast returned to me, whose heart homeless toward the grave did veer. I behold thy face that God hath sent to keep me here.'"

The Old Chief's upper lip twitched as he peered at Caldwell, and he peeled a strip of tobacco off his teeth.

"I opened my eyes—and there she was! The creature sent to me from heaven. Seventeen years old but wiser than any of my political or military advisers ever were, excepting you, Caldwell, if you did ever give me advice, I can't remember now."

"Just once, Chief," said Caldwell. "I suggested you let me execute Santa Anna."

"You did? Well, there were a lot of opinions being tossed back and forth at that moment. But how could I shoot a fellow Mason who claims to get ten erections every day? Don't be upset with me, Matthew, it was just damned politics that saved Santa Anna. But I am in love and had rather not talk politics right now. Let me continue to speak of Mobile. I am lying there, looking up at this darling spirit, yearning to have her for my own, devastated to remember that I am already married to two women. I don't know if I am deliriously happy or utterly miserable—and then I pass out again, from the pain and the strain on my nerves."

He had been revived and carried to the hotel, where a physician diagnosed his knee as having a stressed but not torn ligament and prescribed one hundred drops of laudanum to be swallowed instantly and followed by a bottle of white wine from France. When the general awoke the next morning, he placed fifty drops of laudanum on his tongue while humming a polka tune, had a vigorous scrub in a tub of hot water, with his black slave Andre handling the brush and the lye soap, massaged honeycomb and lard into his swollen knee, wrapped the knee in cotton, shaved and dressed in a blue velvet tunic with a white shirt of fine Georgia cotton and white linen trousers freshly pressed by the hotel valet, and ordered a walking stick of noble quality to be brought to his room. All of that accomplished, the Old Chief drank the rest of the bottle of laudanum and went to eat breakfast in the hotel restaurant, where the customers openly stared at him, this hugely tall and notorious former president of Texas, former governor of Tennessee.

The hotel owner had rushed to have coffee at the invitation of the illustrious Sam Houston, who made inquiries. The girl on the dock was named Margaret Lea, and her mother was a rich widow, known all over southern Mississippi for her fierce rejections of every one of her daughter's suitors as being unworthy. Through the hotel owner the Old Chief arranged a meeting with Mrs. Victoria Lea at her lawyer's office, where he invited Mrs. Lea, who was thirty-eight and quite attractive in a mean-eyed way, to come to Texas to see for herself the prospects for vast wealth in land and cattle and cotton. He was delighted when Victoria and her lawyer accepted, but he was disappointed that they refused to bring Margaret Lea, who was attending school and learning to speak French and play the harp.

The Old Chief twirled a finger above his gray head in the Palace saloon and said:

"What winning graces, what majestic mien! She moves a goddess and she looks a queen! I am going back to Mobile today and marry my Margaret Lea, Matthew, I swear it. Victoria opposes me, but she shall not defeat me."

Caldwell heard the clack of hardware upon a door frame and saw the ruddy, bearded face of Big Foot Wallace ducking to peer into the dimness of the saloon from the yellow heat of the muddy path outside, the Bowie knife on his belt scraping against wood as he craned his body sideways. Big Foot was six feet two, weighed two hundred and forty pounds with hardly an ounce of fat, and he entered the saloon moving softly as a breath. For the past year Big Foot had been scouting from the Ranger station in Boca Chica Crossing, where he shared his one-room house with his dogs, but he had been on a confidential assignment from President Lamar two days ago when Caldwell stopped to report the Mexican battalion that might be marching toward Austin.

"The stout Wallace!" cried the Old Chief. "How da do, man? How da do?"

"I feel almost as good all over as I do any other place," Big Foot said.

Caldwell laughed. He felt affection and respect for his comrade. Big Foot was born William Alexander Anderson Wallace in Virginia to Scots Highlander parents descended from William Wallace and Robert Bruce. Wallace came to Texas three years ago after his brother and cousin were shot by the Mexican army in the massacre at Goliad. He sought revenge against the Mexican army and took payment in blood. On his first patrol after joining the Rangers, Wallace found the track of a cow thief and told his mates, "Boys, that is one hell of a big-footed son of a bitch." Wallace trailed the cow thief and shot the man through the chest from fifty yards. Upon inspection of the corpse, he discovered the thief to be a Kiowa Indian wearing a new pair of handsomely beaded moccasins. Wallace tried them on, and the moccasins fit as if made for him. Henceforth the Rangers called him Big Foot.

The Old Chief thrust himself up to his feet in a sudden burst of energy that surprised Caldwell and waved his heavy, ivory-knobbed cane in the air like the baton of an orchestra conductor.

"You brave hearts join me," the Old Chief shouted. "We are going to sing once again the song that won the day at Peggy McCormick's farm!"

The Old Chief began singing in a roar: "Come, all you reckless and rambling boys who have listened to my song." Caldwell stood and made it a duet with his rough baritone. "If it's done no good, sir, I'm sure it's done no wrong. But when you court a pretty girl, just marry her when you can. For if you ever cross those plains, she'll marry another man. . . ."

The Chief stopped and glared at Big Foot. The Old Chief seemed to grow even taller, rising above Big Foot. Caldwell heard dangerous drunken anger in the Old Chief's voice.

"Damn it, sir, I demand that you sing with us," the Old Chief said to Big Foot.

"I mean no disrespect, Chief, sir, but over where I was we didn't sing 'The Girl I Left Behind Me,'" Big Foot said. "We sang 'Come to the Bower.' Soon as I wet my goozle out of that jug, I'll sing so loud it'll deefen ye."

Big Foot turned up Caldwell's clay jug and swallowed heartily, wiped his mouth and then sang in a clear, thin voice that had a southern mountain accent:

Will you come to the bower I have shaded for you?
Our bed shall be roses all spangled with dew.
There under the bower on roses you'll lie.
With a blush on your cheek but a smile in your eye.

Hearing Big Foot's song made Caldwell remember the black drummer boy beating the rhythm and the German fifer playing on the right flank as seven hundred men, many of them singing, had trotted across Peggy McCormick's farm at San Jacinto at four o'clock in the afternoon of April 21, three years ago. Motts of live oaks and magnolias rose from the high grass. Caldwell remembered the sounds of pounding feet and heavy breathing and the voices rising in song. He felt exhilarated and free. The Texan line was fifteen hundred yards wide. The Old Chief had ridden thirty yards in front of the rest, mounted on his stallion, Saracen. Caldwell saw the Mexicans become aware of the charge and scramble to their weapons, and he saw smoke from cannons and rifles and heard explosions and snapping zings popping past his ears.

A volley had killed Saracen, and the Old Chief had grabbed a riderless horse and swung into the saddle. The stirrups were short for him, so he rode with his long legs flailing. Mexican *escopeta* balls smashed the Old Chief's right ankle and killed the second horse. The general hauled himself onto the back of a third horse and galloped through the smoke and flames and bayonets into the Mexican ranks. Dead Mexicans were piling in heaps on the breastworks of dirt and field packs. Caldwell killed five men with Sweet Lips and stabbed another. The fight was over in minutes, but the slaughter continued. Caldwell had seen the Old Chief, with blood flowing from the hole in his boot, still mounted, shouting, "Parade, gentlemen! Parade!" But nothing could stop the lust for killing. Hundreds of Mexicans tried to escape across a marshy bayou to their rear, but they drowned or were shot. Many who tried to surrender were clubbed or slashed or strangled in the Texans' blood rage.

Caldwell had walked among the dead and wounded, searching for the body of Santa Anna. All around in sulfur clouds Caldwell heard weeping and praying and moaning, and the war whoops of the Texans. He saw the clothing of dead Mexicans being searched for loot. Two dentists knelt among the bodies, filling their bullet bags with teeth they pulled out of skulls. As darkness came, the Texans built fires to dry their clothing and threatened to burn their prisoners. Santa Anna was found in the morning wearing baggy pantaloons of a slave and hiding in a thicket. Sam Houston was lying with his back against an oak tree, weaving a garland of vines to send to Diana Gentry as a surgeon cleaned and bandaged his ankle. The Old Chief had looked up and seen the emperor of Mexico being prodded before him. Caldwell had carefully reloaded Sweet Lips in the hope that the Old Chief would order a prompt execution. Caldwell wanted to pull the trigger. But after allowing the emperor the comfort of chewing a ball of gum opium to make his humiliation bearable, the Old Chief had spared Santa Anna's life on his written word that Mexican armies would retreat to the Rio Grande, and Mexico would never invade the free Texas Republic again.

Out of loyalty to the Old Chief, Matthew had refused to join the rebels who dragged Santa Anna and his officers off a ship in Galveston Bay with the intention of lynching the president of Mexico. The Old Chief, with Caldwell at his side, intervened, faced down the mob and then escorted the Mexicans to Orizambo, the plantation of Dr. James Phelps, twelve miles north of Columbus. For the next ten months Santa Anna and his officers were kept in leg irons, abused, starved. Caldwell had become a Texas Ranger by then, and he heard how poorly the Mexicans were treated, but he had no sympathy for Santa Anna. The Old Chief had finally sent Santa Anna to President Andrew Jackson, who returned the Mexican president to Veracruz. A year ago in Veracruz the French navy had blown off Santa Anna's left leg with a cannonball. Matthew had heard Santa Anna's valets carried the emperor's spare legs in cases like musical instruments.

After Big Foot finished singing in the Palace Hotel Saloon, the Old Chief and Caldwell applauded and the three men sat together at the table and drank crystal snifters of French brandy poured from clay jugs.

"The boys at Boca Chica tell me you're doing a confidential duty for Lamar," Caldwell said.

"Aw, hell, nothing is confidential where you and the Chief are concerned," said Big Foot. "Lamar sent me down here to buy twenty barrels of gunpowder and two oxcarts full of lead for shot and then guard the shipment until it gets to San Antonio. That's one part of my assignment. The other part is, the President told me to find you and tell you he needs to see you on an urgent personal matter, Matthew. Maybe you could give me a hand watching over this cargo on the road, since San Antonio is where our president is holed up at the old governor's palace doing government business and waiting for you."

"The scoundrel won't come to his president's office in Houston City when he knows I am in town," the Old Chief said. "It's to spite me and kill Indians that he's moving the capitol to Austin this summer. Two years from now I'll be elected president again, and I'll see that damned Austin deserted with grass growing in its streets."

Caldwell nodded and scratched his beard, wanting a bath. He believed the Old Chief would let Austin rot if he had the chance. The Congress named the new capital for Stephen F. Austin, a Missouri politician who had founded a settlement of immigrants from the United States on a tract between the Colorado and Brazos rivers three years before the revolution. The Old Chief beat Stephen Austin in the first election for president but named the former Missouri territorial legislator as secretary of state in the first cabinet as a gesture to Houston's many enemies. Caldwell, as elected representative from Gonzalez, voted in favor of moving the capital to Austin. Matthew listened to the Old Chief's diatribe and smiled inwardly. How many towns in Texas could be named Houston?

When the Old Chief paused for a drink, Matthew looked at Big Foot.

"What does Lamar want with me?" Caldwell asked.

"I don't know. All he told me is it's very important."

"Beware of Lamar," said the Old Chief. "Our Republic is worse off today than it was when we fought at Peggy McCormick's farm. We are destitute where before we were only moneyless. The whole United States is in a financial panic and can't help us. Rabble are pouring across the Sabine. Every fool and thug and confidence man in the South is coming here to find his fortune. The land contagion has us in its clutches—even you, Matthew, with your blasted ten thousand acres in Comancheria. Lamar wants to start wars with the Indians to clear out more land to sell, and it's men like you two who will die in the doing of it. You won't find real estate bankers riding headlong into Comanche lances. There is treachery all around. Tens of thousands of greedy second-raters are flooding into our Republic to get fat off the fruits of our struggles. We are surrounded by angry Indians, Mexican armies plunder our out-country and menace our cities, our government is bankrupt, the French and English and Dutch are looking for a justification to move in on us, and our president, Mirabeau Buonaparte Lamar, is a liar, schemer and dangerous man, and besides, he is a damn terrible poet. Have you read any of that sappy nonsense he writes?"

"No, sir," said Big Foot.

"Not me," Caldwell said.

"Consider this place, Austin, that Lamar has chosen for our new capital," said Sam Houston.

"I was at the site with Waller's surveying crew last fall," Caldwell said. "It's a frontier Eden up there. Enclosed by hills in a crook of the Colorado River. Plenty of flowing water, springs, timber, fish and game. The elevation makes a healthier climate than here in Houston City. Lamar says it is a natural hub for roads that will run from the Red River to Matamoros and from the Gulf of Mexico to Santa Fe."

"How many miles is it from Austin to what Lamar claims as our Republic of Texas westernmost outpost, the city of Santa Fe?" asked the general.

"About eight hundred miles," Caldwell said.

"And how many forts or even settlements do we have between Austin and Santa Fe?"

"Well, none, as you know," Caldwell said.

"Now let's tell the truth about Austin, with its abundant water and game and magical scenery, the favorite resort and spa for the whole Comanche Nation for thousands of years. Do you not agree that establishing our capitol building in Austin will provoke an all-out war with the Comanches?"

"Chief, I fall in with Lamar on that one. We're going to have to fight those Comanches to the death. I ain't against all of the Indians, not by any means. Your Cherokee friend Chief Bowl is doing fine in East Texas. But we're going to have to whip those Comanches. They've killed or captured three hundred immigrants along our southwestern border in two years. I found another family hacked to pieces a week ago. If building Austin will make the Comanches come out and fight, I am in favor of it."

The Old Chief laughed. "Come out and fight? If the Comanches would all join together and come out and fight, it would be like twenty thousand of Genghis Khan's Mongol cavalry howling down on helpless villages. How big is San Antonio? Maybe two thousand residents, less than half of them

Anglos? And what do we have in Austin to face the Comanches—a thousand lawyers and land speculators. What can you put in the field against the Comanches, Matthew? Two hundred Rangers?"

"About a hundred and sixty right now," Caldwell said. "We've had some people hurt."

"Then there is the Texas army," said the Old Chief. "Maybe six hundred are left, but there's no money to pay them. I furloughed the rest so they wouldn't form a mob behind Felix Huston and try to invade Mexico. Don't count on the Texas army to help you Rangers defeat those Comanche warriors. Two or three years ago you could have gathered a militia of civilians to help you. But now our civilians are rabble from the east who want to buy and sell land, not fight for it."

"Well, then, I'm glad the Comanches aren't organized, because we are going to have to fight them," Caldwell said.

"Tell me, Matthew, if the Indians could send feathered chiefs to our Congress to vote as landholders just like the white man, what do you think would happen at our next assembly?"

"Which Indians?" asked Caldwell.

"The Indians that live in our Republic—the Cherokees, Comanches, Apaches, Kiowas, Alabamas, Shawnees, Karankawas, Tonks, Delawares, Kickapoos, Patawonatres, Caddos, Creeks, Wacos, Pawnees and all the rest. What if they had the vote, like we do? What would happen?"

"They'd vote our ass right out of Texas," Caldwell said.

"Lucky thing most of these tribes hate each other worse than they hate us. Otherwise, they could destroy our republic in a week," said the Old Chief. "The only way Texas can maintain itself against its enemies is to join the union of the United States and call upon the U.S. Army to do the bloody work."

"I fought to become a citizen of the Republic of Texas, and I will fight to remain so," Caldwell said. "But I will not fight for the United States. My place is here."

"Ah, but you will fight for your ten thousand acres, will you not?" the Old Chief said.

"Unless you can sweet talk the Comanches into turning it over to me, I will," said Caldwell.

"Matthew, you're an imperialist at heart. You want your own kingdom," the Old Chief said.

"I stand for a free and independent Texas," Caldwell said.

"I'll drink with ye on that," said Big Foot.

"I daresay you would drink with Matthew on anything," the Old Chief said.

"You know me well, Chief," said Big Foot.

"That's what we're all doing here, ain't it, Chief?" said Caldwell. "Building a republic?"

"Drink to Texas," the Old Chief said. The three men drained their snifters.

"Sam Houston, you swore to me you would go to bed and get a full night's sleep, but I can plainly see you chose to stay up all night and get even drunker with your fellow sots," said Victoria Lea.

A tall woman, wearing white, with a broad-brimmed hat to protect her face from the sun and a net hanging from the brim to fend off insects, Victoria Lea stood in the lobby entrance to the saloon. Behind her was a soft, plump little man with side-whiskers, wiping his face constantly with a handkerchief, looking as if the slightest relaxation of inner tension would cause him to wilt into a puddle.

The Old Chief shot up abruptly from the table, knocking over their brandy jugs and breaking their crystal snifters, standing up straight and tall as if he were reviewing troops, huge in his blue tunic and his white cotton shirt, now torn open to the waist, revealing a chest crisscrossed with scars.

"The beautiful Mrs. Victoria Lea, may I present two heroes of the Texas Republic? Captain Matthew Caldwell, a congressman and our senior Ranger, and the famous Ranger scout and warrior Big Foot Wallace."

Caldwell and Big Foot scrambled to their feet. Mrs. Victoria Lea studied Caldwell with interest, then glanced at Big Foot and back at Caldwell. Though he could hardly see her eyes through the mosquito netting, Caldwell felt them exploring his body.

"And the puny gentleman is her esteemed attorney, Mr. Ned Boodle, Esquire," the Old Chief said.

"Victoria, please, we're going to miss the steamboat and have to spend another day in hell," said Ned Boodle.

"General Houston, I have decided to invest a large sum in Texas. I shall require you to accompany Mr. Boodle and me back to Mobile to sign the necessary documents," Victoria Lea said.

"He'll make us late. We can do it without him," said Boodle.

"Why, Mr. Boodle, you think too short of me," the Old Chief said. "My man Andre is sitting behind the hotel at this minute with my bags packed and a pony cart to take me to the dock. I was returning to Mobile today in any case, dear Victoria, to propose marriage to your darling daughter, Margaret Lea."

"I don't want you for a son-in-law," said Victoria. "You're old. You're crippled. You're no longer a president or a general or a governor. You have no power. You are not rich. You stink of whiskey and tobacco. I do want to buy the land you are representing and will appoint you as my agent for buying a cattle herd. But you will never marry my daughter, you stinking old drunk." Victoria Lea whirled on her heel in a flutter of white and marched into the lobby, closely tailed by the miserable Boodle.

The Old Chief looked back and forth from Caldwell to Big Foot. He straightened his shoulders, sucked in air and stuck out his chest. He made a formidable figure, as fierce a sight as any Comanche warrior.

"Do either of you see my hat?" the Old Chief asked.

"You don't have no hat, General Houston," said the bartender. "You give it away yesterday as a souvenir to some little child."

"So I did. Quite right. Andre will have me another hat," the Old Chief said. He shook hands with Caldwell, then with Big Foot. He clutched each man on the shoulder in a powerful grip. He looked them in the eye.

"Texas can be heaven on earth if we love her well," the Old Chief said. "I'm leaving Texas in your care, my noble friends, while I go woo the sweetheart of my life. You brave Rangers remember what I tell you—beware of Lamar. He will sacrifice your lives to serve his greed and ambition. I'll find you a different piece of land, Matthew, a better piece, bigger, your own empire. Stay alive until I am elected president of Texas again, and we'll do things right next time. The streets of Austin shall once more become the feeding place for buffaloes and the hunting ground for red men. Don't risk your scalps for that damned hole called Austin! Adios, my comrades."

Letter: May 29, 1965, on Writing *Blessed McGill*

Sterling Lord became my literary agent after Annie Laurie Williams retired. Sterling was, and is, among the best. He represented me on *But Not for Love, Blessed McGill,* and *Strange Peaches.* We parted ways when I quit *Sports Illustrated* to go to Hollywood. Cindy Degener, Sterling's wife, had been my movie agent for *J. W. Coop, Kid Blue,* and *Nightwing.* She was three for three for me. But I felt I needed a bigger agency on the West Coast. Willie Nelson had just signed with Jim Wiatt at ICM and recommended I do the same. Willie and I were trying to get the movie *Songwriter* (at the time it was just an idea we were talking about) made. I thought ICM would help, and they did. Wiatt spent several years hustling for *Songwriter.* But I was careless in the way I broke up with Sterling. He got hurt and angry and quit speaking to me. I don't blame him. I regret it. The fact is, ICM helped me get lots of movie work. But when Cindy sold a script, somehow the movie got made.

This letter to Sterling is talking about what was going to be the story of six Americans in Rome during the beatification of the first American saint. I was working on the novel one night in my apartment on Fifteenth Street in New York. I came to the part of the story where I had to name the first American saint. There had never been one, so who would it be? I figured it would be someone from the deep Southwest where the Catholic religion collided with Native American beliefs very early in our history. I started making notes about this imaginary saint, and I found myself writing his memoir.

I realized the story of the saint was better than the story of the Americans in Rome. I had spent a few weeks in a small walk-up hotel on a narrow street near the Spanish Steps in Rome while I was writing *But Not for Love.* I used to watch the tourists at the café tables and wonder why they were there. I made up stories for them. Their book was called "These Happy Occasions." But they fell by the way. The saint took over. The new book became *Blessed McGill.*

Bud Shrake works on his novel *Blessed McGill* in Acapulco, 1966.

Dear Sterling:

I know when you read this you are going to think you are dealing with a lunatic, and perhaps you are—especially in view of all the squabbling I raised over that 15,000 words of THESE HAPPY OCCASIONS. But I have thought about it constantly for the last three days, and it has struck me that I am writing the wrong book. If you agree, after you have read the new idea, please withdraw that other manuscript. There are a lot of good things in it that I can use later.

The way this came about was I was working out the story of McGill, the Beatified, and I realized his story was the one I really wanted to tell. His story is the strongest. The other—about Dabney Patch and all that—has a couple of inherent flaws that have not showed up yet but are waiting down the line. They could be fixed, and maybe will be in a slightly different book.

But I thought I might write one called THE SECRET JOURNAL OF BLESSED McGILL. In an introductory note it is explained that Peter Hermano McGill was one of the first Americans to be declared Blessed, as a martyr to his faith, and that it was thought he had left behind no writing. But this journal was discovered in an abandoned adobe house in the Taos mountains. The journal was written as McGill prepared to go to death. It comes out as the story of a wild, brawling, gambling man who became a saint in spite of himself, and for different reasons than those supposed by the Church. . . .

Letter: September 8, 1966, on Visiting Chihuahua

This trip into the canyons of Chihuahua not only became a *Sports Illustrated* piece but was the source of much of *Blessed McGill.*

Shel Hershorn was an outstanding photographer who shot for the Black Star Syndicate and worked regularly for *Life* magazine when it was famous for its pictures. Not long after this Chihuahua assignment, Shel suddenly put his cameras away for good, moved into a small adobe house outside of Taos, and began making custom furniture by hand and milking goats. It was a great loss to photojournalism, but his furniture is lasting and beautiful.

Shooting pool in Creel, Chihuahua. Photo by Shel Hershorn.

Dear Missy:

... The elegant pool hall shot was took in Creel, Chihuahua, during an 8-ball match between myself and Shel Hershorn (who took the photo). When we started playing 8-ball the pool hall was empty save for Shel, the barkeep and me. Shortly after the first game was finished I looked around and there were eight or ten people watching. By the third game, there were forty or fifty. By the fifth game I was wobble-legged from drinking tequila (the duty of the winner) and so handed my cue to a Mexican and requested him to beat that white man's ears off, which he did. But in Last and Dramatic Bloody Final Game, Shel arose magnificently to beat the Mexican, the local champ, in a fine and courageous display, after which we stumbled together out into the dust, staggeringly avoided hordes of chickens and pigs in the streets, were helped onto a train by some friendly Tarahumaras and rode to Los Mochis. Or at least that is where we, amazed, discovered ourselves after paying a $36.00 bar bill on the train and frightening several passengers with our visages. ...

The Tarahumaras: A Lonely Tribe of Long-Distance Runners

Sports Illustrated, January 9, 1967

Here's the *Sports Illustrated* story on the Tarahumaras—the same tribe that appears in *Blessed McGill*.

The Indians began to come in as the sun touched the ridge west of where the Río Cusarare bends in a clear stream past a place called Cabañas Barranca del Cobre. The first we knew of their approach was when Shel Hershorn, the photographer, glanced up from our game of crazy eights and said, "It's a classic. A face in the window. Don't look over your shoulder." So I looked over my shoulder and saw framed in the window a pine tree and the nape of a chalky hill, nothing more.

"Perfect face," Shel said. "Brown. White headband. Black hair. Curious oval eyes. Apache-looking. Too bad you missed it. However, if you could look up just now, carefully, without letting them know what you're doing, and turn your head very slowly, then suddenly snap around, you could see three more."

I looked around again, and there were five. Rather than popping out of sight, these five—now seven, all wearing cotton headbands, dressed as if they had been sent by Cochise—grouped at the windows and peered into the room where we sat at a table near the fireplace. Those faces, black eyes following each movement of card or cigarette or coffee cup, awoke some ancient memory that caused a certain creeping of the flesh. Mollie Lowther got up and opened the door. Bundles of cloth lay on the hillside beyond Río Cusarare as though someone had tossed his laundry out of an airplane. Since early afternoon we had heard the bells of the Indians' goats and had caught an occasional ghostly motion up in the rocks. Now the Tarahumaras were showing themselves, coming in for the fiesta we had decided not to have that day. "Must be at least 50," Mollie said. "Somebody's going to have to explain this to them."

We had been passing the word for the Tarahumaras to come in some morning and had been assured by Juan Safiro, a mestizo from a valley known

In Chihuahua, 1966, while on assignment for *Sports Illustrated* (and research-ing for *Blessed McGill*). Photo by Shel Hershorn.

as the Place of the Eagles, that they would. But an Indian is not obsessed with counting time as we are. When you say morning he thinks you eccentric if you expect him before dusk. We went out on the porch of the Cabañas Ba-rranca del Cobre, which is a long wooden cabin divided into rooms. An old blind man in a loincloth was walking down the road toward the lodge, pok-ing up dust with his stick. Behind him wandered a small boy wearing only an unbuttoned red shirt. The old man sat down against the Lowthers' pole fence. The boy came to the porch and looked up at us.

"*Chu-mu rewe?*" I said, exhausting one-seventh of my knowledge of phras-es in Rarámuri, the language of the Tarahumaras.

"*Nejé rewé Juan Batista,*" said the boy.

"Terrible name to stick a kid with," Shel said. "Give him some candy."

The boy unfolded a bandanna, placed our peppermints inside with several jellybeans of dubious vintage and refolded the bandanna. He kept looking at us. They were all looking at us, the ones who had been at the windows and the ones on the hillside and a dozen more who were coming down the canyon from the direction of the waterfall and perhaps another dozen who had appeared on the ridge in the sunset. They were not talking. They were just looking at us. Even the goats were looking at us. They were all waiting. They could wait all night.

Shel picked up his Polaroid color camera, and we went out to the pole fence, where an Indian woman in a white cotton dress sat with two babies and a dog. All three were in her arms, wrapped in a red shawl.

Shel shot her picture. Many of the Tarahumaras have never seen their own reflections. The Polaroid was our device for introduction. Shel gave the woman the color print, and she held it upside down, as other Indians did later. Shel righted it. She examined the photo and began to make the mental connection between the red on the paper and the red of her shawl. She tapped the photo, tapped the shawl, tapped her face and looked up at us. "That's you, ma'am," Shel said. She grinned in a sudden burst of pleasure. She started stroking her hair and smoothing it back, looking into the photograph as if it were a mirror.

Mollie, meanwhile, was informing the Indians through one who spoke Spanish as well as Rarámuri that the fiesta would be put off until tomorrow at San Ignacio. The reason, she told them, was that it was getting too dark for pictures. Having come to expect baffling behavior from us, they nodded. By now they knew Shel as Loquito, or Little Crazy One, because he lay in the dirt or hung from rocks a mile above canyon floors to point his black boxes. We broke open a crate of animal crackers and passed them out and watched the Indians disappear into the evening, goat bells tinkling, dogs barking, bundles of cloth vanishing into the pines.

This was the barranca country in the southwestern part of the state of Chihuahua, Mexico, about 400 miles south of El Paso and 180 miles west of Chihuahua City. We had come down to find the runners of the Sierra del Tarahumara, a stretch of the high mountain range called Sierra Madre Occidental. The Indians for whom the Sierra del Tarahumara is named refer to themselves as Rarámuri, a word that means "foot runner." Anthropologists class them as Uto-Aztécan, related to those fantastic runners of the southwestern U.S., the Apaches. It was not extraordinary for an Apache to run 75 miles in a day, leaving his horse far from the scene of a raid and approaching on foot. The origins of the Tarahumaras are unclear, but a band of Apaches living northeast of the Gila River in Arizona were called Tarasoma by the Pimas. Among the Tarahumaras is a tale that they came down from the Apache land, although there persist old men who say their people descended from heaven with corn and potatoes in their ears.

The Tarahumaras were driven into the mountains by the Spanish and by other Indians, including the Apaches and the Yaquis. Over many of their canyon paths it is safer and faster to go on foot than by horse or even by burro, and running developed as a mode of transportation as well as a game. "There is no doubt they are the best runners in the world, not for speed but for distance," says Professor Lamberto Alvarez Gayou, an authority on Mexican sport. Forty years ago an emissary went to a Tarahumara chief to invite him to send runners to a marathon race in Kansas. When told a marathon was a mere 26 miles, the chief ordered three girls to run it. In 1927 Professor Gayou clocked two Tarahumara men in 14 hours 53 minutes for a distance of 89.4 miles between Austin and San Antonio, Texas. Two Tarahumara sisters ran 28.5 miles in 4 hours 56 minutes—not astonishing for speed or distance in terms of the Boston Marathon, but a fair jog for two teen-age girls in long dresses. Several Tarahumaras were on the 1928 Mexican Olympic team, and others have come forth for a trial now and then, but the Indians have never done well when brought down from their high country and made to behave like athletes. When they run, it is to get someplace or to win a bet. Recently a Tarahumara messenger ran 50 miles through the mountains, stopped at several villages for reports on the Indians' food supply—which, as usual, was scant—and returned to the Jesuit mission in Sisoguíchi. He made the trip in six hours.

To reach Tarahumara country we flew from Juárez to Chihuahua City, coming in over patches of brown desert sprinkled with the green of sage and cactus, the jagged mountains blue in the distance. From Chihuahua City we rode southwesterly on the Chihuahua al Pacifico, a remarkable railroad that goes through 72 tunnels and across 33 bridges and twists over the Continental Divide three times before it arrives at Los Mochis, 400 miles away on the Pacific coast. Vaqueros and children herding goats and sheep watched the train go past as it climbed higher into the mountains, into a vast, lofty country of pines, oaks, aspens, boulders and great swollen batholiths. The rivers have carved the area into five major canyons, or barrancas, and many lesser canyons over an area of 10,000 square miles. Five of our Grand Canyons would fit into the barranca country like five stewpots into a bathtub and leave rattling room on the sides.

The rivers that have sculptured the barrancas come together into the Río del Fuerte, which breaks out of the Sierra Madre Occidental southwest of the Divisadero near the town of Choix, said to have been named for a French soldier who deserted from Maximilian's army after the Emperor of Mexico was overthrown in 1867. In the time of the conquistadores, gold and silver were packed out on burros along the Río del Fuerte and then north to Alamos for smelting. For centuries men have searched western Chihuahua, eastern Sonora and northern Sinaloa for the lost Jesuit mine of Tayopa, which 17th century records prove to have existed, perhaps on the Yaqui River, but which now exists in tales, in faded maps, in mysterious lumps of gold that turn up in trading towns and perhaps in the secrets of the Tarahumaras or the Yaquis. Within the past two years an archaeologist from California discovered 24 suits of 16th century Spanish armor in perfect condition in a cave outside Sisoguíchi, on the headwaters of the Río Conchos. He says the huge ovens he found may be evidence to verify a Tarahumara legend concerning a race of giants who lived in the mountains, and had much gold.

Clearly, one could not enter such a country without a certain amount of dreaming. I went up to the head of the two-car Fiat Autovia train to discuss with Shel what problems enormous riches might cause us. Shel was standing between two engineers and watching as the train clattered toward a black mule that was dining on the track.

"Hey, there's a mule on the track," Shel said finally to the chief engineer.

"Oh, we kill lots of mules," said the engineer, making a duck-quacking motion with his fingers and looking at his assistant as if to say these Anglos know nothing of how to run a railroad.

The mule rose up large in the windshield. At the last moment the engineer honked his horn, and the mule walked off the track. "Pardon me," Shel said. There was a dull banging sound and a jolt. We looked out and saw a pig tumbling off into a ditch. "We kill lots of those, too," said the engineer, and we went back to our seats as the train came into Creel, a lumber town 7,000 feet high on the Continental Divide, six hours by rail from Chihuahua City.

The little station was crowded with Indians in diapers and headbands and Indians in jeans and straw hats. They boarded the train to carry off the bags.

A lumber truck went by, and dust hung over the adobe houses and wooden shacks. An old Indian woman sat eating a Popsicle under a *Tome Pepsi* sign outside a cantina. Chickens and pigs foraged in the streets. A butcher was cutting up a cow in front of his shop. We found the face of Joe Lowther, brown skin stretched tight across his cheekbones, under a felt cowboy hat. We piled into Joe's station wagon with his driver, Salvadore Molino, and set out on the bouncing 12-mile drive up a lumber road past Lake Arareco to the Cabañas Barranca del Cobre, or Copper Canyon Lodge. Joe Lowther, a cowboy, and his wife Mollie built the lodge because there is only one other tourist hotel between Chihuahua City and Los Mochis and that one lacks private baths and even running water in the rooms.

To get permission to build on Indian land, which is divided into sections called *ejidos,* each ruled by a governor or chief, Mollie had to promise that her lady guests would not wear shorts or stretch pants, a sight the Tarahumaras consider indecent. The lodge has six inches of dirt on the roof for insulation, is lit with kerosene lanterns and warmed with wood fires. "There's no use in women wearing makeup around here after dark, because you can't possibly see it," Mollie says.

Mollie is not the sort to worry much about makeup. When she was a girl her parents packed her off to Sarah Lawrence College in Bronxville, N.Y. to polish the Texas off her. The night before the term was to begin she put on her fur coat and went to the Madison Square Garden rodeo for a date with a bull rider. That night a steer got loose on Eighth Avenue as Mollie and her cowboy were coming out of the Garden. He grabbed the steer and wrestled it to the pavement, Mollie handed him a rope to tie it with—and the scene was preserved in photographs on the front pages of New York newspapers. After seeing the papers, Mollie's parents gave up on Sarah Lawrence and ordered her home. Joe Lowther grew up in Montana, breaking horses and guiding hunting parties and fighting on Saturday nights in a circle of pickup truck headlights. "People drove in from several counties to try to whip me," Joe says. "Nobody ever did it, but I sure got puckered up some."

In August of 1965, as the lodge was being built, Mollie was caught in a flash flood on the Río Cusarare with her children, Alden and Zoe, and their friends, Sellen and Kay Bickers. Several Tarahumaras came along and escorted them to a cave to wait out the flood. The Indians could not understand why the Anglos would be discomforted by the prospect of missing a few meals. One Indian, pointing at the sky, asked Mollie if she had noticed the odd star that moved across the heavens every couple of hours. Mollie told them it was a space capsule with two astronauts inside.

"That machine goes across the sky and crashes on the other side and two men die," the Indian said, "and it happens over and over."

"No," Mollie said. "The earth is round and the same machine just keeps going around it."

Being too polite to tell her she was wrong, the Indian said, "It does not matter if the machine crashes into the earth. The purpose of life is to be relieved of suffering. That is what death does, so death is good."

The Tarahumaras are intimate with death. Four out of five Tarahumara children die of disease or malnutrition before they are 5 years old. Those who survive are very tough people—short, thin, shy, dignified nomads who live in caves or log-and-stone huts called *garí*. They roam over 35,000 square miles of mountain country, including the barrancas, moving into the valleys in winter and into the high places in summer. There are about 35,000 Tarahumaras, or one per square mile, which is not enough land to have supported the horse Indians of the southwestern U.S. The Tarahumaras raise corn, beans and squash in small plots, kill a few deer and rabbits, and they endure, walking in the snow in rubber sandals made from tires abandoned by lumber-truck drivers, starving when there is drought, eating pinole (corn mush) and drinking *tesgüino* (fermented corn sprouts) when there is some. They do not encourage visitors. Unless in a village, they usually hide or become stony silent at the approach of strangers, waiting stolidly for them to go away. But there are means of getting their attention.

Our first morning in the lodge we were out of our blankets at daylight, had a breakfast of pancakes, eggs, chili peppers and hot chocolate while listening to Benny Goodman on a transistor radio, and went to find the Indians. For the next week we explored the canyons of Urique, Batopilas and Cobre, going in Joe's station wagon over lumber or mining roads so precipitous that a 56-mile trip to La Bufa silver mine took 12 hours, twice the time it took the Indian messenger from Sisoguíchi to run a similar distance. Or we went on horse and mule with José Esquivel, a mining engineer who has spent 50 years in the mountains, and Santiago Parra, a Tarahumara guide. Whenever we rode up to a cave or hut back in the mountain country, where the wild diapered Indians are called *gentiles*, the occupants would disappear. We went to Sisoguíchi, where the Jesuits operate a hospital and a school that broadcasts in Rarámuri and Spanish to 84 radio sets scattered through the mountains.

The information somehow was getting around that we were harmless, funny-looking, gave away colored images on paper and had pockets full of animal crackers, chewing gum and pesos.

In the side of a cliff at Csiteachi we found an ancient burial cave with clay bowls to hold food that was to have supplied happy passage for the bones on the floor. There was no armor. "This was sealed up before the priests came," said Santiago.

There are a few old Mauser rifles, left over from revolutions, in the barranca country, and the Indians bargain for them to kill the bears that damage their crops. As any Tarahumara knows, a bear is good not only for soap and medicine, but its skin guarantees the chastity of the wearer and overcomes lust. The fat meat of peccaries is a gourmet item. The coyote, killer of goats and destroyer of green corn, is trapped. The Indians hunt wolves with rifles or poisoned arrows but have no use for the meat or pelts. There are otters in the streams of western Chihuahua, bobcats in the forests of the canyons, and opossums, gray foxes and coatis. Skunks are killed for medicine. Gophers and rabbits make a nice stew. Field mice, pack rats and big storehouse rats are roasted or boiled. Jaguars and cougars prowl the barrancas and kill sheep and cattle, but they are wisely avoided by hunters armed only with rocks or arrows.

Deer, though, are prime game. The Tarahumaras form teams to run down a deer, pursuing it for days in relays until the animal falls of exhaustion. One trick is to find a deer trail and hammer pointed stakes into the earth just beyond a fallen log or other natural barricade. Dogs are starved for several days and used in the hunt to find the deer's scent, at which time the animal is chased down the trail, leaps the log and is impaled. The hunters eat peyote in the belief that it makes them sharper and faster in the hunt—and maybe less morose if the hunt fails.

When game is scarce, or when drought or hailstorms ruin the crops, the Indians starve. They rarely eat their domestic animals but when absolutely necessary will kill a pig or goat by stabbing its heart with a pointed stick or slaughter a cow by thrusting a knife into a neck artery. Mushrooms, berries, peaches, apples, toads, lizards and rattlesnakes are utilized as food. If a hunter is bitten by a snake, he is cured by having tobacco smoke blown into his face, by eating peyote or by having his friends hold the snake while he bites it back.

Three hundred years of contact with Spaniards and Mexicans have yet to have much effect on Tarahumara culture, except that their ceremonies are a strange mingling of the Catholic and the pagan. The Mexican government and the Catholic Church are trying to educate the Indians—a mixed blessing—but it is a big country and funds are short. Two young government teachers in Cusarare want to teach their students to play baseball but lack the money for balls and bats. When we gave those two teachers a crate of brown soap, they declared a school holiday and took their pupils to Río Cusarare for a bath. It was the first soap they'd had in a year. For the price of one bombing raid in Vietnam every Tarahumara in the barrancas could have food, soap and medical supplies. But that, of course, is not the way things ever work, and so to brighten their lives the Indians turn to *tesgüino* and peyote, games and fiestas. A fiesta is a catharsis and an expression of hope. There are fiestas for the curing of illness, for dedication of crops, for births, for deaths and for the harvest. The Indians give thanks for a good catch of fish by grinding narcotic roots and placing them before a cross. At each festival except the one celebrating death there is a game.

The most important and festive game is the kickball race called *rarajípari*. A major race is always held between runners of different *ejidos*: They run barefoot or in sandals, kicking a ball made of oak or madroño heart that has the team markings on it. The course, called a rarejípama, is designated by cutting crosses in the bark of trees. The chiefs of the competing teams decide the time and place and length of the laps, anywhere from three to 12 miles. If it is a small race, such as one between individuals, no training is required. But for two to five days before a major race the runners must not drink *tesgüino*, must have no contact with women and must eat no fat, potatoes, eggs or sweets.

Magic is vital on the eve of a race. A chief will go to a burial cave with two kickballs and exhume a shinbone from a right leg. A jar of *tesgüino*, bowls of food, the kickballs and the shinbone are placed in front of a cross as a request for the dead person to weaken the chief's opponents. Other human bones are carried out and hidden in places where runners must pass. These bones are known to produce fatigue, and the chief tells his own runners the spots to avoid. Herbs are scattered in the wind or shaken to poison opposing runners. For each enchantment there is an antidote. Turtle and bat blood, powdered and mixed with tobacco, is smoked to counteract cheating.

A shaman, or medicine man, is always consulted. He helps the chief rub the legs of the runners with herbs, smooth stones, goat grease, oil and boiled cedar branches, and he waves the witches away. The water the runners will drink is placed beneath a cross, and candles are lit on both sides. Runners carrying their kickballs line up beside the cross while the shaman sings *The Song of the Gray Fox*. All food and drink are supplied by relatives. The runners make ceremonial turns around the cross in the number of laps they must run. Then all runners sleep beside the cross with an old man watching their victuals, since old people can see even if asleep.

Winning is hardly ever a result of who is faster or stronger. It is a result of bewitching. One anthropologist was seen taking the temperature of a runner, and all the opponents quit, certain they were having their spirits injected into him. And, as in any game, bribery is not unknown. Each group of runners has six supervisors, some of whose duties are to keep drunks off the course and to prevent pregnant women, who are a bad influence, from watching the race. The supervisors also try to keep the runners from tripping each other or booting their opponents' kickballs away. The runners are watched for any sign that they are chewing the dried leaves and seeds of the *riwérame* plant. It is said that a *riwérame* chewer can blow his breath into the face of another runner and cause him to collapse within half a mile. Supervisors are responsible for blocking off the bettors who will race along with a runner to urge him on or to discourage him by suggesting that his wife is up to no good at that moment.

The afternoon of a race is occupied with betting. Poor as they are, the Indians bet bows, arrows, belts, clothing, spools of thread, maize, sheep, goats, cattle, *tesgüino* and, very rarely, money. Two or three hundred people will gather at the betting place, drinking and bickering, until all bets are settled. The runners are wrapped in blankets, and their legs are rubbed with warm water. A number of stones corresponding to the number of laps are laid on the ground and studied by bettors. Each bet is certified by a chief, who is not allowed to write it down. After all bets are made, the governor of the home *ejido* makes a speech and warns the runners that anybody who throws his kickball by hand automatically goes to hell. At a signal, suddenly, the race is on. The runners jump up, shrug off their blankets and begin a race that may take three days and cover up to 200 miles.

Many of the runners chew the tips of *jíkuri* and peyote as a stimulant. Nearly all have some sort of magic with them—a glowworm, bird feathers or heads, a rattle of deer hooves and bamboo that helps keep them from falling asleep. The runners of the different *ejidos* are distinguished by the colors of their headbands or by other symbols, such as the white plaster worn on the faces and legs of those from Batopilas. They move out at a steady trot, laughing at the game, for the first 40 or 50 miles. Crowds run along cheering and pointing where the kickballs went, since for a team to lose its kickball means disqualification. Women give the runners warm water and pinole. Pine torches light the course after dark. Within 50 miles some of the runners begin to drop out. Usually the race comes down to a contest in which only the strongest runner from each *ejido* remains. In a race that was matched for stamina rather than laps, early last spring the runners went from Friday afternoon at 5 until Sunday night at 11 and ran about 170 miles until there was only one man left.

The winner gets no prize but becomes immensely popular with the ladies, a questionable reward for a man who has been running for three days. The custom is for a bettor who has won a cow to give two pesos to the father of the winning runner. For a goat, the father gets half a peso, or about 4 cents. Other winners may chip in a spool of thread, a piece of cloth, a jug of *tesgüino,* whatever their pleasure moves them to contribute. When the big race is finished the Indians go back to a life that one described as: "I get up in the morning and eat pinole, if I have it. I sit on a rock all day and watch my goats. At night I pen the goats, eat more pinole if I have it, and sleep. And sometimes there are races."

Letter: October 4, 1967, on the Publication of *Blessed McGill*

Ken McCormick was a gentleman who belonged to the now all but vanished school of editors who believed in long literary lunches and actually loved writers and good writing. When I left for Europe to write *But Not for Love,* Ken gave me a satchel to carry my manuscript in that had belonged to Sherwood Anderson. Just touching that satchel gave me confidence.

But Ken was sorely disappointed in me for writing *Blessed McGill.* What he had wanted and expected was the further adventures of the characters in *But Not for Love* as they got a couple of years older.

So my penalty was that Doubleday wouldn't promote the new novel. The awful jacket copy was my tip-off to our coming divorce.

Dear Ken:

I am sorry to have to tell you this, but I was stunned when I read the jacket copy for *Blessed McGill.* Not only was the copy full of errors—even to the misspelling of the name of one of the major characters, the misplacing of the book in time, the misplacing of McGill's birthplace, etc.—but the copywriting was utter garbage. I don't think I am being too vain when I say this, but this is a very complex novel that does have many levels to it, successful or not. One of the things that gives it strength below the surface is that it is an allegory about Jesus and Peter, for example (though God knows I would not tell that to anybody but you and Doatsy). It also is about the need for dope-smoking, about religious mysticism, about the similarity between the religious experience, the drug experience and death, etc. It is about a lot of things, although I have made sure they are not obtrusive so that the novel can function purely as an adventure story or as a semi-history of how it was in the West in this period. The copywriting, however, makes it sound like a Max Brand Western. I hope to Christ it is not being presented as such to the booksellers, but I fear that selling it from the jacket copy, which I know is important, will sink this book before anybody ever reads a page of it.

Hence, I have written some new jacket copy which is herewith enclosed. I hated to do it because I hate to talk about or try to explain myself in such a way, but I had much rather have no jacket copy at all than the copy I read in the Doubleday office today. This copy that I have hastily written at least gives some sort of idea what sort of book this is or tries to be. . . .

I appreciate that you have been very busy. Maybe a drink soon?

Going into Chihuahua

From *Blessed McGill* (1968)

What grand country that is down there! The only places I have ever been happy are in the hills of central Texas, up here in the Sangre de Cristo Mountains of Taos and Santa Fe and in the mountains of Mexico. Our ride out from Chihuahua City took us through the sorts of country that I prefer. First we rode through a land that is like central Texas—hilly, full of meadows and pastures, with a wide clear sky where hawks float. We saw children herding sheep and goats. There were many of the small black Spanish cattle that have Longhorn blood in them. We passed several ruined haciendas. Revolutions had all but wiped out the grandees. The country was in political chaos, with large sections lorded over by Indians and bandits. The governors of the states lacked the strength to enforce what authority they had. The federal government, in Mexico City, had its own problems and was pretty useless in dealing with remote areas. We were a thousand miles, more or less, from Mexico City, and the way between lay blocked by mountains, deserts, and hooligans of the lowest type.

Leaving the Texas-like country, we entered a land that is more like northern New Mexico Territory—high, mountainous, with castle rocks and purple peaks rising above the pines. And going on from there we at last approached the barranca country. The mountains in the barranca country are not overly high, seldom beyond 10,000 feet above sea level. What makes them so dramatic is the plunge into the barrancas. You can look at a mountain that seems nothing special until you round it and descend into the barranca and then look up again and cannot find the peak, lost in the clouds two miles above you.

We went along with some caution. We had brought a mozo to guide us to the town of Creel, which is near Cusarare. The mozo trotted ahead of our horses, mules, and burros. He was a Tarahumara, and so the twenty-five miles a day that we covered was merely a pleasant job to him. No Nose had begun to complain of feeling ill. Her eyes were indeed red and her flesh was hot to the touch, but she found some jakuri roots and made a tea and seemed to improve. Barney, Badthing, and I took turns scouting out front. There had been a number of Apache heads on poles before the prison in Chihuahua City. The Apaches were being frisky and we did not wish them to catch us.

We had one close turn some miles from the town of Sisoguichi. I was on scout and was coming up to the Río Conchos, where we intended to get water, when I got a warning from my instincts. I dismounted, hid White Foot in some brush and crawled to a bluff above the river. There below me were a dozen Indians of some motley band. Several were Lipans. A few looked like Yaquis, and two wore sombreros. They were a party of bandits, bathing and drinking. Their sentinel was on the bluff opposite me. I did not dare move.

As I lay there, a mere fifty feet from them, I suddenly felt a tickling on my right forearm. As it was a warm day, I had taken off my jacket and rolled up my sleeves. When I looked down, I saw a wicked gray scorpion common in Chihuahua had crawled upon my arm and was inspecting me. Any motion to brush him off might have alerted the sentinel on the other bluff. I lay sweating and watching as the scorpion calmly and with what I would almost swear was amusement lifted his stinger tail, curved it down and shot agony into my arm. The gray devil stung me until he was satisfied. I looked into his eyes. I lay and bit my lips for what seemed an hour. When at last he was finished, he crawled off into the grass. My arm throbbed as the poison rushed through my veins. My arm began to swell and turn blue. I was very glad when those Indians mounted their runty ponies and rode north. I could barely make it back to our little group. No Nose and Badthing wrapped my arm in a hot prickly pear poultice. I spent a feverish night but was ready for traveling the next morning.

After some slow and delicate moving, made so by No Nose's recurring illness, we reached Creel. There we decided to keep our mozo. He was called Valentine and was quiet and a tireless worker. We stayed one night in Creel to get fresh supplies, though it was dangerous there. The news of our arrival was bound to spread through the territory and reach Apache ears. But we could not hope to keep our presence forever secret and considered ourselves lucky to have come that far without detection.

From Creel we went southeasterly to Cusarare and reached the place in half a day. For hours we lay on a cliff above the village and watched for sign. The little stream called the Río Cusarare ran through the valley below. We saw Tarahumaras moving about their cave dwellings and crude huts, tending their goats. The old Jesuit church with its broken-down walls sat silent in the middle of the valley. Once late in the afternoon we heard Tarahumara drums thumping from the mountains beyond, but our mozo assured us the drums were only part of a peyote ritual and had nothing to do with us. Although

I had seen Apaches near Sisoguichi, these Tarahumaras did not seem concerned. They were, after all, too poor for the Apaches to bother robbing them and in January too scrawny from hunger to bring much as slaves.

We tried to pick out the mountain from which we could see the peak that guarded the canyon of Tayopa. There was no outstanding mountain. The cliffs around Cusarare were of uniform height, with an occasional high knob where eagles nested. Studying the map, Barney decided that we should go down to the church. From there, it was his idea we could look up in the general direction the map would indicate and could spot the viewing point. It made sense to me that the map would be so oriented. Once we found the viewing point, we could turn our map to match up roughly with the landmarks and should be able to pick out the proper peak, though reaching it would no doubt be a difficult matter.

At dusk we descended to Cusarare. The Tarahumaras who saw us paid no heed. We opened the door of the church and took our animals inside. Father Higgins would not approve of that, I am sure, but we had to have our animals out of sight. The night was becoming cold, as happens in the high country. Inside the church we could build a fire. We quartered our animals near the altar and took them out one by one to drink from the Río Cusarare. There were many old paintings, peeling and dusty, hanging from the walls of the church. They seemed almost alive and moving in the shadows from our little fire. But there was nothing else of value in the church. Any altarpieces, crucifixes, or cloths had long before been looted.

We put Badthing and his wife, who had become rather sullen and sluggish, into the bell tower as lookouts and settled down. I read the third of Ellen's letters that night. It was more tender, less formal, than the first two. The mind can do wonders with desiring. She still did not speak of love, but she signed it *sincerely* rather than *your friend*. I began to muse upon becoming rich and marrying her. I would ride up to her uncle's house in a carriage like the one that belonged to my mother's cousin in San Antonio. Her aunt would be overwhelmed. The neighbors would come to watch. No ruffian, this McGill. I slept well.

Before daylight, Barney woke me. He had been outside for his morning ritual, balking at performing such an act inside a church. He had heard horses and, peering over the stone wall of the church, had seen several riders at the river.

"It was too dark to be sure, Hermano," he told me, "but I think they are Apaches."

Almost at once, Badthing came scrambling down the ladder from the bell tower.

"Eight of them," Badthing said in Tex-Mex. "My woman was sick again and I was washing her face and did not see them approach. They don't know we are here yet."

Taking my Henry, I slipped out of the church and kept into the darkness along the wall and crawled to a tumbled mound of stones in a field of gourds to the south of the church. From there I could see them clearly. They gave me quite a shock.

I had expected the same band of Apaches I had seen on the Río Conchos. But these were different. And I knew them as surely as they would know me. They were warriors from a big family of Kiowa Apaches that had a *ranchería* in the Chisos Mountains—the very coons I had circled wide to avoid, the very ones who had sworn to kill me because of the six scalps I had taken from their kin who were torturing old James Santiago. Now this was a disgusting turn of affairs. I watched them filling their buffalo paunch water bags in the river. They were tall, graceful for the most part, with long black hair. They wore headdresses of crow feathers, owl feathers, and cow horns. They carried lances and bows and wore their arrows in quivers of Mexican leather. I knew that most of the warriors in that family—it was not uncommon for a large family of Kiowas or Kiowa Apaches to live together in a private place, intermarrying brothers with sisters-in-law and so forth until they were a numerous mob of brothers, sisters, uncles, cousins, fathers, mothers, and whatnot—were members of the Crazy Dogs Society, a pretty high-up warrior organization. Some were even Koisenkos, sworn never to retreat. Once that family had joined two other families to form a band of a couple hundred, but they had broken up after a battle with the Rangers and some cowherders near Presidio, and this family had gone into the Chisos Mountains and established a stronghold that nobody had ever tried to penetrate.

From the indolent way that they loafed about the stream, it was clear they had not been informed of our presence. It was possible they would water up and go off. They must have been inside the church on dozens of other raids and would know there was nothing of value there. I could hear them laughing. The sun began to appear over the rim of the valley. My breath blew white in the morning as I lay among the gourds and rocks. Two warriors had a wrestling match beside the river, each trying to dunk the other in the cold water. Both wound up drenched. I lay there, wanting coffee and a cigar, and studied them. They had no firearms, which was a good thing. They had about twenty horses and mules with them but little booty that I could see. Tied to the back of one mule was a silver candelabra, stolen from Lord knows what church or hacienda. Otherwise, their expedition had produced nothing of obvious worth.

Three warriors stripped off their shirts and leggings and marched naked up and down the stream, waving their arms and calling for the Tarahumara maidens to come down from their caves. The others laughed. The three climbed into the cold water and bathed. Two more squatted on the bank in view of all the Tarahumaras and did their morning easement and called out strange clattering yells to the valley walls. But none appeared in a mean or warlike humor. In time, I found myself getting tired of watching them. An hour after sunup, they mounted. They rode in a circle around the valley, shouting challenges up to the caves, and then went up a trail to the west and rode out of the valley, heading toward a blue ridge that was marked with a cross, as the Tarahumaras do to protect travelers from the devils. I lay there until they were out of sight and then, relieved, got up and went into the church. Barney came in, too. He had been lying behind the stone wall west of the church. Badthing had been in the tower. Valentine had been sitting on the altar. No Nose was lying on a blanket in the corner with her teeth clicking.

"Thought we were in for a fracas," Barney said.

"I sure wanted breakfast first."

No Nose was in no condition to cook, so Barney handled that chore. The woman had a fever and her eyes were teary. Her skin seemed miscolored, but it was hard to tell, as she was of a darkly uncertain complexion anyhow and had been much exposed to weather. Badthing assured us she would be all right, that she was in the time of life when a woman is subject to these minor ills. We sent him back to the bell tower to keep watch. After breakfast of bacon, beans, and biscuits we all felt better, though No Nose could eat little. Barney and I went out to the church yard with our map. We lined it up the way it had to be, with the line pointing into Cusarare. We decided the viewpoint we wanted was on the valley wall to the north. We searched and debated and at last settled on a high bald rock near the valley entrance. If there had been a higher mountain there once, it could have fallen. There were rocks and rubble below it, indications of an old landslide. We packed up, put No Nose astride a mule and went up a steep trail on the north wall, seeing a few Tarahumaras—the men in diapers, shirts, and headbands, the women in long dresses with shawls—who came out of their caves to stare at us.

It was well past noon before we reached the bald rock. We approached it through a stand of pines and cedars. Once there, we were hardly better off. Looking to the southwest, we saw ridge after ridge, several marked with crosses, with canyons between, and a few mountains that reared up but none higher than the others. We all got interested in the project, except for No Nose, who lay down and wrapped herself in her blanket. Finally Barney and I agreed that we had to decide on something. Valentine came up with the information that he had heard of gold being near a certain mountain that he pointed out, although he informed us he would under no circumstances go there. The mountain he pointed out looked like an alligator lying against the sky. With his compass, Barney took a reading on the alligator's nose. He wrote down some computations to keep us straight in our journey and drew lines between our current location and the nose of the alligator if that was truly it on the map. We determined to set out at once, rather than spending another night in the church. The problem was whether No Nose could travel.

Thinking about her, I heard an odd snorting cry and turned to see that we were trapped.

The eight Kiowa Apaches, two of whom held No Nose by the arms, were behind us and we had only the cliff to the front. Preoccupied as we were with our map and our dream of gold, we had laid our rifles on the ground some feet away. Not that the rifles would have got us anything but death, for the Kiowa Apaches had arrows fitted to bow strings and were aiming at us. The arrow devoted to me had an iron tip made from a barrel hoop, and I recall thinking that wounds from such arrows almost always got infected.

"Well, well, this is a very sorry deal," Barney said.

The leader of this troop of cretins had put on a long sash that showed he was a Koisenko. He was almighty pleased with himself. Doubtless, he had not grinned much in his life, for the act seemed to stretch his face out of shape. He stepped forward, muttered some guttural rubbish, and the two coons who were holding No Nose tossed her over the cliff.

"Mother Mary," Barney said.

No Nose cried out sharply once. Then the cry broke as her body bounced off a rock. The leader looked at Badthing, who had not moved. In near perfect Spanish, the leader said:

"I have heard of your magical powers, dwarf. Call your woman back to life. Fly her through the air and plant her feet on this earth in front of me, and I will worship you and make you rich."

Badthing cleared his throat. His emotions must have been quite strong. "What is done is done," he said. "I would not ask the spirits to undo it. However, I will ask them special favors pertaining to you, to assure that all your children are crippled, your mother is blind, your wives have lung fever, and the dogs eat your face."

The leader laughed. "I thought you were a fake," he said. He turned to me. "I have heard of you, also," he said. "The Enemy"—by which he meant the Comanches—"call you No-Die. They say they have shot arrows into your heart and have stabbed you and beaten you with clubs, and yet you live. They say they have cut you into little pieces, and you re-formed yourself, like an earthworm. They say you are now a particular enemy of our Forest People and have cursed us as you did the Honey Eaters, who are shamed. They say you are to be feared. None of this I believe. But we will find out. You killed my brothers and cousins. So we will see if you can die."

They gathered up all our weapons, including those on our bodies. One of the coons covered us with my Henry rifle. The leader, the Koisenko, motioned for us to stand away from the cliff. The other six arranged themselves in a corridor leading to the cliff, three on each side, facing each other in a staggered pattern.

"It appears," Barney said, "that we are to have the privilege of running the gauntlet and if we survive that we have the joy of falling off the cliff."

"Some fine reward," said Badthing.

PART 3

Mad Dogs and Outlaws

The Best-Kept Secret in America

From *Willie: An Autobiography*, by Willie Nelson
with Bud Shrake (1988)

I was playing golf with Willie Nelson at his course west of Austin, and he
said he had been offered a lot of money for an autobiography. "I don't want
to do it myself," he said. "But if you'll do it with me, we'll split the money
and have a good time while we're at it."

I spent the next few months with Willie on his bus, on the airplane he
owned at the time, on various golf courses, and at live-music venues all
over the country. It wasn't all that different from the life I had been living,
anyhow—except that I turned on a tape recorder and got about forty hours
of Willie and others, reflecting on their desires and adventures.

When it came time to write the book, I suddenly thought: Hey, I don't
know how to do this. Then I thought: Sure you do, you've been doing this
for years. Just think of it as about twenty-five *Sports Illustrated* bonus pieces
like the as-told-to biography of Titanic Thompson that I did for the magazine. For some reason I started writing the manuscript in longhand on yellow legal pads. It turned into 150,000 words. I've still got a knot on my right
index finger from this.

I was in sort of the same situation I had been in ten years earlier. My band
would fill a Texas dance hall. We were stars in Texas. But in Nashville, I was
looked upon as a loser singer. They wouldn't let me record with my own band.
They would cover me up with horns and strings. It was depressing. But as
some athlete said, I hung my head high. . . .

As soon as I signed with Atlantic, I moved back to Texas, looking for
something like the Happy Valley Dude Ranch. First we had to pick a town for
headquarters. We considered Houston. I even put a deposit on an apartment
in Houston. But then I went up to Austin and looked around. My sister Bob-
bie was playing a gig at a piano bar on the top floor of an apartment building
near the capitol. She and her husband Jack were living in Austin with their
kids, Freddy, Randy, and Mike.

The more I got to thinking, I liked the idea of living in Austin more than
Houston. Who wouldn't? Houston was too hot and too crowded. Austin was

a very pretty place. My friend Darrell Royal was the football coach at the University of Texas, and he told me I'd be crazy not to move to Austin. He said Austin had a lot of people like me, brothers under the skin, and I would find it out.

Austin had lakes and hills and plenty of golf courses, and it also had Big G's and the Broken Spoke and other good halls to work.

And Austin had a new redneck hippie rock and roll folk music country venue in an old National Guard Armory. They had painted the walls with portraits and scenes by Jim Franklin, Gilbert Shelton, Michael Priest, Jack Jaxon, and other Austin artists who were becoming well known in the hippie underground. My friends in Mad Dog Inc. had an office near the stage where they did "indefinable services for mankind." The roof was hung with acoustic shields, and the crowd mostly sat on the floor like at the Fillmore in San Francisco.

There was a strong Austin to San Francisco axis in those days. The towns reminded me of each other. If San Francisco was the capital of the hippie world at that time, then Austin was the hippie Palm Springs.

This new Austin hall I'm talking about was sort of like San Francisco, but at the same time it was pure Austin. It was called the Armadillo World Headquarters.

You need to understand what Austin was like when we moved there in late 1971 and rented an apartment on Riverside Drive.

If you stand downtown and look west across the river to the limestone cliffs that rise up abruptly on the other shore, you are looking at the place where the West literally begins.

The cliffs are a tall wall of rock that runs in an arc from Waco south to Del Rio. The old cotton economy of the South ended where it struck those limestone cliffs. Farther west beyond the cliffs is the Hill Country, which used to be the Comanche territory.

Built on seven hills in a river valley where pure artesian water flowed from the rocks and with a mild climate and deer and other wild animals roaming through the oaks and cedars, Austin was like Palm Springs for the Comanche nation long before the Anglo real estate developers turned it into a town in 1840. Houston had been the capital of Texas until then. The brazen act of building a new capital right in the middle of the Comanche's centuries' favorite resort started the bloodiest Indian war in Texas history.

You know the Indians lost, but it was hard to tell in Austin in the early sev-

Doatsy and Bud Shrake at Willie Nelson's 1976 Fourth of July Picnic.
Photo by Scott Newton.

enties. A hell of a lot of young people wore feathers and beads and necklaces and bells and doeskin pants and skirts with fringes and moccasins and long hair and headbands.

It was cheap living. Low taxes, no traffic to speak of. Billie Lee Brammer, who wrote *The Gay Place*, a novel about Austin, was legally blind without his glasses, but Billie Lee was forever taking a bunch of acid and losing his glasses and driving safely all over town in the middle of the night. Austin was a stable place that depended on the state government offices and five universities for much of its economy.

There was no way to get rich in Austin. Only half a dozen houses in town would be allowed in Beverly Hills. People who did have money didn't show it off. Car dealers and beer distributors were big socialites.

You couldn't legally walk around Austin smoking weed or eating acid or mescaline or peyote—dope was very much against the law in Texas—but it seemed like you couldn't walk around Austin for very long without at least being offered a joint.

Every few blocks in Austin you saw some new, unexpected vista—a Victorian house framed against the water and the purple hills, a pair of hawks circling above Mount Larson, a Mexican family eating dinner on the front porch of a house painted pastel yellow with statues of Jesus and the Virgin in the front yard behind a little iron fence.

Barton Springs was the greatest outdoor swimming hole in the country. You could fish and swim in the river right beside your house. You could go out on Lake Travis in a houseboat and putter around hundreds of miles of shoreline for days before somebody found you.

For a population of about 250,000, Austin was a real piece of paradise, an oasis, the best-kept secret in America.

The most famous musician in Austin when I got there was Jerry Jeff Walker. Janis Joplin had sung for years at Kenneth Threadgill's place in Austin, but she'd gone to San Francisco to make her reputation. Jerry Jeff and I had some wild nights and days partying and picking in joints and people's homes around Austin. Everybody wanted Jerry Jeff to play his classic "Mr. Bojangles," but he never did like to be told what to play or when to play it. If some host asked Jerry Jeff to play "Mr. Bojangles" or anything else at the wrong moment in the wrong tone of voice, he was liable to whip out his dick and piss in the potted ficus plant, and the fight would start.

There was more live music played in joints in Austin every night of the week than in Los Angeles.

Rock bands like Shiva's Head Band, the Conqueroo, and the Thirteenth Floor Elevators were going from Austin to San Francisco and back to the Armadillo World Headquarters. The Armadillo World Headquarters was a center for the arts. You could buy jewelry and leather goods there as well as beer and good food cheap. They booked acts from the Austin Ballet to Ravi Shankar to Bette Midler. Eddie Wilson, who was the ramrod of the operation, would try anything. Rednecks and hippies who had thought they were natural enemies began mixing at the Armadillo without too much bloodshed. They discovered they both liked good music. Pretty soon you saw a longhair cowboy wearing hippie beads and a bronc rider's belt buckle, and you were seeing a new type of person.

Being a natural leader, I saw which direction this movement was going and threw myself in front of it.

My first show at the Armadillo World Headquarters was August 12, 1972.

In the spring some promoters had put together an outdoor concert called the Dripping Springs Reunion on a ranch west of Austin. They had bluegrass, Loretta Lynn, Tex Ritter, Roy Acuff, Kris Kristofferson, Waylon Jennings, Billy Joe Shaver, Leon Russell, and me—with Coach Royal onstage. The promotion lost a bundle, but it had the seed of a sort of country Woodstock and got me wondering if I could do it better.

After my show at the Armadillo, I started getting bookings at college auditoriums. A new audience was opening up for me. I phoned Waylon in Nashville and told him he ought to come play the Armadillo. Waylon walked into that big hall and saw all those redneck hippies boogying to the opening act, Commander Cody, and he turned to me and said, "What the shit have you got me into, Willie?"

The Screwing Up of Austin

Texas Observer, December 27, 1974

No matter what year you moved to Austin, you just missed it. Somebody will tell you this was a really great place to live until shortly before you arrived. This was my pass at telling how much better it used to be. The country musician that for some reason I didn't name is Willie Nelson. And by the way, it *did* used to be better.

The other night I was talking to a country musician about the screwing up of Austin, and he had what seemed at that hour to be a pretty good idea. This country musician hisself had moved here from Nashville a while back and had in fact set off a near to stupefying rush in this direction of musicians and semi-musicians, as well as literally hundreds of hairy vagabonds loaded down with Nikons, videotape machines, cowboy hats, electric mouth organs, and deer-horn coke scoops. This country musician was only about half pleased at what he had helped to attract, but that was no bother at all (even semi-musicians don't like to knock down curlycued old houses or pour concrete) compared to what was coincidentally going on in the screwing up of Austin.

"Well, the only way I can see to handle it is to build a big tall electrified bob war fence around the place and give out numbers to the folks inside," the country musician said. "I suppose I would probably be about number 217,156. Anybody with a number higher than 250,000 has to leave town and can't come back until they get hold of a number under the limit, say by their old uncle leaving it to them in his will, or maybe by winning it in a card game, or buying it outright, or sticking a pistol up aside somebody's ear and hijacking their number. Anyhow, we can plainly see there's just too damn many people flocking in around here for what is good. If they was deer, we could declare a harvest and send a bunch of their meat overseas."

We can see what a struggle that would be, placing numbers on people and shoving thousands of the poor bastards off toward Wink or Graham. It would require vicious dogs at the very least, and you would have a hell of a time explaining to the exiles why you were demanding that they do the right thing. Pick up any outlander newspaper or magazine these days, and you are liable to read about the peculiar appeal of Austin. They're catching on to it out there, partly because of these honkytonk heroes and motion picture gypsies who are slipping in, and partly because a number of greedheads discovered they could make a living out of Austin by chopping it down.

For years Austin has been a stopoff on the hippie railroad between the Left Coast and the Right Coast; *Rolling Stone* called Austin "the hippie Palm Springs," which didn't help any, but after all, hippies didn't hurt anybody who didn't ask for it, and they sure didn't get together to put up parking lots. The hippies realized, as generations of college students have understood, that Austin is the best place in Texas to be, and that there are precious few places in the whole of the U.S.A. that have got the odd magic that Austin has got. Some of the very things that make that true—cedar hills, water, unexpected vistas, a sultry mañana way of moving—are the things that have to get torn up to make room for the people they seduce.

Just about my favorite place to go in Austin is out on our back porch. From there I can see as far as I can look. At night the flashing light straight

Bud Shrake at his home in Austin, 1974. Photo by Sarah Pileggi.

ahead is the airport miles away, and the flashing light off to the right is Berg-strom. I can see the Tower, the Stadium, the Capitol, Westgate, and that gold firecracker that bank employees have to work in, and there's squirrels and possums and birds walking around on the porch, and I can see down to Bee Creek and a little piece of the river. Except one nice fall day not long ago, I walked out on the back porch and could see only a greasy orange smaze right on the other side of the river where the town should have been. I took this matter up with a neighbor who is a psychiatrist, and he told me the smaze was blowing up from Houston. Well, Houston money is buying up land around Austin so fast it figures a herd of smaze would come along with it. The third day of the smaze a friend told me about a small plane that almost hit an air-liner at the airport because the pilots couldn't see each other. The fifth day of the smaze I called the Air Pollution Center and asked what was this smaze the newspapers kept reporting as clouds or haze. The Air Pollution Center said it was "smog." I asked how we could blow it back to Houston. We can't do that because it is our very own smog, said the Air Pollution Center. I said why don't they report that in the newspaper? "That doesn't come under the heading of Good News, does it?" was the reply.

So I called the newspaper. The city editor wouldn't speak to me. Having worked for several newspapers before I retired to the ministry, I could un-derstand why a city editor might refuse to speak to me. When I was sitting in as city editor at a huge metropolitan daily, I finally had to quit speaking to a guy who knew the real story about the moon, how it got there and what was underneath its crust, etc. He had studied it out, but I had criminals and bureaucrats and reporters to mess around with on several deadlines a day, not to mention an uncommon number of women who wanted photographs in the paper of their eight-foot-tall hollyhocks.

So I didn't have time to listen about the moon. The sixth day of the smaze my friend Jap came over and called the newspaper and said he was a Colonel from Bergstrom and could not lay his airplane down neatly any more because the air that got in front of his windshield looked like apricots. Next day the paper did a story, on about page eight, about Austin having "smog." Smog, do you hear that? The worst part of it did blow away, and I don't want to make a big deal out of it. I repeat only because I urge you *Observer* readers flung out there through the hemisphere to forget about moving to Austin. Stay in Dayton! There's swell people in Pasadena! To be frank about it, Austin doesn't need you here.

Anybody who can concentrate as long as it takes to answer the doorbell knows Austin doesn't need 50,000 university students, either, just as Austin doesn't need a bunch of nice clean new factories that are going broke anyhow, and Austin doesn't need roads bulldozed through the parks and hills to accommodate cars that won't run without gasoline. But the people who gave us Dallas and Houston are trying to present us Austin. In this case that means jobs and lodging for plenty of nice young people who can dance pretty good to loud music and procreate in clapboard Camelots thrust out over the pastures only a gallon or two from the office where everybody is very goddamn hip because Austin is where you go if you're hip now that San Francisco is about to fall into the ocean and Taos has run out of water and John Denver has moved to Colorado.

Listen, let me tell you, it used to be hip to be in Austin, but it's not anymore. San Angelo is hip. Dripping Springs is hip. Alpine and Dime Box are hip. Fort Worth is hep. Austin is engaged in a death-grope with real estate developers, and there is nothing less hip than that. It will take severe measures to save the city, even beyond issuing numbers and putting up a fence. New rules, for example. To apply for a license to build, sell, or develop new real estate properties, as opposed to peddling or improving existing ones, an agent or developer should have to spend as much time in training as a tooth dentist does. An agent, developer, or builder should have to study humanities and aesthetics and certainly ethics, should not be allowed to vote or hold elective office, and then should have to stand before an examining board which would automatically refuse the license. That would put the developer-agent in a pertinent place in society.

Twenty years ago when the *Observer* was born and Ronnie Dugger began to be viewed with ever greater dismay in board rooms, the coalition of greedheads who thought up such public disasters as MoPac and the Loop had not yet been turned loose. But somehow they got out among us, and first thing you knew they had not only laid unnecessary and hideous concrete runways through some of Austin's leafier neighborhoods, they had even got cooking on one of those notorious doubledecker dodo paths, that starts in the air and goes nowhere along what is called IH 35. In so doing, they wiped out a good chicken fried steak cafe and other shrines that were worth more to the quality of the city than all the freeways that will ever be built here. Could there be a poetic payoff when MoPac is turned into the world's longest rose garden? Could we be rescued from ourselves by forces from the East?

But, then, why wait to be saved by the Big Bustout? Put up the fence. Pass out the numbers before, as Willie Morris says, "the dirt is all ruint and the wine's drunk up." They're barring people from Oregon already. St. Petersburg announced nobody else is welcome. I admit to being selfish about this, and as usual incapable of moderation. But listen to me, dear readers out there: stay home or go to Indiana. If you move here, Austin won't happen.

Letter: December 16, 1969, on Mad Dog, Inc.

We were more serious about some aspects of Mad Dog, Inc., than we were about others. One thing we were definitely serious about was publishing Candy Barr's prison poems. But as with most Mad Dog projects, the publishing venture never died, it just sort of trailed off.

Dear Prof. King:

. . . I guess you've heard about Mad Dog Inc by now. It is far too complex at this point to explain in writing, but we automatically put you on the board of advisors, and you can be president of any department you can think up. (There is a vacancy now as head of the Ornamental Shrub Company, a subsidiary, and also as chairman of the How Dare You Squad.) Our first project, outside of buying a ping pong table for the office, is the MAD DOG MASKED BALL, to be held maybe on Valentines Day. At the Vulcan Gas Co. MAD DOG INK, our magazine, will devote its first issue to Candy Barr—her life, framed by the oligarchy, etc. and will print the poems she wrote in prison. . . .

Bud Shrake at the Armadillo World Headquarters, 1974. Photo by Sarah Pileggi.

The Regenerator Erection Laboratory

From *Peter Arbiter* (1973)

Joe Fox, an editor at a major New York publishing house, came over to my table at Elaine's restaurant one night and asked to sit down. "I've just read *Peter Arbiter*," he said. "It is terrible. If you publish this your career as a novelist is finished."

Until that moment I hadn't thought I actually had a career as a novelist. I was a sportswriter who wrote a novel occasionally. I thanked Joe for his advice and went ahead with trying to publish this takeoff on *The Satyricon.* But after a couple more rejections, I packed the manuscript away until I was back in Austin, where my old friend Bill Wittliff read it and said he would publish it at his Encino Press, with classy woodcut illustrations by Barbara Whitehead.

Bill put out a beautiful book, except for the small type, but I doubt it had any effect on my future as a novelist. Very few people read it.

I wrote about half of *Peter Arbiter* on my little Smith Corona Skywriter while I was on a long assignment for *Sports Illustrated,* traveling the Far East. I wrote this chapter during a fourteen-hour flight from Singapore to Kuala Lumpur. They served four elaborate meals, but I typed through the second two.

The Regenerator Erection Laboratory was on the eighth floor of a downtown hotel. I had to wait a long while for an elevator because the hotel was accommodating a convention of automobile dealers. Though it was not yet noon, the lobby was packed with conventioneers and thick with whisky fumes, and every elevator was jammed with short-haired, red-faced men wearing badges on their suits. Their hard Midwestern voices buzzed around me, and I felt many an eye, hostile or speculative, regarding me, my clothing, the length of my hair. This increased my nervousness.

Finally I forced myself into an elevator full of these people. Bodies mashed against me. I kept my gaze directed at the flashing numbers as the elevator rose. Everybody on the elevator was a male, and they were pressed together like cigars in a box.

"Don't wiggle that thing if you don't mean it," someone said from the rear of the elevator, and there was general giggling.

"I don't dare face the front," said another.

"Or the rear!"

"If you reach back to scratch your ass, you better not smile!"

"Who brought the Vaseline?"

"In a place like this, who needs girls?"

"Oh Charley baby, jam it to me!"

Thank God, the eighth floor arrived. I pushed out of the elevator.

"Toodleooo darling!" someone said as the doors shut.

Could this be America? I wondered as I found the sign and went down the hall to a door that had the name of the laboratory on it and a slogan that read YOU CAN'T KEEP A GOOD MAN DOWN.

The waiting room was typical of a hotel suite. Utrillo on the wall, a shabby green couch, a television, red drapes, venetian blinds on the windows, a radiator, grease spots, musk. I rang a bell and then sat down and looked through a copy of *Argosy* that explained why the U.S. government had hushed all attempts to reveal the secret of the Yeti. After a few minutes a door opened and a fat, redwigged old lady, about seventy, in a white nurse's uniform with crepe-sole shoes, came out. I stood up. I started to say my name but she waved a hand for silence.

"Him sick in his dickie?" she asked.

"Well, I've had this certain . . ."

Deftly she unzipped my pants, burrowed inside and produced my tool.

"Oooooo, him dickie sick!" she said.

A tall, thin woman with very black dyed hair appeared in the doorway. She must have been six feet four, and she also wore a nurse's uniform.

"I am Dr. Claudine Babcock," said the tall woman. She held one hand behind her back. "Strip naked, handsome."

"Shouldn't we discuss the problem?" I asked.

The hand shot out from behind her back, and she slapped me with a quirt that had been concealed there.

"All talk and no action, that's the problem!" she said. She brandished the quirt in my face as the fat woman began removing my clothes. "This here Apache Sex Starter Upper may be what you need a taste of. Then again maybe not. Come on, Nurse Heinz! Get the patient ready and bring him into the lab!"

"Oooo, this dickie's no use to nobody," said Nurse Heinz.

"That sort of talk hardly builds confidence," Dr. Babcock said.

They took me into the next room, which did resemble a doctor's sanctum, and had me lie down nude on a table. Before I knew what they were up to, they strapped my wrists and ankles to the table. Then a color photograph of a beautiful naked girl popped onto a screen in the ceiling. Dr. Babcock put her ear on my member.

"Nope. Nothing. Try the next slide," she said. The following slide was of a beautiful naked boy. "Still nothing," said the doctor. Now came a slide of two girls and a boy engaged in a fleshy arrangement. "Nothing again." The next slide was of a rosy pig.

"Hah! You damned pervert!" Dr. Babcock said, striking me across the stomach with her quirt.

"I didn't like that one!" I said.

"No? I was sure I heard something." She poked my member into her ear and listened. "Perhaps not. Next slide, Nurse Heinz."

In order the screen showed old men playing chess, a Peeping Tom view through a window of a girl undressing, naked teenagers on rollerskates, a duck, a motorcyclist wearing black leather and carrying a chain, a fashion model, a drag queen, a nude mother powdering a nude baby boy, a nude father powdering a nude baby girl, a German Shepherd dog, Nurse Heinz on the toilet, Rita Hayworth in a negligee in *Gilda*, football players nude in a locker room, a Green Beret with a rifle, a box of chocolates, a racing car, the Lone Ranger on Silver, Dale Evans tied to a tree, Nurse Heinz performing fellatio on a Mexican with drooping socks, a close peek up a bum, the ocean, a Chinaman, money heaped on a table, two men masturbating, a rocket, naked savages with dangling testicles and sausage breasts, a stout motherly woman in a girdle, oil derricks, nudists playing volleyball, redneck whores, Frank Sinatra in a sailor suit, a milk cow, a blonde family in a sauna, a drawing of Popeye screwing Olive Oyl, marching WAACs, several handsome men and women copulating in a living room with a pool visible through the door, a chicken, a jet fighter, a high school girls' basketball game, a bag of doughnuts, gang rape on a car seat, the dead body of a woman with her skirt pulled up, a cop beating a longhaired kid, a Gila Monster, a pregnant woman, a pile of feces, a cowboy lighting a cigarette, a tattooed woman with a python, a man wearing a garter belt and high heels, and so on. Dr. Babcock flipped a switch and the projector turned off.

"Well, Nurse Heinz, we've got us a hell of a tough case here. He don't like any of the normal stuff," Dr. Babcock said.

By this time Nurse Heinz was sucking my toes and pounding on my knees with xylophone hammers.

"Goddamn Heinz, cut that out! I said we've got a special tough case here! Pay attention to business," said Dr. Babcock.

"Sometimes that works," fat old Heinz said.

"It never has worked," Dr. Babcock said to me in a confidential tone. "Never has worked once. She just likes it is all."

"I learned it at nurse school," said Heinz resentfully. Nurse Heinz straightened her red wig while Dr. Babcock paced about the lab.

"We have it established that this one definitely is not normal. That means he's a pervert," Dr. Babcock said.

"He's one of them?" said Heinz. "Gagh! I'd never of sucked his toes if I'd known that."

"Dear old Heinzie, what a heart you've got," Dr. Babcock smiled.

"Let me up from here," I said.

"Just like that? Oh no! This laboratory has a solid reputation. We'll not have it spoiled by a pudding peter like you," said Dr. Babcock. She tweaked my ear. "Tell you what. Be a good boy and respond to treatment, and I'll let you have a piece of me. If you've not had me, you've not had the best."

Nurse Heinz came out of another room nude wearing an enormous pink rubber dildo with a red head. It was strapped to her ruddy, tracked-up old body with an elastic harness. A recording of *The Sheik of Araby* was placed on a phonograph and played at 78 rpm while the nurse laced her fingers behind her head and obscenely revolved her hips. Dr. Babcock sprinkled me with powder from a leather bag and then began to tap my groin with a handful of nettles she had produced from a drawer. Meanwhile they chanted:

Rise up and play
I mean today
I'll have my way
Or you will pay.

The nettles stung and I groaned and hauled against the straps, exciting Nurse Heinz into a leaping frenzy. Red welts spread across my abdomen. The slide show began again on the screen in the ceiling. Nurse Heinz sprayed me with perfume from an atomizer. The stinging of the nettles did cause my member to swell somewhat, and the two women croaked with glee. At that sound a fat goose wearing a rhinestone collar waddled in from the next room and hissed and spanked its wings as though dancing with Nurse Heinz. The women had lost all reason. They capered around the table and littered my body with powders and ointments. Nurse Heinz tried to mount me with the dildo but lost her grip and fell backward onto the floor where she was assaulted by the hissing goose. Dr. Babcock now had a vibrating machine in one hand and was attacking herself with it rather than me, although she continued to lash me with the nettles. I had started to fear for my life. The old phonograph was playing Martin Denny jungle music. Nurse Heinz grappled with the goose and cried what struck me as Druidic incantations. Dr. Babcock collapsed across my body kissing and slobbering and sneezing—part of what she had tossed onto me were ground peppercorns—and ripped open her dress to expose a modest phallus.

This revelation gave me the strength to tear my right arm loose from its binding. I pushed Dr. Babcock off the table, quickly undid my left, then sat up and freed my feet. The doctor and the nurse wallowed together, each attempting to do the other, and as I leaped down onto the linoleum the goose charged and bit a painful bruise on my shin. I caught it under the breast with a nice kick—rather call it a punt, as one punts a football—that lofted it against the far wall with a satisfying *thamp!* and scattered the room with white feathers.

I fetched my clothes and ran into the outer room to put them on. My member was puffy but not rigid and I felt as though tiny ants were crawling on my groin.

As I was jamming my feet into my loafers, Dr. Babcock came in, buttoned and proper.

"I see you are one of those laymen who have no faith in or respect for the medical profession," said Dr. Babcock.

"Well, it's not that exactly," I said.

"Then too there's the fee. Ten dollars please. I think you'll agree that's not out of line," said Dr. Babcock. I placed the money on the coffee table atop a copy of *National Geographic* and walked rapidly to the door. I could hear Nurse Heinz in the other room carrying on about the state of the goose. Dr. Babcock followed me to the door. Her gaunt face with black-ringed eyes was the last thing I saw before I shut the door.

"Have we meant nothing to each other?" asked Dr. Babcock.

Peter the Home Arbiter was closer than my apartment, so I went to my office for a drink. My assistant tried to say something to me as I entered, but I ignored him and went into my own sanctum where I found, at my desk, an old school mate, Harvey Smedley, perhaps the last person on earth I would have chosen to encounter at that moment.

Harvey was wearing Indian moccasins, Levis, a brocade vest with buckskin fringes, several strings of beads and a half dozen rings. As I entered he removed his wig of shoulder-length hair, scratched his cropped scalp and grinned at me. When I had known him best, he had been Harvey Smedley, third string fullback and sophomore flunkout. Now he was Sergeant Smedley of the Narcotics Bureau. The drawers of my desk and filing cabinets were open.

"Couldn't find nothing to smoke," Harvey said.

"Please, Harvey, my nerves are shot," I said. I poured myself a half glass of scotch and drank it down.

"Shoot, Pete, don't be nervous," said Harvey. "I just did a light search to keep in practice. Hell, I didn't even break the door open or nothing. I know you don't have no marijuana."

"Never shoot the stuff," I said.

"Hell, I said I know it. If you'd been the kind to smoke drugs or sniff that damn hashish, it would of come to my knowledge. Think we don't know what you citizens are doing? Shoot! Damn! Son of a gun!" He shook his head with a proud smile. "Damn fags and dope fiends, we latch onto their ass before you could say poot."

"Oh yes?" I said, looking very closely at Harvey and pouring another drink.

"Sure, buddy! If you'd been one of them, why, teammate or no teammate, I'd of stuck your butt in the penitentiary for twenty years. Might of broke my heart but a good officer has got to do his duty and uphold the law, and the law says twenty years for fags and dope fiends. Frankly, some think we ought to kill em."

"What do you think?" I asked.

"I give it lots of study," said Harvey. "I'm a expert in this, of course, been to the academy more than once, and I say, naw, there's no need to kill a man just for putting marijuana in his arm. Twenty years is enough to teach him to do right. Same for fags. I've been blowed before, in line of duty, lots of times really, still work that trick on my day off now and then to help out, and it's disgusting but you kind of feel sorry for some of them fairy bastards and don't even hit some of them."

"You have compassion," I said.

"Shoot yeah, man, you think I'm a savage skunk without a heart in his breast? I've got a family. Look, here's their picture. The one on the left in the bathing suit is my wife. Between you and me, she's the best piece of tail in America. This one here's my little boy. If he grew up to be a queer, I'd blow his brains out. Think it can't happen! Remember old Mossy that used to play tackle? Had two kids he was damn proud of, damn proud. The little girl grew up to be all-state third baseman and high-scoring forward on the Roaming Queens, and the little boy turned out to be a champion drum major. Like to of killed old Mossy. How about your family, Pete? Your old Mama still cranky as hell?"

"Yeah," I said.

"That's good. And how's your old Daddy?"

"Still dead."

"Too bad. Listen, Pete, I'll tell you actual why I come here today after all this time. Set down there. This place bugged?"

"I don't know," I said.

"Can't be too careful these days. What ain't bugged by the CIA, FBI, NSA, IRS, damn federal narks and private cops is most likely bugged by us, but of course we only bug citizens that we got reason to think is up to some crime or another. Except sometimes for fun we'll bug a hot motel room or bridal suite, you know, and get some photos for the boys. But you got no cause to be worried unless you're a damn criminal or a suspect."

I sat down and carefully scratched my groin.

"Why I'm here is this," Harvey said. He reached inside his moccasin and laid a little plastic bag full of green herbal matter on my desk.

"Parsley?" I said.

"Shoot! Guess again!"

"Oregano?"

I was prepared to run for it as soon as they came through the door.

"It's Irish tobacco," I said.

"Boy!" laughed Harvey. "You are one pure goddamn innocent son of a gun!" He leaned across the desk, peered at me with small yellow eyes, and whispered, "This here's Mary Wanny."

"What?"

"You know, Mary Jane. Boo. Grass. Speed. Horse. Reefer."

"I don't understand."

"Damn, I'm trying to tell you in code in case the place is bugged. Think now. You know what I mean—weed, monkey, spike, cactus. Do I have to spell it out for you?"

"I guess so."

"Well, this here is marijuana," Harvey said petulantly. "I guess we'll have to take our chances with the bug. What you see in this bag is what the dope fiends in India call Cannibal." He hefted the bag in his palm as if judging the weight. "Just this little bit here is worth more than two hundred dollars on the dope fiend market. With this right here you could roll forty cigarettes— they call them joints, or fixes—and sell them for five bucks each. A dope fiend has got to have a fix of this stuff two or three times a day. Some need five or six. And this is not your real hard dope like your damn hashish, the Big H. You've saw pictures of damn Chinamen laying in their bunk beds smoking hashish and shooting it in their arm? This ain't that powerful. You can get addicted to it, but it takes a while. Took me a couple of months in fact." He began rolling a cigarette out of the green matter, using a package of Bambu papers. "It's a hazard of being a cop. I been a cop on the Nark Squad many years, but it was only two months ago that I finally got trapped into smoking this damn stuff—kids was getting so slick that I had to learn their ways—and now I smoke it ever day. Oh, it's okay, since I'm a cop I'm allowed."

"Where do you get it?" I asked, watching him lick the cigarette and suck it into form.

"This here Baggie I took off a kid I caught eating banana cream pie at an all-night diner. You see one of them longhair freaks at a all-night diner eating banana cream pie at 3 a.m., you've caught yourself a dope fiend! I just rousted him out of there and took his dope. Used to, I would of hit him on the head and put him in jail, but I let this one go because I needed my fix."

"Harvey, I'd rather you didn't smoke that in here," I said.

"I told you, I'm allowed."

"Not in my office."

"Don't be a damn square, Pete."

"But what if the police break in?"

"Damn, you are thick-headed. I told you already. I am the police. I can do what I please."

"What about me, though?"

"You're why I come here, Pete," said Harvey, lighting the cigarette. He held his breath for a moment and then said, "I must be getting soft lately, but I come here to help you. Getting soft! Oh that's good! Getting soft! One thing this stuff does is make me funny as hell!"

My groin was itching terrifically. I poured another drink.

"I learned from one of my sources that you can't get it up no more," Harvey said.

"What?"

"Never mind what certain place I seen you leaving or who told me, but I know. So I brought this stuff. This weed is supposed to turn you into a real sex maniac. You know, rape. Orgies. All that. It don't work that way on me. Just the opposite in fact. But they told me about it at the academy. Hell, everbody knows about dope orgies. Now, take a puff."

"Harvey, this is too much. My nerves are ruined. I want to go home."

"Just take a deep drag and hold the smoke down, Pete."

"I'd rather not."

"At first you may not notice nothing. But two or three drags and you'll see. Come on, Pete. This is mighty fine stuff. It's real Panama Green."

"You promise you won't arrest me?" I said.

"Arrest you! Hell, I'm your friend! I come here to help you! You're as paranoid as some of them dope fiends."

Harvey giggled. He held the joint out toward me, but as I slowly reached for it a new expression came across his face. He squinted. He frowned. Keeping the joint a few inches from my fingers, he studied me as though suddenly he no longer quite recognized me.

"Wait a minute," he said. "Level with me, Pete. Who do you work for?"

"For myself. This is my shop."

"Yeah?" He looked around the office, became involved for a while with his reflection, then looked back at me. "Yeah, you'd say that, wouldn't you? Pretty damn sharp, Pete. You almost had me."

"What do you mean, Harvey?"

"Sergeant Smedley here?" he said loudly. He took his wig off the bust and talked directly into the ear of Socrates. "Sergeant Smedley doing his duty!" He lowered his voice and chuckled ironically. "I've got to hand it to you guys. Damn clever. Perfect setup. Ingenious web you spun. I can see why you claim to be the best in the business." He clapped the wig onto his head and snubbed out the joint. "Might as well save this butt . . . ah . . . roach. Tell me, Pete, your boys waiting outside?"

"Harvey, I don't have any boys."

"Strictly pro, hah? Pro to the end! Merciless with a friend as with a enemy. I shouldn't be so surprised. I'm a good cop, too, Pete. A damn good cop. Tell them that."

He patted the pistol butt that stuck out of the brocade vest when he stood up. Putting his back to the wall, Smedley opened my office door a crack and peeked out. "Very good," he said.

"Very smart. Two in drag. I make it the one dressed like a old lady with blue hair and the young one with the big shades. My hat's off to you, Pete. It'd take a real pro like me to make that pair, and then only because I got wise. Got a sense for danger, you know. Don't last long without it. Like a fox." Harvey smiled tightly and again showed me the pistol butt. "You gonna let me walk out of here, or will I have to use this?"

"You can walk out," I said.

"How can I trust you?"

"We're old friends, Harvey. Besides, you're a good cop."

"Thanks for nothing, baby," he said and slid out the door.

I went out and watched him edge down the sidewalk. He bought a newspaper from a rack and held it in front of his face until he arrived at a Volkswagen bus, painted with flowers and circles and stars and sloshed with Day-Glo, that was parked at the curb. Swiftly he jumped in and drove off down the street at eight miles an hour with people honking at him.

"Crazy hippies," said my assistant.

"Ronald, I don't feel well. Take over for the rest of the day."

"You've been sick a lot lately. I'm getting worried about you," he said. Knowing Ronald was watching, I tried to keep from diving into my crotch with both hands until I could reach my Alfa-Romeo and put at least a block between me and that shop.

Letter: August 1, 1969, from Zihuatanejo

I have always been fascinated by Mexico. The summer after we graduated
from high school, my friend Ed Poulsen and I rode the train to Mexico City
and rented an apartment on the Calle Edgar Allen Poe, the very name of
which filled me with literary longings. I fell in love with the place. The air
was clear then—you could see Popo the volcano looming over the city—and
you could smell the flower gardens in the windows.

I went back to Mexico often for months at a time. I wrote part of *Blessed
McGill* in a rented villa overlooking Acapulco Bay. It was not the house I talk
about in this letter, but Dan and June Jenkins were there with me then, too.

After I hung out at Tres Vidas for a while researching a story for *Sports
Illustrated* and got some ideas for my novel *Strange Peaches*, my wife Doatsy and I drove up to Zihuatanejo to see how Gary Cartwright was coming
along on his new novel.

Acapulco, 1965. From left: Fletcher Boone, Bud Shrake, and Dan Jenkins.
Photo by June Jenkins.

Cartwright, his wife Jo, and their very young son, Shea, had gone to Mexico to hide out from various distractions. The town of Z was a wild place, small and isolated, on the edge between the Pacific Ocean and the jungle-covered mountains. We drove down a dirt road and found the Cartwright adobe in a grove of palm trees overlooking the ocean. Hammocks swung in the soft air. The door was open, but nobody was around. I saw a portable typewriter on a table with a sheet of paper rolled into the platen. I went over to see how far he had progressed in the months he had been gone. On the paper it said this was page six.

That called to mind a fellow who lived in the gatehouse of the Acapulco villa where I had worked on *Blessed McGill*. His name was Norris. On his wall was an oil portrait of Norris in his full-dress uniform as an officer in the Scots Guards. Norris had retired from the Queen's service and moved across the sea to Acapulco to write a novel about his adventures in World War Two. Twenty years later he had written about 100 pages. "It's this bloody, balmy weather and the beauty of the place," he said. "When I sit down to write, I go to sleep. But the truth is, mate, I'd rather keep living here than finish this damn book."

Dear Prof. King:
We just last night returned from our month in Acapulco—in a big, rambling, old, seedy, classy, beat-up, elegant house that meandered down a mountainside into the Pacific—and the impressions are still so strong and fresh that in my head we have not left the place, and I wish we never had to. The house looks like a set for a decadent fucked-up in the Tropics Tennessee Williams fantasy; in fact, the tour boats that regularly went along Boca Chica Channel past our place broadcast announcements to their passengers that: "The big white house with the red tile roof is the private home of that fabulous Meskin actress, Dolores Del Rio." So we and the kids painted up, on a bedsheet, a sign that said dolores says hi to all our boys in khaki and now and then hung it on the railing of the pool where it could be seen by all aboard. There were piles of us in the house: five Jenkinses, three Japs, four of us (including my two kids) and for a week a fellow from Houston . . . and for another stretch Skidmore arrived with Miss Nancy Greene and pocketsful of strange white tablets.

Not that we needed much heart medicine. Jap had a large supply of Pure Green Overkill. Also Jap and I spent about 10 days of going through the elaborate dealing protocol, with many meetings with mysterious folks, journeys to strange places, lots of beer and tequila consumed, etc. and finally came out of it with a stack of newspaper-wrapped material that was green and seedless and could in a twinkle turn your wonderful God-fearing college-educated Amurikan into a piglet. It will be clear to a wise fellow like yourself that there was not any really terrific amount of work done. Dan did finish his golf book, I did rewrite about 70 pages of my current project, and Jappo did do a lot of mighty pondering and some typing as well, but none got anywhere near as far as had been loudly promised. The month, though, was beautiful. Got brushed by one hurricane, went deep sea fishing a few times, had some hearty adventures, went to several parties (got thrown out of one), got sunburned and lazier, you can imagine.

And now what? I guess I'll be coming up to NY in a month or so, about the time you set up house in Boston. Perhaps Miss D and I can visit up there for a weekender. We're not going to move up for the entire five or six months this year but I'll probably be there for 2 months or so, and Miss D for somewhat less. Firstly I got to finish this book—called bone yard, a rewrite of *The Satyricon* that I set in modern Texas. I'll be finished next week, God help. Our fren Golb at Harper Press read about half the first draft and greeted it with remarks such as "trash . . . a waste of time . . . a conceit . . . Willie thinks so too . . ." Not to me did he utter these atheistic remarks but to [my agent] S. Lord, who likes the book and so is perplexed. Only reason Golb ever saw it in the first place was his own insistence upon doing so. Same sadly defiled ms went over to Doubleday and they are buying it, says Sterling, with enthusiasm and promises of no more McGill type shitting-upon. This book is not really a novel any more than *The Magic Christian* is a novel but it's not less of one either; it's supposed to be funny, is no doubt dirty (narrated by a switch-hitting interior decorator from Dallas), is I guess perplexing. Golb was I think looking for Western Gothic and got instead a faceful of faggots and it made him jumpy. He told Sterling I could call him up and talk to him about it if I wish. I think I will go ahead as I have been and talk to my frogs and ducks and whenever possible to a horsey.

What you said about B. McGill is very much appreciated. In my infrequent periods of dejection and despair (about five or six per day when I am trying hard) I will read that again and again and say aloud old doctor king sure knows what he is talking about! Then swaller a pill and get to typing. It did in fact amaze me how what I thought that book was really about was not what others thought (the movie guy who called me about the screenplay last month said, 'of course we had to take out all that religion shit') and one respected fren said he was surprised the book had not a trace of humor in it (when I thought much of it humorous and all of it ironic) and anyhow you got down to it and what you said in the letter is precious encouragement.

This fantastic unrelenting nonflagging rightness that a writer has got to keep up does get me down, is especially outlandish for a dopefiend to maintain when it is to him plain as the nose on an armadillo that writing is the freakiest most utterly egotistical endeavor a man can undertake; who could be so sublimely arrogant as to think ever that anybody would care to use the time and effort necessary to read an entire book that this here arrogant person wrote, to have eyeballs drift across maybe 100,000 words, not to mention phrases and to be sure sentences and even paragraphs and whole pages are put together haphazardly into ideas, or in rare cases vice-versa, by guys who are writing books. . . .

Scenes from *Kid Blue* ("Dime Box")

Final shooting script, September 20, 1971

Filmed as *Kid Blue,* starring Dennis Hopper, Warren Oates, Peter Boyle, Ben Johnson, Lee Purcell. Bud Shrake had a small part as "Town Drunk."

The making of *Kid Blue* was an experience that changed my life. The Mad Dogs drove down to Durango, Mexico, in a motorhome with a NO FUMAR sign on it to fool the cops, and in a Ford van. The first place we tried to cross the border we were turned away because of Pete Gent's long hair. Sixty miles away we found a different crossing. We arrived in Durango and walked straight into a bizarre meeting at Dennis Hopper's rented mansion where we found people on acid with pistols. And soon the chief narc of the district landed in a helicopter with armed soldiers and let us know our lives would swiftly get very dangerous unless our producer, Marvin Schwartz, paid him $25,000 in protection money. Marvin looked like Buffalo Bill, but he was a wise man, and he paid.

Kid Blue changed Marvin's life drastically, too. He fought with the bosses at 20th Century Fox during post production until eventually they threw him off the lot. The last fight he lost was over the title. The bosses at Fox said "Dime Box" sounded like a dope movie. So they changed it to *Kid Blue.*

Marvin phoned me on his last day at the studio. I could hear the banging as his furniture was being carried out. Through the window Marvin could see his name being painted over on his parking space. Marvin went to Europe and traveled as a middle-aged hippie. He walked across Africa. He went to India and Tibet. Years later he turned up at my front door in Austin as a smiling, beatific, serene, Buddhist monk called Brother Jonathan. He helped build a monastery near San Francisco, where he died while kneeling at prayer.

And how did the *Kid Blue* experience change my life? It made me want to keep on making movies and being around movie people. The show business game brings out the best and the worst in just about everything, and abrupt change is the rule. I liked being part of intrigues and trying to duck the double-crosses. Also, to lift a line from *Songwriter,* "he did it for the love but he was not above the money."

Reading this bit of the script, I am surprised at the lengthy descriptive paragraphs, very novelistic. I had never written a script before and didn't know that most directors don't want this much description. The only time this much description is used is for the version of the script that is to be read by studio people who need to see the picture in their imagination while deciding whether to make the movie. That the long descriptive paragraphs survive into the shooting script shows Jim Frawley was trying to shoot this script as I wrote it.

Setting: Dime Box, Texas, 1902.

Scene 7

EXT. STREET—NIGHT

Bick [Dennis Hopper] is walking along the street at twilight. He passes houses with little fences and burnt flower gardens. A skinny dog barks at him. Bick comes to the livery stable. Sitting on the ground, leaning against the wall of the livery stable, are THREE FIGURES that catch Bick's attention.

Scene 8

EXT. LIVERY STABLE

The three are INDIANS. They are dressed in white men's discarded clothing. Two wear hats and one wears a greasy headband. All have long, black, dirty hair. Two of them have faces that tend to look Oriental. The one with the headband has some Latin blood. All three incline toward being squat and bowlegged. They are Comanches—former "Lords of the Plains"—who are supposed to be on a reservation up in Indian Territory (in what five years after this, in 1907, becomes the state of Oklahoma). They have a corncob pipe that they are passing back and forth, and one has a deerskin pouch hanging from his neck. Bick is fascinated. He stares at them. They stare back with stoned eyes. Bick hunkers down beside them, very curious.

BICK

My daddy told me Texas used to be crawling with Indians, but they run all you fellows up north to the reservation before I was born.

The three Comanches look at each other. With an almost imperceptible shrug, MENDOZA, the one with the headband, drags on the pipe, grunts as he holds his breath, and then hands the pipe to Bick. Bick thinks this is some kind of peace pipe ceremony, which in fact it is but not the sort he has heard about. Bick puffs at the pipe and has a coughing fit. Another Indian, JOE CLOUD-MAKER, reaches for the pipe, which Bick gladly surrenders. Cloudmaker begins to drag on it. All three Indians are in danger of dozing off. They look red-eyed at Bick.

BICK

Listen, my name is Bick. Bick, you savvy?

MENDOZA

(speaks English with a Tex-Mex accent)
That's good.

BICK

(delighted at getting a response)
My daddy used to hunt buffaloes . . .
(realizes this is the wrong thing to say to an Indian)
But that business kind of wore out . . .

Cloudmaker's head falls back against the wall with a whomp! The third Indian, OLD COYOTE, takes the pipe.

BICK

You got a village someplace? You live in a teepee?

MENDOZA

We live in the stable.

BICK

Yeah, I guess it's warm in the stable.

MENDOZA
Very warm. All summer. Cold as hell in winter.

OLD COYOTE
Hell is hot.

MENDOZA
You don't know.

OLD COYOTE
(nodding wisely)
Hell is fire. Is fire cold?

MENDOZA
(to Bick)
They talk to a man who tells them that. A God-Shouter Preacher. He
is making a machine that will fly up to heaven.

As Bick takes the pipe again and puffs on it, he seems to be gently covered
with smoke that rises from his person like morning fog. The Indians are looking directly at him, and everything appears lightly golden in color, the gold
slowly deepening into sunset-gold before gradually fading again. Now Bick
can definitely tell something strange is happening. But it doesn't worry him.
He coughs and spurts smoke.

BICK
Fly to heaven! Whew!

He whistles. Mendoza leans over and removes the pipe from his hand. With
effort, Bick begins to stand up. The Indians roll their eyes upward to remain
fixed on his face. Now he is on his feet . . .

BICK
Thought I'd never get here! Whew! God dawg! What did you say? . . .
Oh yeah, that's right, heaven! Listen, it was a pleasure. I don't know
another soul in this whole damn town that a man would want to
know . . .

The Indians watch curiously as Bick walks on to continue his tour of the town. He goes along the street, grinning and occasionally saying whew! He slaps his leg.

> BICK
> Real Indians!

While grinning and thinking about seeing the Indians, at the same time slightly puzzled as to why he feels better than when he left the boarding-house, Bick happens to look up at the sign on the building he is standing in front of. The sign says confectionery. Bick is no great reader, but he knows what this means. He whistles to himself, chuckles and enters.

Scene 9

<u>INT. CONFECTIONERY—NIGHT</u>

Inside the Confectionery, there is a glass counter full of cookies, cakes, pies and tarts. There are three tables. Two are empty, but at the third sit Reece and Molly Ford, sipping iced drinks. Reece smiles and nods. Bick does the same. A MAN comes out of a back room and looks at Bick from behind the counter. Bick is studying the pies and cakes.

> BICK
> (momentarily confused, glances at table where Reece and Molly sit)
> Give me what they got.

> COUNTER MAN
> Iced lemon phosphate?

> BICK
> (enormously pleased)
> Iced lemon phosphate!

COUNTER MAN
(flattered)
We're the only place in sixty miles that's got it. You'd have to go to
Austin.

The counter man opens the ice box and chips off a piece of ice. It is very hot in
the store and the ice looks unbearably good to Bick. The counter man pours
the lemonade from a pitcher he takes out of the ice box and squirts the phosphate from a bottle. Bick looks around and smiles again at Reece and Molly.

REECE
Won't you join us?

COUNTER MAN
(handing Bick the drink)
Five cents.

BICK
I just want one glass.

COUNTER MAN
Prices gone up.

Bick goes to the table. He pulls out a chair, touches his hat brim when he looks
at Molly, smiles at Reece and sits down. There is a true Texas inarticulate
moment when none of them can think of anything to say. They smile quite
pleasantly at each other, though; and finally Bick speaks.

BICK
Hidy.

REECE
I'm Reece Ford. This is my wife Molly.

BICK
(shaking hands with Reece)
Bickford Waner.

REECE
You from around here?

Bick is sipping his lemon phosphate with great, obvious, stoned pleasure.

BICK
Huh?

REECE
I said you from around here?

BICK
Naw. Up yonder.

REECE
Indian Territory?

BICK
Naw. Just North Texas. Fort Worth.

REECE
I guess you got family up there.

BICK
My mama's been dead a long time. My daddy used to hustle cows at the Stockyards in Fort Worth, but he got in a fight with some rough old boys and they stomped him to death. I think. Hard to tell whether it was the stabbing or the stomping that done it.

MOLLY
Did you go after them?

BICK
Who?

MOLLY
The men that stomped your daddy.

BICK
(with slowly creeping incredulity)
Me?

MOLLY
Did you bring them to justice?

BICK
My daddy was a pretty rough boy, too. If he couldn't handle them fellers, there ain't much chance I could.

REECE
Molly's been reading adventure books. She looks for everybody to walk around with a pistol in their belt.

MOLLY
(to Bick)
Do you have a pistol?

BICK
Used to have a shotgun. It got broke, though.

Bick gets up goes to the counter. Molly and Reece also rise.

BICK
Gimme one of them skinny cookie deals with ice cream in it. Strawberry.

He also picks up a small paper bag of candy and puts it in his shirt pocket.

REECE
Molly's from Dallas. She thinks everybody out in these parts is a wild savage.

MOLLY
Well, there's panthers in the streets of Fort Worth, they tell me.

BICK

Not in the daytime.

(to man)

How much? Candy too.

Bick tosses him four cents and they all leave the Confectionery.

A-9

<u>EXT. STREET—NIGHT</u>

The three of them start walking down the quiet street . . .

REECE

When we got married I decided to come down here and work in the new factory. But I ain't sure how much Molly likes it.

BICK

What is a factory, anyhow?

REECE

A factory is where a lot of people make products . . .

Bick still doesn't understand.

REECE

You see, America is growing fast and we gotta have a lot of products for people to buy.

BICK

People buy these products with the money they get for making these products?

REECE

That's about how it works.

BICK
How come you don't make this here product your own self and then keep it? That way you don't have to work in no factory.

REECE
(patiently)
Because you can't make these products if you ain't got a factory.

BICK
Well, what kind of factory is this?

REECE
The Great American Ceramic Novelty Company. I work in ashtrays . . .

As Reece explains, Bick's puzzlement grows into disbelief and finally into amusement.

REECE
. . . little clay bowls that you put your ashes in . . . from your cigar or your cigarette.

BICK
Man, you throw your ashes on the ground.

REECE
Not indoors.

BICK
Nobody smokes indoors. It stinks up the house.

REECE
Mr. Hendricks says they smoke indoors up East. Even women. He says everybody in America is gonna be needing ashtrays . . . to hold their ashes.

BICK
(chuckling)
You can believe that if you want to.

REECE
Somebody must buy these ashtrays. This place is booming. Mr. Hendricks says good American know-how is gonna change this town so you'd never recognize it if you been gone in the wood a few years.

Letter: November 4, 1973, on Larry Mahan

I met Larry Mahan when he played a rodeo cowboy in *J. W. Coop,* a movie Gary Cartwright and I wrote. Larry made an immediate impression on me. He flew his own small plane from rodeo to rodeo, sometimes making two in one day. It was a natural progression that I would someday write about him in *Sports Illustrated.*

I still get a little shiver when I remember going through that gas station at 100 mph. But it didn't rattle Larry at all.

After this story appeared, I was at the National Finals Rodeo in Oklahoma City and two cowboys approached me in a saloon with the angry complaint that I might have been calling them Communists when I wrote about them traveling together and sharing everything. Mahan appeared out of the crowd and calmed the situation. Believe me, I know better than to call a rodeo cowboy a Communist.

Dear Dr. King:
. . . Was in Austin a few days ago and The Flying Punzars appeared in full outfits at a party. . . . Then I came out here and have been running around with world champion cowboy Larry Mahan. We only been arrested once. So far. He drove through a gas station about 100 mph, taking a little shortcut around a stop sign, you know. I decided right then maybe I shouldn't have given him his first snort of coke about 10 min. earlier . . .

Horsing Around with Bull

Sports Illustrated, December 3, 1973

We passed through the gas station at maybe not much over 100 miles an hour. Concern was detectable on the face of the attendant as he threw down his hose and flung himself against the wall. What he should have understood was if we didn't get to Redwood City pronto we might miss something down there. Anything could be happening in Redwood City at that very minute. By driving through the gas station we could go around the stop sign, cut an angle across the intersection and save precious seconds.

Nothing to it.

The man at the wheel in the white beaver hat, Navajo necklace and lizard-skin cowboy boots was a finely trained athlete at the peak of his powers. Plenty of nerve, reflexes of a great middleweight, the night vision of some kind of panther. As we bounced off the first curb and went sideways through the intersection, it briefly occurred to me: *Are you sure about nothing to it? This man has spent half his life in plaster of Paris.*

But by then we had hit another curb. That turned out to be convenient, because it meant we had almost quit rolling when the police surrounded us and jerked us out of the car.

"We were just on our way to Redwood City," I explained.

"Right now you're in Brisbane, and it looks like you're gonna be here for several days," the cop said, searching my person for dangerous substances, which I, of course, was innocent of.

Brisbane is down the road south of the Daly City Cow Palace where the last rodeo of the season still had three nights to go. The last rodeo before the National Finals, anyhow. Daly City is just south of San Francisco. The mayor of Daly City used to be Bob St. Clair, who was well known for being a 49er tackle and for not needing a cooking fire to prepare his dinner.

"Who does that guy in the white hat think he is?" the cop said.

"He thinks he's the world champion cowboy," I said.

"He's Larry Mahan?"

"He thinks so."

Damaging information was not being given away. There were already half a dozen cops around Mahan, and they had his driver's license and were starting to put together his name with the events at the Cow Palace.

The cop looked at my driver's license. "You guys both from Texas?" he said.

"Yeah," I said. Mahan carries a license from Oregon, where he was born, but I didn't know that, and besides he now lives in Dallas in a house in the suburbs where he keeps horses on the lawn.

"Then you don't know any better," the cop said.

Two or three cops were peering in the windows of the station wagon. Inside they saw Mahan's rigging bag, the three briefcases he totes his business papers in, boxes of books (*Fundamentals of Rodeo Riding, The Mental & Physical Approach to Success* by Larry Mahan), bull ropes, halters, rosin, spurs, more hats, loud silk shirts and a pair of patchwork leather chaps that had roused a cry of admiration from a girl hitchhiker we had picked up that afternoon. "Wow! You ought to be the champion just for dressing like this!" she had said.

So I looked at him now, the All-Around Champion Cowboy who had just clinched that title for a record sixth time. Most of the good riders are about Mahan's size—5' 9", 165 pounds. The really big cowboys are the calf ropers and steer wrestlers.

The cops had Mahan with his back against the hood of a patrol car. They told him to stand on his left foot, raise his right foot in the air, extend both arms, then slowly bring his right forefinger forward and touch the tip of his nose. He did what they said and stuck his finger an inch up his right nostril. *Nothing to it.*

Mahan grinned. He can sell almost anything, but what he sells best is himself. The cops picked up a few Larry Mahan ball-point pens that he passes around ("Hidy, hidy, I'm Larry Mahan, this thing's real handy for writing down somebody's phone number") and said we could get on down the road if we departed at a slower pace. They said that there was hardly a thing in Redwood City we needed to see strong enough to take a shortcut through a gas station. So we went on down there, and if we missed anything I don't remember what it was.

Larry Mahan's nickname is Bull. A lot of the other riders call him that, and he likes it. *Bull*, in fact, is the title of his biography, now being written by Doug Hall, author of a new book called *Let 'er Buck!*, which is also mostly about Mahan. Hall lives in New York and has long hair and a beard. He dresses like one of those cosmic-fantasy cowboys. When he traveled with Mahan on the rodeo tour, he was known as the Freak. Not that appearances matter as much as they used to. One young cowboy said, "We might be the biggest traveling hippie commune in the world."

He was laughing when he said that. But the cowboys do travel together to as many as 200 rodeos in a year, and they share everything from gas and hamburger money to girls and information on bucking stock. They swap their Going Down the Road clothes. One bull rider travels with nothing but a toothbrush in his pocket. Mahan borrowed a pair of jeans from him once and found five different laundry marks in the pants, none of them the initials of the last rider who'd had them. Mahan flies his own twin-engine Cessna to many rodeos. He has crowded five cowboys into it and flown over the Rocky Mountains. Sometimes they stay six or eight to a motel room or borrowed apartment. Living like that, they get pretty well acquainted with each other, and the attitudes of the younger ones soak through the structure. But of course the old rodeo cowboys lived the same way. They just used different words for it. Instead of calling it community, they called it freedom.

"Most of the guys are out here because they love to be around animals, love to compete, love the life," Mahan said. "They don't want to be stuck in some town all their lives at some dull job. The adrenaline flows pretty fast out here. Plenty of guys get hurt, but you worry about a good ride more than about your safety. I figure if I ride three more years, I'll be up on 1,500 more head of bucking stock. Now it's not reasonable to think you can ride 1,500 head of bucking stock without going to the hospital, so you just put that idea out of your mind and think about riding and winning and loving the life. I love it more every day."

At 30, after 10 years of competing in big-league rodeos, Mahan is approaching the end of his riding career. Only a few rare individuals like Freckles Brown, the famous bull rider, keep on trying to sit on a wild animal as a regular matter after their middle 30s. In the bull riding at the National Finals this year, Mahan is cast as the aging star against a brilliant new generation that includes the year's leaders, 22-year-old Bobby Steiner and 20-year-old Don Gay, both from Texas rodeo families.

"Bulls are the meanest, rankest creatures on earth," Mahan said. "Horses don't try to step on you when they throw you off. They don't want to trip. Bulls love to step on you, or whip your face into the back of their skull and break your nose and knock out your teeth. Getting your hand hung up in a

bull rope is about the most dangerous thing in rodeoing. You have to trans-
form yourself into some kind of a small beast. When I can't reach down and
pull up a bunch of want-to out of myself, I'll know it's time to quit."

It is no myth about rodeo cowboys being tough. Mahan has had his jaw
smashed, three vertebrae cracked and his foot broken. After he broke his foot
a few years ago, he put on a plaster cast and kept riding. Then he broke his leg
in two places during a bareback ride. On the night I joined Mahan down in
the basement bar at the Cow Palace, a cowboy had been thrown and knocked
cold in the arena. He awoke on a stretcher as he was being carried past a bar
upstairs. "I'll get off here, fellows," he said, and went in and ordered a shot of
bourbon.

"I'm not superstitious," Mahan said as the dancers shuffled around the
Cow Palace Bar, "but I try to put bad thoughts out of my mind. If you only
think about good things, maybe good things are all that will happen."

Just about then Dennis the bartender decided he had listened to enough
mouth from a cowboy standing a few feet from Mahan. Dennis leaned across
the bar and punched the cowboy in the face. Then Dennis leaped up on his
knees on the bar and pounded the cowboy three or four more splats before
some other cowboys pushed in and got in the way.

"Nice going," Mahan said to his neighbor. "You didn't spill a drop."

The cowboy with the bloody face walked right back up to the bar and
ordered another drink as if nothing out of order had happened. Dennis
fixed it for him, rang up the dollar and not another word was said about the
incident.

In the alley beside the chutes on the final night of the Cow Palace rodeo,
Mahan was fretting. He was already $16,000 ahead in the all-around for the
year and couldn't be caught no matter what happens at the National Finals,
but he wanted to finish at the Cow Palace with a good ride. His first bareback
horse the previous week had been a rough one named Necklace. Mahan had
phoned ahead to find out what horse he had drawn. "When I heard it was
Necklace, I got that sick, empty feeling in my stomach," he said. "I spent four
days psyching myself up for that ride. I rode Necklace in my mind hundreds
of times. I went through every trick Necklace could possibly pull on me, so
when he came out of the chute I was ready."

But his last bareback horse this week, Blue Sky, had a reputation for taking three jumps and bolting. A cowboy can't make a good score on a horse like that. The two judges each can give 25 points to the horse and 25 to the rider. If the horse doesn't buck it doesn't matter how well the rider performs for his eight seconds; the score will be low.

"This horse shouldn't be in the finals of a big rodeo," Mahan said, looking at the big white horse waiting in the chute. "It's three jumps and whoopee-ki-yi, head for Tulsa."

Bareback riding is the most punishing event in rodeo, according to Mahan. "Your hand in the rigging is the only point of control between you and the horse," he said. "The jerk and strain through the hand and arm to your body are tremendous, and you keep spurring as wildly as you can. You look like a big flying bird that's hooked onto the horse."

Mahan was digging through his bag and preparing his equipment while other cowboys paced up and down in the alley, nervously smoking and doing knee bends and checking their rigging. There was the warm smell of dung and fear. Mahan was trying to work up that sick, empty feeling in his stomach, but Blue Sky had not inspired him. He pulled out his rigging. A bareback rigging is a curved piece of leather with a handle. Mahan powdered rosin on the rigging and on a goatskin glove that he cinched to his right wrist with a leather strap he pulled tight with his teeth. He tucked in his pants and tied a leather strap around his boots to keep them from flying off. He checked the rowels of his two-inch spurs. The rowels have to be dull, but they need to spin. He put on a pair of chaps that fit snug around the thighs; and then he walked over to another rider, Rusty Riddle, to ask again about Blue Sky. Riders keep book on horses and bulls like pitchers do on hitters.

"He's bucked good before. I've seen people get upside down on him," Riddle said.

"My motor just started running," said Mahan.

Mahan did a few pull-ups and climbed onto Blue Sky for the cinching, first touching the horse gently with his feet to let the horse know he was coming. He picked burrs out of Blue Sky's mane and formatted it so the spurs wouldn't catch. The rigging was cinched with a hair pad underneath, the halter and flank strap were put on. The flank strap is leather covered with sheepskin. It is tied around the ticklish flank of an animal, and when the strap is pulled the animal should buck from irritation. A horse in real pain will usually stand still instead of bucking.

Now Mahan was on Blue Sky in the chute and nearly ready. He looked out to where the previous horse was out of the arena and the catch-pen gate was closed. If you happen to ride a bucking horse into an open catch pen, you could be in for a terrible wreck. Mahan looked to see that the judges were watching. He looked to see that the flank man was behind the chute with a hand on the strap. A few days earlier, thinking somehow to promote Doug Hall's book, Mahan had yelled "Let 'er buck!" as a signal to the chute man and had torn muscles in his ribs on the ride. This time Mahan just said, "Go!"

Blue Sky came out with a big jump. Mahan leaned back with his chin tucked and his free arm bent at the elbow, his spurs well out over the animal's shoulders, his eyes on Blue Sky's head and neck. For two more jumps it looked like a good scoring ride. Then Blue Sky quit kicking and started running. Mahan looked disgustedly back to the alley. "A score of 55 on that ride," the announcer said. Get very many 55s and you'll have to start working for wages.

After that, it was still close to a month before the National Finals, plenty of time to rest and heal up. Mahan thought about it for a moment and grinned. "Well, this week I'm going to Dallas, then to Portland for a banquet, and down to a rodeo in Brawley, California," he said. "Not much money down in Brawley, but we have some kind of time."

Rafting the Big Bend

Sports Illustrated, April 15, 1974

Paddling a canoe for hours into a hard wind on a bitter cold day is about as miserable a way to spend time as I can imagine. But that was only one day on this trip. The beauty of the canyons and the excitement of running the rapids made it worthwhile. Many people make this trip over and over and love it. Once is plenty for me.

I am having a hard time reading this notebook because it got very wet, but I can remember that it was about a year ago when Don Kennard asked if I would like to paddle a canoe 90-odd miles down the Rio Grande through what he promised would be spectacular canyons. He asked it one sultry midnight at a party in Austin, Texas. At that hour almost anything sounds like a wonderful idea, and I have promised to do a lot of things then that I never got around to. A little twang inside my head told me Kennard wouldn't forget about this in the morning, but I kept listening anyhow.

"We're going to see, feel, taste and record that section of the river," he said, flushed with what I assume was enthusiasm. "We'll be the first working scientific expedition to go through there since the Hill Expedition in 1899. There are thousands of prehistoric Indian sites no scientist has ever looked at, and Lord knows how many rare plants to be found, and the geology is fantastic. Besides that, there are some pretty good rapids to run, and some good old boys to sit around the fire with, and at night the stars are right in your face."

Kennard is a robust, speckle-bearded fellow in his early 40s who played football at North Texas State University and was for 20 years a member of the Texas legislature, where he set a senate filibuster record of 29 hours, 22 minutes. To use up the time, he proposed a Texas Hall of Heroes and discussed 460 candidates for membership before two senators finally surrendered the votes he wanted. Now Kennard was with the Lyndon B. Johnson School of Public Affairs, working on a wilderness preservation project.

"We're going to explore the area in more than a cursory way," Kennard said. "It'll be a trip you'll never forget, you can count on that. How much do you know about canoeing?"

"You paddle on one side and then the other."

"Sure. It's easy. You'll catch on. When you turn over, what the hell, everybody does."

"Everybody turns over?"

"Sooner or later everybody tumps over. Nothing to worry about if you don't get caught under the canoe against a rock, or hurt yourself too bad. What do you say? Got the sporting blood?"

"Sounds like a wonderful idea to me."

Kennard didn't forget. He phoned and brought over a couple of U.S. Marine surplus waterproof packs. "Here's how this thing started," he said, while I was wondering what to put into the packs besides my knife and sleeping bag. "The Parks and Wildlife Commission, the General Land Office and the Texas Historical Survey Commission asked the LBJ to conduct a survey of areas of Texas that should be preserved. So we're beginning to look at 14 natural and rare sites and write them up from the standpoints of botany, archaeology, zoology and geology. Graduate students from all over the state will follow up and do a more thorough job on what we begin.

"In the next five or 10 years we hope to cover 150 sites that should be protected as parks or wilderness areas. But this is the first one. We've got some strong people on this trip—Stephen Spurr, the president of the University of Texas, Bob Armstrong, the Land Commissioner, Jenkins Garrett, a member of the Board of Regents, Clifton Caldwell, the chairman of the Texas Historical Commission. They'll be in a position to draw attention to what we're doing. Of course, we'll have a little pure fun in the Peggy Eaton Appreciation Society style."

For many years Kennard and a group of lawyers, politicians and other Texans have gathered to ride horseback through the mountains, float rivers and generally step around on nature. Once they climbed Sentinel Peak, the highest mountain in northern Mexico. Sitting up there, they decided to form a society. They named it after Peggy Eaton, who ran a boardinghouse with her mother in Washington, D.C. during the Andrew Jackson Administration. Peggy Eaton was married to an officer who spent too much time overseas. She took to messing around with a Cabinet member, and there was a scandal. But Andrew Jackson kept inviting her to dinner anyhow. "She was a free spirit, and we admire that," said Kennard. The slogan of their society is: Any Friend of Andrew Jackson's Is a Friend of Mine.

Society members like to go places by all sorts of conveyances. A couple of years ago a number of Peggy Eatoners and several members of a group called the Gosh Awmighty Fellas chose to ride their motorcycles to Mexico City. An El Paso lawyer, Jesus Ochoa, who had never been on a motorcycle before, had somebody show him how to shift gears and twist the throttle, and he made it all the way to San Luis Potosi before he and the famous criminal lawyer Warren Burnett both wrecked at the big traffic circle and broke several bones.

About that same time Kennard was taking a trip on a boxcar. He and a few others, including his teen-age daughter Karen, hopped a Texas & Pacific freight from Fort Worth to El Paso. Kennard fell off and caught the moving train nine cars back. At the first stop, a few miles outside Fort Worth, Kennard ran up to join the others. The train started up suddenly. Kennard grabbed a ladder and fell again, this time into a bar ditch, where he lay with torn clothes and bleeding knees watching the train depart for West Texas. He took a taxi home. The phone rang. At gunpoint the cops had rousted Karen and the others off the train in Weatherford, 30 miles away. Kennard drove out and brought them back to Fort Worth. But two members of the group returned to the railroad, caught the 11 p.m. freight to El Paso, rode another freight back to San Antonio and flew home from there—a performance in the Peggy Eaton tradition.

I drove to the home of Anders Saustrup, field director of the Rare Plants Study Center of the University of Texas, and threw my two waterproof packs in the back of a pickup truck hitched to trailer hauling six aluminum canoes. "See you on the river," Kennard said. He and Geologist Dwight Deal and graduate student Carl Teinert got into truck for the all-night drive down to Black Gap at the edge of the Big Bend. I was to fly down next day with Bob Armstrong in his Beechcraft Bonanza. The weather was clear and warm. A lovely Texas spring.

The trip [from Black Gap through the canyons] could be disastrous if someone broke a leg. There would be no way to get an injured person out other than to float out over a period of several days. It would be extremely difficult to float an injured person out in a canoe without capsizing several times. The discomfort of being thrown into the rapids with a crudely splinted broken leg can hardly be described. For this reason, my strict instructions to members of the expedition before leaving are don't break no legs.

—Bill Kugle, member of the Texas Explorers Club and a Peggy Eaton founder.

EMERGENCY EXIT FROM THE CANYONS: The Border Patrol flies these canyons every few days, and you could possibly signal them with a mirror.

—Bob Burleson, member of the Parks and Wildlife Commission.

"I hear Anders has refused to let women go on this trip," said the hostess at a dinner party. "You know why? Macho stuff, that's why. He doesn't want to be sitting at the Scholz Garten drinking beer and bragging and suddenly hear some girlish voice pipe up, 'Oh, I did that trip last Easter, isn't it fun?'"

"Well, I saw some of the canoes today," I said.

"How'd they look?"

"They had a lot of dents."

The lovely Texas spring suddenly turned nasty. It began raining before dawn. At noon Bob Armstrong called. "How's your courage quotient?" he said.

"I'll just let it ride along with yours."

"I don't mind this rain," Armstrong said. "Flying on instruments is fine. But there's a few thunderstorms between here and Pecos. It probably won't be too bad. It just won't be good, is all."

The General Land Office in Texas controls 22 million acres of land and mineral resources, an area larger than Maine and only slightly smaller than Indiana. Armstrong, who is about 40, was elected Land Commissioner in 1970. He rides a motorcycle to the office, skis, backpacks into the mountains, plays the guitar, raises cattle, is a good photographer and a good canoeist. His wife Shannon used to teach canoeing someplace. The words that would have told me where she taught are a blue muddle now in my notebook.

A young woman from the Land Office picked me up in her car. "Last year they took 20 canoes down that part of the river you're going on," she said cheerfully. "Only three or four didn't turn over. I think Kennard turned over twice."

We stopped at a big white wooden house on a street with many trees. Dr. Spurr came to the door and looked out at the rain. "Some of these guys may not be very well organized, but we'll bungle through and have a good time," Spurr said. "I've canoed about all the canoeable rivers in Michigan and Minnesota. Been on a lot of float trips around the country. But I can't say I'm an expert whitewater canoeist. It's by guess and by God with me. How about you?"

"I can't remember whether I've ever actually been in a canoe before."

"Oh. Well. You're in for an interesting time, aren't you?"

Spurr is a forester with a Ph.D. from Yale. He taught and did field research for 19 years at the University of Michigan. Later he became a compromise dean at Michigan following a campus political struggle. He was hired by Texas in the midst of another political fight which at the time of our trip was nowhere near over. Spurr picked up a small bag, put on a straw farmer's hat and kissed his wife. "If they fire me here," he said, "we can go back to the woods and be just as happy."

The 2-½ hour flight to a landing strip on a ranch outside the town of Marathon wasn't bad, considering it rained most of way and the plane iced up. Clifton Caldwell met us at the airstrip with his truck. He is president of the committee that puts up historical plaques and attempts to protect old buildings. Caldwell is a West Point graduate who flies his own plane and owns some ranches. One is 7,000 acres out in the Big Bend, which Caldwell says is not enough land to make a living on in that kind of country. The main ranch is outside of Albany, Texas, on the Clear Fork of the Brazos River. "My nearest neighbor is 11 miles," Caldwell said, "and it's 35 miles from my house to a bottle of beer."

The truck sped along a highway cut through greasewood and cactus. The mountains turned gold and purple in the dusk, and, beyond, higher mountains rose across the river in Mexico. Caldwell told about driving into this area looking for a place called Stillwell Crossing. "At the river we ran into a snaggletoothed old man and asked if we were at Stillwell Crossing. The old man said if we had an airplane we could just fly right over that mountain and be there in no time. If we didn't have an airplane, go 75 miles back down the road and turn left. The old man thought that was really funny."

We entered Black Gap and descended on a rough road toward the river at Maravillas Canyon. "This is about as remote a place as you can find in Texas," Spurr said. Up ahead we saw a campfire. We could hear the river. The first rapids of the trip was 50 yards away.

Most of the others were standing round the fire. They were playing guitars and harmonicas, singing, talking, drinking whiskey. But always we could hear the river like a wind blowing.

"You done much canoeing?" Caldwell asked me.

"None."

Caldwell nodded. What I didn't know at the time was that he had read a Sierra Club report on the trip we were about to take. It dwelt on the difficulties and dangers of the river, warned that under no circumstances should the trip be attempted by a lone canoe, and said no one should paddle that stretch of the Rio Grande who was not an expert canoeist in excellent physical condition.

If I had seen that report, there might not have been a story like this.

The Rio Grande rises at the Continental Divide in southern Colorado and flows 1,800 miles into the Gulf of Mexico. It goes south down the center of New Mexico, enters Texas at El Paso and turns southeast to form the border between Texas and Mexico. At the Big Bend the Rio Grande turns and runs north, northeast and east for more than 200 miles before dropping southeast again. Most of our trip would be north and northeast. It seemed to me it would be harder to paddle north than south, but what did I know? I was assured it wouldn't make any difference unless a good north wind came down into our faces.

Long stretches of the river are often dry enough to walk across. Farmers in New Mexico irrigate from the Rio Grande. Santa Fe, Albuquerque, Las Cruces and El Paso, among other cities, take water from it. The Rio Conchos flows from Mexico to replenish the Rio Grande at Presidio, but Mexico has built a dam on the Rio Conchos to irrigate sections of the Chihuahua Desert. The Mexicans pretty well control the level of the Rio Grande for hundreds of miles through the Big Bend. After the river turns south again, past Langtry, another big dam at Del Rio creates the Amistad Reservoir, an enormous twisty lake that looks like a tidelands bay.

Some of the canyons on the river have never been named on official documents. The area we were to go through is usually called Reagan Canyon, or Bullis Canyon, although in fact several canyons enter the river there. The walls are steep and there is seldom a place to climb out. Where the canyons are less vertical, an occasional smugglers' trail may be seen. There is a steady, illegal business in smuggling the candelilla plant into Texas for the making of high-grade candle wax. Now and then you come across remains of a camp marked by the presence of 50-gallon drums used for boiling down the wax. The occasional goatherder's camp is always empty, although the coals may be warm. Marijuana and peyote no doubt come through there sometimes, but it is difficult country for a smuggler to cross.

Temperatures in the Big Bend go up to 140 degrees in the summer and down below freezing in winter. This was April, and I figured it would be hot all day and cool at night. But the cold look of the rainy morning back in Austin had persuaded me to borrow a long underwear top. God bless it. The first morning at the camp on the river I was huddled behind a truck with a coffee cup shaking in my hands. My sleeping bag lay crumpled in dark wet grass. I was wearing everything I had brought with me. Palms red from the hot cup but fingers blue. We were camped beside a huge midden, a mound of dirt, stones and cooking utensils built up by Indians over centuries. Anders Saustrup walked past in a T-shirt, suspenders and baggy pants, brushing his teeth.

"What the hell is this with the T-shirt?" I said. "Don't you realize it's about to snow?"

"It's not cold. It's very nice weather. Beautiful weather, in fact," said Anders, fog blowing out of his mouth.

Anders was born in Denmark. What business does a Dane have telling a native-born Texan whether it's cold or not? This might have been a pleasant spring morning on the Arctic Circle, but for this time of year in Texas it was cold. I could hear that first rapids roaring. Caldwell came by wearing a yellow rain suit. I asked if he thought it was cold. "The water sure will be," he said.

My first canoe partner was Bill O'Brien, a young, hairy-faced architectural engineer from Fort Worth. He is a son of Davey O'Brien, who was an All-America quarterback at TCU and set passing records for the Philadelphia Eagles 30 years ago. Bill went to the University of Wyoming and likes to climb mountains. He didn't let on if he was worried we might dash into the rocks.

"After the first two rapids you'll know what to do," said Jenkins Garrett. "Just remember when you run into cane and salt-cedar branches that grow over the river, don't pull away from them and upset the canoe. If you hit something in the water, lean forward, downstream."

In the morning light the air was so clear that mountains across the river in Mexico looked fake. The dry air does tricks with distances. Canyons that appear only 500 feet high will in truth be three times that high. A wall you think you can hit with a rock you might not be able to reach with an arrow.

We put into the river just up from Maravillas Creek, which is 100 miles long, has a bed that would accommodate the Hudson, and is usually dry. Bill and I looked at the narrow, boiling channel of the rapids. "Might as well," he said. We got up a bit of speed, entered the current and whanged into a rock.

There was a scraping sound like tin tearing. The current began to swing the canoe broadside to the flow of the river. "Use your paddle like a lever," Bill yelled. I stuck my paddle between the boat and the rock and yanked. We popped loose from the rock, shot down the channel, crashed through some overhanging cane and were past the first rapids. It was not one of the monster rapids of North America, but I will remember it fondly.

The second rapids, we raked bottom rocks. The third, we went too far left and I shoved at a boulder with my hands as we slid quickly past. It was not a classic move. But anything you need to do to keep a boulder from knocking you into the water has to be acceptable.

By now it was warm enough to peel off my windbreaker, wool shirt and long underwear top. The water moved us along with easy paddling. The land, called Outlaw Flats, was fairly level for a while before it climbed toward the mountains. Up ahead in Mexico was a sheer, flat-topped butte that shone red in the morning sun; it is known as El Capitan and is supposed to hold a clue to a lost mine.

Several little girls and a woman were fishing on the Texas bank. Were they, too, intrepid explorers? A man and his son had pulled their outboard onto a gravel bar a mile farther on. "You turn over yet?" the man yelled in greeting.

During the day we stopped and climbed a rocky slope. Curtis Tunnell, the state archaeologist, pointed out broken Indian tools on a large midden. Round mortar holes had been dug into the rock for the grinding of grain. Flints lay on prehistoric scraping sites. Buzzards floated above the river. Marshall Johnston, a University of Texas botanist who had been working for months in the Chihuahua Desert, which is nearly as large as all of Texas, pulled up a wild tobacco plant with yellow blossoms. Creosote bushes and candelilla grew all around. Dr. Johnston broke open a plant called leatherwood, or dragonroot, which Indians used as eye medicine. It pours blood when uprooted.

Then we entered the canyons. First the wall rose on the Mexican side, and we hit some rapids. Then the wall of Reagan Canyon soared on the Texas bank. For the next 40 miles we would be in the canyons, and the walls would get higher and closer as we went downstream. When we landed to make camp, I dragged my two U.S. Marine surplus waterproof packs up the bank onto a grassy bluff and began to unload them. Packing is a tedious chore, especially when done in the cold early morning. The straps make your fingers

Shrake taking notes during his rafting trip along the Rio Grande, 1974.

bleed. Unpacking is a lot better. When you dig toward the cognac bottle and the sleeping bag, you feel you're getting something done.

I spread my air mattress and sleeping bag and looked at the stuff I had brought. Knife, mess kit, spoon, cup, water jug, canteen, three paperback books, two pairs of Levi's, sneakers, windbreaker, two T-shirts, one wool shirt, long underwear, tape recorder, batteries, life jacket, straw hat, towel, two Flair pens, a notebook, three cassettes (including, accidentally, an old tape of Janis Joplin singing in Austin at Kenneth Threadgill's birthday party where a girl got bit by a rattlesnake, and another old tape of Tom Landry talking about God and football).

And food, of course. Kennard and I were splitting rations. We had cans of chili, cans of Salisbury steak, cans of stew, a bag of rice, many boxes of raisins, milk chocolate, vegetable soup cubes, powdered potatoes, onions, Vienna sausages, potted meat and crackers. I looked at that mound of food lying there, patted my sleeping bag and knew a great contentment.

Then I looked around the camp. My God, it was Brasilia! Orange and yellow and green and blue nylon tents had sprung up everywhere. Inside the tents were air mattresses and puffy sleeping bags and hunks of foam rubber and candle lamps for warmth and light. All over the place little Swiss cooking stoves were burning.

Bill O'Brien was preparing a hot meatloaf dinner with vegetables. Jenks Garrett and his son Jenkins Jr. were dining on soup, tea, lasagna and banana pudding. Dr. Spurr and Clifton Caldwell had opened a crate packed with dry ice and removed a couple of filet mignons for dinner. Except that he scorned the use of a tent, Dr. Spurr was elaborately equipped for the trip. I asked him at different times for tweezers, a hand lens, suntan lotion, a saw, a can opener, a Brillo pad. He had them all. He even had packets of sugar from the Coconut Grove, Ambassador Hotel, 1968 Rose Bowl. The only thing I asked for that he didn't have was a piece of watermelon.

But where had all this stuff come from? How had they crammed it into the canoes? Well, a whole pot of lasagna with plenty of meat fits into an envelope now. The cooking stove folds into nothing much. You can almost stick a new sleeping bag into your coat pocket. A tent doesn't take up as much room as a pillow. But I had not been into a sporting goods store in a long time, and my old sleeping bag occupied as much space as Alex Karras doubled over.

In the middle of the night the wind struck. Tents clapped and wires whined. The wind itself sounded like rushing water. "The Mexicans have let water out of the Rio Conchos!" someone yelled. But no, it was just a blue norther. It was what a friend of mine would call semi-miserable. In fact, it was halfway an ordeal. It was cold to begin with, and the wind wouldn't let up. As we went down the river again, the wind stayed in our faces. We had to dig water to move. I was thinking I wouldn't do this again for $1,000.

In the afternoon we came to Arroyo San Rocendo, the biggest canyon entering the Rio Grande from Mexico. We had passed Asa Jones pumphouse, a cabin stuck against the top of a steep cliff, with broken water pipes sticking down toward the river. Bill O'Brien climbed to the top, just as he later scaled a cliff to rescue a baby goat trapped on a ledge. After the pumphouse we heard the rumble of rapids around a sandstone corner. At San Rocendo is Big Hot Springs Rapids, named for the hot springs on the Mexican shore.

They say it is not advisable to run Big Hot Springs. We got out and lined our canoes down through the rocks to a pool between two sections of the rapids. It was hard, wet work, crawling over slippery boulders, dragging canoes and equipment. When the last canoe was in the pool, we were tired and shivering.

I found a place that was sheltered on three sides by thickets and a cliff. Kennard set up his tent to block the wind from the fourth side. We built a large mesquite fire. Down by the river a hot spring opened into a natural rock tub about 15 feet across. We soaked in the spring for a while. For dinner we heated cans of chili, chopped a couple of onions and cooked some rice on the fire and then stirred the mess up in a pan. It was as good as anything I ever tasted.

For the first time on the trip I used enough breath to blow up my air mattress; I wrapped my life jacket in a towel for a pillow. Stuffed with chili, rice and onions, smoothed out by a little bourbon and a cigar, I lay in my bag just outside the firelight, listening to the talk, hearing the river and the wind. The stars were down in my face, all right. Orion, the Pleiades, Arcturus, the North Star, the Big Dipper. Moonlight spread over the canyon wall high up. Whoever said this was an ordeal?

I changed over to Bob Armstrong's canoe the fourth day out. We were going to catch up with some canoes that had gotten far ahead. Bill O'Brien wanted to hang back with the scientists. Armstrong was a little bothered because I weigh a lot more than he does, and also because he didn't want to turn over with his $1,400 worth of camera equipment. But he kept up a cheerful attitude about it.

"I guess you know how to reach and pry," he said as we set out alone.

"What's that?"

"To reach, you reach out with the paddle and draw it toward the boat. If you reach to the right, it swings the front end to the right. To pry, you push out with the paddle, and the boat moves in the other direction. If you don't mind my asking, how did you manage to come 40 or 50 miles without knowing that?"

Up ahead was a noisy rapids. Armstrong stood in the rear of the canoe to study the flow. I thought you were never supposed to stand in a canoe. The good canoeists appear to do it whenever they want to. "Hit this one on the left and go like hell," Armstrong said. The canoe leaped ahead. Armstrong cried for me to pry on the left and I did. It was like a miracle. This boulder that I would probably have poked with the paddle or shoved desperately with my hands, this boulder flew past inches away with a satisfying hiss and gurgle. Then we were bouncing in haystack waves and spray. Then we paddled hard in an eddy before coasting in a current.

"See what I mean?" said Armstrong.

It had taken me several hours the first day to realize the person in the bow could help at all, steering in the rapids rather than merely providing locomotion. The person in the rear is the captain. He does most of the steering and, if the person in front does not stay alert and keep glancing back, the captain is liable to rest too much. But now this new knowledge about reach and pry gave me power. So an hour later we cracked into a rock and turned sideways. The canoe filled with water. We jumped out and fought to keep the boat from going over. You figure a canoe full of water weighs about a ton. Put the force of the current against it, and you can see why it is nice to have several people around to help.

We wrestled the canoe to shore and began bailing. Armstrong hammered out the dent. I had learned one lesson I didn't know I had learned until that night. The lesson is, no matter how cold and early it is in the morning, don't be sloppy in packing your waterproof bag.

Some things have blurred in my mind, but I remember a few places very well. I remember castle rock formations, keyholes to the sky 1,500 feet above our heads, side canyons hardly wide enough for a man to walk into. I remember climbing to a cave where the ceiling was black with centuries of cooking smoke and the floor deep in stones and scraping tools. There was a Campbell's soup can near the entrance.

Most of the rapids are no longer distinct to me. I can't even recall at which rapids the notebook escaped from my pocket and tumbled into the current. We found it 200 yards downstream. At another rapids I knocked off my eyeglasses while changing hands with my paddle but reached back with my left hand and grabbed the glasses as they disappeared under water. All my life I have been dropping things with my right hand and catching them with my left before they hit the floor.

Into the wind again. All day long. Hands have swollen and their backs split open. Neck and shoulders are riddled with needles. Keep head down, stare at water. Think about Oxford vs. Cambridge on the Thames. Terrible idea. Clang, bang, hit a rock, the hell with it. We run a rapids near a sandbar, and the wind blows sand into our faces. You can run a rapids and get a dirty face? Armstrong remarks that adventure and fun are not necessarily the same. For a mile ahead I can see whitecaps whipped up not from current but from wind. I discover something. Each stroke appears to move us three feet. That means 1,760 strokes will move us through these whitecaps. If the wind keeps up for the 30 miles left to go, that's only 52,800 strokes to home, boy. Let's hit it. That's two . . . three . . .

"If you start counting strokes, you'll go crazy," Armstrong says.

In all, the expedition examined more than 60 historic and prehistoric Indian sites that had never before been officially recorded. Archaeologist Curtis Tunnell says Indians occupied the canyons for at least 12,000 years. About the only litter they left was burnt rocks, pieces of flint, dried bones. At one place the floor of a cave is deep in buffalo bones. It is near a cliff off which the Indians used to stampede the beasts. When you sift through the floor of the cave, you find a 4,000-year gap between layers of buffalo bones. That means either the Indians forgot how to stampede buffaloes for a long time, or else the buffaloes went away for 4,000 years. It is less than 100 years now since the last great buffalo slaughters of the West. So maybe buffaloes will come back again sometime.

Of the 6,000 species of plants that grow in Texas, about 50 are found only along the river. Each time one of those species dies out, it disappears from the earth. The Rare Plants Center puts exotic plants of this sort in courthouse squares, garden club plots and state parks, as well as greenhouses. "Of course, the only rational way to preserve the plants is to preserve their habitats," says Marshall Johnston, director of the center. He took more than 200 plant samples on the river and in the canyons. To protect the canyons, the state could buy scenic easements along the river, or the Department of Interior could declare the river a wild scenic area. But something else that might happen is that a third Rio Grande dam may be built at Sanderson Canyon. If it is, everything we saw will be gone except the tops of the canyons.

On our last night on the river, after laboring into the wind all day, we camped on a knoll and waited for the wind to die after dark. But it kept on blowing. Caldwell and Spurr fried the last of their steaks and shared them. I found a spot where the wind was muffled by a canebrake and the rock wall. I settled into my bag, and then I heard a little scrabbling noise in the cane. Borrowing a flashlight, I saw I was lying beside a tunnel about five feet high that had been trod through the cane. Wild pigs, maybe. Deer, coons, coyotes, no telling what all. I moved over two feet and went to sleep happy and incredibly comfortable.

I read the Sierra Club story about the ferocious rapids and the need for physical conditioning. Caldwell and I talked it over. We decided the rapids and the paddling had been strenuous but not what you would call supremely difficult.

"I guess we're finished with the bad rapids," Caldwell said.

"Only one really tough one left," said Armstrong.

"I don't see it on the map."

"That's why it's known as Horrible Surprise Rapids," Armstrong said.

For the final few miles, the wind lowered and we paddled lightly. Terns flew in formation above our heads. Thousands of swallows skimmed the river, dipped their beaks in the water, and collected mud from the bank to build nests against the cliffs. The land was spreading out on either side. And there it was ahead of us: the Texaco sign nailed to a tree that marked the take-out place, Dudley Harrison's camp.

Only one more rapids. We drifted into some rocks and got out to look. The current swung close against a rock outcrop. Spurr and Caldwell got into their canoe and went into the rapids. They clattered against the outcrop. Spurr's paddle left his hands and looked glued to the wall for an instant. He grabbed it again, and they headed to shore. Armstrong and I had a choice of running the rapids or walking the canoe through a few feet of very shallow water. We walked.

We drove in Caldwell's truck for an hour across dusty brown land, scaring up a few sheep that took off toward the mountains. We stopped at a general store in the town of Dryden. The owner wore a baseball cap. "Wouldn't be surprised if you fellas got kind of cold on the river," he said. "Had a big freeze the last few days. Wiped everything out. Hell, it snowed over in Alpine."

We ate at the Big Bend Cafe in Marathon. Caldwell placed what he said is his usual order at a place that serves Tex Mex food—six enchiladas and three tamales. They didn't have any tamales, but they brought the enchiladas stacked up on the plate like a mound of pancakes. I had three enchiladas, three tacos, tortillas, butter and a little bowl of jalapeño peppers. As we were leaving, the woman behind the counter asked if we were some kind of a scientific outfit. We said yes ma'am, we were about halfway scientific.

"Then you must of heard about it," she said. "Down the road south of here they just dug up a 60-foot-long monster skeleton with a big fang buried in its neck. You didn't hear about it? Well, go down there right now and look at it. Tell them Sally at Marathon sent you."

PART 4

Night Never Falls

Letters to Larry L. King, 1978–1983

January 7, 1978

I spent the best years of my life trying to get a statue of Larry L. King erected in a prominent public place—or, actually, in any place at all. After repeated failures, I was fired from the statuary committee. The silver lining to that cloud is that I was able to sleep late from then on and stopped begging for money from strangers who had never heard of Larry or thought he was the guy with the talk show on television.

The movie I am talking about in this letter became *Songwriter*.

Texas Walk of Stars induction ceremony on Austin's Sixth Street, 1987.
From left: Gary Cartwright, Larry L. King, Bud Shrake, and Dan Jenkins.

Dear Perfessor King:

I have tried to phone you several dozen times over the past few weeks in order to inform your ass that we are hard at work on the big fine statue of you that will stand on the site where I discovered the East Pole.

We are following your drawing of what the statue should look like, as closely as possible, I mean. The 14-inch waist, Wilt Chamblerlain's cock and Henry Fonda's face have been no particular problem, but our stonemason keeps misspelling "intellectual" in the carving at the base of the monument. He got "Trick Fucker" in upside down, which he claimed is the only hep way to do it.

I hear now that the reason you never answer your phone is you are (1) too famous (2) too rich (3) busy singing and reciting on the stage (4) getting married (5) busy making Bobby Baker famouser (6) stoned (7) degenerated beyond human help, etc., etc.

Anyhow, I have heard from folks who have saw your Broadway show [*The Best Little Whorehouse in Texas*], and all I have heard from claim to like it very much. This is dangerous, as us writers know. The Hollywood people on the killer bats movie claimed I have wrote the near perfect script and they love me to a nub as a person, which is why the producer had his secretary call me up and fire me off the movie on Christmas Eve, thus jacking me out of the $50,000 bonus I would of got had I been the only writer employed on the movie as of March 1.

But that are show biz, perfesser.

Now it looks like I am writing a script about country music—a original, as we say—that Willie and Waylon are putting up the front money for, and are going to star in along with Mary Kay Place and Dennis Hopper (Jacky Jack got mad and said count him out but I think he will want back in). I been with Willie and Waylon for more than a week now, here and in Houston. Willie has "blowed my brain," to use the hepcat phrase, and Waylon's personal conduct makes Jacky Jack and Hopper seem pretty calm.

I got to go now to other daily big deals, but I want you to know I got lots of little tiny midgets putting together your monument pebble by pebble, just like they built the Sphinx. . . .

December 5, 1979

No harm in telling this story now. During that 1979 season of *Monday Night Football,* Don Meredith and I were writing a country song one line at a time, one week at a time.

He would phone me from the booth and we would decide on the line. Then Don would say the line on the air. Usually it didn't make sense in the context of the game. Howard Cosell would say, "What? Old Danderoo is losing his marbles up here."

We did it for six or eight weeks before the thrill wore off.

King, meanwhile, was starting into his wealthy years with the huge success of *The Best Little Whorehouse in Texas.*

My wife Doatsy and I had gone with Larry to LaGrange on his first trip researching what was then a story for *Playboy* magazine. A character in the show is called Doatsy Mae. During the football game in the second act over the public address you can hear me throwing a touchdown pass to Gary Cartwright, or maybe it is vice versa. We got the notoriety instead of the cash. Notoriety lasts longer than cash, as King explained it.

Dear Barbara:

It is kind of disturbing to me, one of the last of Larry's friends, to see a ex-Ivy League professor and one-time Broadway flash become so eat up that he would write me a letter full of raw envy and, even worse, misunderstandings, about such a common event in my life as having my name proclaimed to hundreds of millions of people on the Monday Night Football.

It could be that the strain of having to hang around and watch you endure and bring forth a beautiful baby girl has finally snapped the old fart's synapses.

Clearly it is true that the Jets-Seahawks game was not the big event of the year in the sporting world on TV. But for Prof. King to claim that it was degrading for me to have my name spoken on the TV for the Monday Night Football during such a lowly game, only indicates to me that he has got no grasp of the Show Business. Prof. King states that he could have his name spoke on TV during the first quarter of the Super Bowl if he wanted to call in favors owed to him from his old (?) homosexual days. What he don't understand is that basic principle knowed to people like you and me who have studied the Show Business: you don't need to call upon the star quality of a big name to promote a star vehicle. I can appreciate that ABC knew they was in trouble with that game and had to call out the big guns—namely me—to try to grab the audience by the throat and make the suckers keep listening to see if my name would be proclaimed again.

"Bud Shrake" is, after all, the name that was proclaimed on the Monday Night Football—not "Professor Lawrence such-and-such."

"Willie Nelson" is the other name that was spoke in connection with mine, and also the phrase "good ole boys." I of course didn't see it myself, being involved in lecturing on *The Truth of Fiction* to a hand-picked group at the Quorum Club, but fans did start to rush in and gesticulate. Ironically, the first thought I had was: I hope Larry didn't hear that, for it might be the final blow for such a fragile ego.

I do treasure your husband's friendship and don't want to hurt him, so I have requested they not speak of me any more on the Monday Night Football unless they really need the ratings. On his last visit to Austin, the advice Prof. King gave my fiancée . . . showed the poet in him that we love. "Don't be stupid and hang around with that sumbitch, he ain't anywhere near good enough for you," was the way he put it. Could Auden have done better? [My fiancée] and I have pretty much come to agree that Prof. King struck with a poet's perception to the heart of the matter; but she is coming up to New York with me anyhow on this coming Sunday. We are going to stay with the Jenkinses for a few days, and on Monday night Bill and Sally Wittliff (Bill, who Larry might remember, is a very nice fellow and a wonderful writer and book publisher with integrity, who Larry pushed off the porch) who are there coincidentally to do enormous global movie deals, have got four tickets for WHOREHOUSE and so it looks like I will have to go see it again for the FIFTH TIME! I have not seen my own Mother five times! But I am not the sort of person who would write Prof. King a letter revealing sacrifice; no, I would rather drink some gin and smoke some sticky dope and sit in the theater and grin like a goon and flap my hand like a retarded person.

Once again, also, Prof. King wrote to me complaining about the paucity of gifts I send him. This has been a long-standing complaint of his. I could point out that I have never written to him begging for presents, but I don't want him to get shaken with the notion that I are more secure than he; when one's name is proclaimed on Monday Night Football, the tributes arrive. No begging required. I have got so many gifts piled up in my house now that sometimes they fall with great crashes & have come close to smashing me underneath. I would be glad to send a bunch of gifts along to Prof. King if it wasn't for you, Barbara, and that pure little baby daughter, who would have to watch the awful sight of a down-deep West Texas savage ripping the tissue paper and ribbons off and then plunging hairy arms through the lids of enormous boxes.

If you get in real trouble with him, kid, don't forget that I am a minister and a Doctor of Metaphysics, and don't be put off by the fact that I am real famous.

Love, Bud

July 29, 1980

This is a classic case of what Darrell Royal calls "the Re-Re's"—regrets and remorse, when you sit on the edge of the bed the next morning and say, "Oh, no, did I really . . . ?"

Dear Dr. King:

No sooner had I wrote you that last letter about how I had got off of the whiskey, and how much better I felt, than I went to California for five days of not drawing an undoped or undrunk breath. Then I come home and got off the plane and drank with Fletcher from midnight until noon at his house (without ever once heading for the roof)—and for the three days since then I been sitting in my big orange chair squinting at my TV and wondering if I sank my career last week, or if I done good. It was one of those weeks in which I went to two big Hollywood parties and two Willie Nelson concerts at the Universal amphitheater and several meetings at Paramount, and whatnot, and most everbody seemed to think I was entertaining (I thought) at the time but later in remembering what I could of the events I had to ask myself: how could they have thought that? A idiot, is more likely what they thought. I do remember one girl whose eyes got real big and she ran from me as I was trying to explain something to her at a Hollywood birthday party about 3 a.m. I also remember sitting at a table at another party, wondering if I was going to throw up, and Casey Tibbs came up and offered me a swig out of his tequila bottle—and of course I turned her up to my lips. The instant the tequila hit the other garbage in my stomach I whirled and threw up on a coke dealer and his tight-pants slut at the next table (a boy don't ever throw up on the table where he is at).

Anyhow, I have given the plumbing three days of rest again, and now tomorrow I got to go back to LA until Friday or so. We keep on creeping closer to getting *The Songwriter* into production. If that happens, I will be pretty well fixed for a while and intend to take up golf and get a suntan. For two and a half years now, trying to force *Songwriter* into being has been like trying to cram a carload of spaghetti through a keyhole. I've got one more movie to write—for Fox, on inventing the A-bomb at Los Alamos with a bunch of brilliant cuckoos—plus a couple of pending deals with Dan T. Jenke [Jenkins], and then I hope it is back to the big fat Indian book [*The Borderland*]. To leave Hollywood and retreat to the mid 19th century sounds like spending the winter in Palm Beach, the way I feel now.

Perfesser, I am too tired to type any more at the moment. I must flee back to my orange chair and peer at the 24-hour TV news channel on the cable until I fall asleep so I can get up and go fling myself into the breech or maw or whatever awaits in Hollywood. . . .

July 11, 1980

This letter sounds as if I was about to hit the wall, but it didn't happen until four years later and then I hit it again the next year.

Dear Professor King:
. . . After reading your letter—which took a week to get here—I started pondering what us old boys are up to. That very day I had spent six hours driving around looking for just exactly the right nightstand that had just exactly the right drawer at just the right height to hold my pistol near my hand while I sleep. Nothing really wrong with that, your honor—the sons-of-bitches are really out there, you hear em? I do know I've been drinking way too much—I don't get cute so much anymore as I get stupid and red-faced and hollow-eyed. Since you left town I've been on the wagon all but two days (those two were killers). I had started feeling like I was about to die, and not caring

much if I did. I didn't feel suicidal but I did feel like I didn't give a shit . . . I don't know why I'm using the past-tense. I'm sure I'll feel that way again. But without a hangover and a headful of Who-hit-John, it is a different light I see. I remember what Bear Bryant said after he had quit hard liquor: "This is the first time in 20 years I don't wake up mad at everybody." As of right now I feel real good because I haven't had a drink since night before last, when I knocked off a quart of Boodles gin. I hope I don't get to bragging on myself so much I wind up down in the bunker at the Quorum looking for the ghost about daylight. . . .

August 12, 1980

I was getting closer to hitting the wall. Gulping down the big glass of kerosene at the Squirrel Inn, thinking it was scotch and water, probably should have killed me. I would have died in the Williamson County Jail if the lady bartender, shortly before we were arrested, had not rushed up to me with a gallon of goat's milk and told me to drink it as an antidote.

Dear Professor:

By the time you get this, I suppose you will have been given your graduation papers from Whiskey A&M—I mean I *hope* you will have been graduated, for I know how oft foul fortune intrudes on the finest of intentions. . . . On the lush test you sent, I only scored 11 out of 20. On question #20, I take "institution" to also mean "jail," which gives me a solid yes—since I have been in jail for drunk and disorderly at least five times I can recall offhand, most recently when they clapped Jap and Phyllis and me in the Williamson County Jail the night I accidentally drank a glass of coal oil at the Squirrel Inn in Theon; by far the most glamorous being in Buenos Aires when the Nazis sat on me.

Anyhow a score of 11 don't match up to your 19 yeses and one perhaps— but still an 11 is . . . wait, I just recounted and my score is up to 12 . . . and some might argue that I should answer yes to #7, too. . . .

It may be a blessing that I have terrible hangovers, steadily worsening now, and so am forced to lay off a while after big bouts with them little fruit drinks. But no matter the score, I got the message in your "serious" letter and I appreciate it. I know I'm heading for real trouble if I don't lighten up some with the whiskey and the dope—and I swear I will in no way contribute to any backsliding on your part if I can help it. If you notice me doing so, slap my face. But not hard, please. . . .

I would like to know [of] any ideas [you have] for making it better—and also this should take your newly-clear mind off your own problems so you can devote yourself to worrying about me.

November 11, 1983

Two years after writing this letter I was at the British Open at Sandwich, in Kent, at a big house party. I sort of accidentally drank a big glass of vodka and was off and running again for a while.

Dear Perfesser:

. . . I decided once and for all I'm through with dranking and nose candy. Ain't had any liquor in a year now. And I feel better than I can ever remember feeling. So what, I ask myself, was the point of getting loaded so I could think I was having a good time that cost aplenty in body and brain damage, not to mention cash money. My latest test—last week—shows even my liver is back to normal, blood pressure down, etc . . . I'm convinced I would be dead now and writing you from heaven if I hadn't stopped when I did. For years I'd been half-scared I couldn't write without being drunk and wired. Untrue! In fact, my work is better now—and even easier. Am writing this from a rehearsal [for the film *Songwriter*]. They are actually saying most of my lines and what new ones they've thrown in are so good I claim I wrote 'em.

I know all this good stuff that's happening ain't just coincidental to stopping the whiskey. Odd, too, a half-dozen people have come up to me on the movie and congratulated me on being sober (god, I musta really been a case before) and said they are now, too. In the last year a lotta notorious drunks and dopers I know have straightened up. The hell of it is—they *all like it this way*. Drunks tell me I must be bored now. The truth is, I might be boring but I've never been as busy—or as happy, by god. . . .

Scene from "Pancho Villa and Ambrose Bierce"

Dennis Hopper and I spent a year or more hustling people and concocting schemes to raise the money to make "Pancho Villa and Ambrose Bierce" as a film with Dennis directing.

We failed.

Then I turned the movie script into a play called *Pancho Villa's Wedding Day.* At one point Tommy Lee Jones was going to direct it and play Villa as the opening event for the new Bass Concert Hall in Austin with music by Beto y los Fairlanes. Tommy Lee was living in Austin then, down the hill from me on the shore of Bee Creek.

That grand project fell apart when the authorities at the University of Texas heard our budget request from Tommy Lee. The budget was not at

Bud Shrake and Dennis Hopper at the helm of Mad Dog Productions.
Photo by Doatsy Shrake.

all extravagant at $500,000, it seemed to us, compared to what it cost to do a show on Broadway, but the authorities decided they'd rather have a sure winner, like a concert singer or a ballet.

Then it rained in biblical amounts, Bee Creek flooded, a drowned body washed up in Tommy Lee's yard, and he abruptly moved to San Antonio.

Next, Nick Kralj and others from the Quorum Club formed a production company and got the play produced at the Zachary Scott Theatre, where it had a successful run. Sidney Brammer, daughter of the novelist Billie Lee Brammer, was working as my assistant. She produced the play. Stupidly I didn't even see the whole show until dress rehearsal. I had made sure they had scripts that were bound in spiral plastic so they couldn't change anything, another foolish move. But the play drew sold-out houses for weeks. Following that, *Pancho Villa's Wedding Day* moved to the Austin Opry House for another few weeks.

During the run at Zach Scott, my script of *Songwriter* was being filmed in Austin at the same time. I was pretty happy with myself. When the play moved to the old Opry House, I was standing in the lobby, grinning and greeting people, and suddenly I got dizzy and sweaty and passed out cold. In the dressing room after they threw water on me to revive me, one of the actors, who was a diabetic, thought to take out his meter and test my blood sugar. It was more than 500, a deathly dangerous level. I had already quit drinking by then at least once, but I hadn't been taking my diabetes seriously. I thought a gallon of ice cream covered with trail mix was health food. For a diabetic that kind of diet is poison. After this incident, my eating habits changed.

EXT. COUNTRYSIDE AND HACIENDA—DAY

It is a great, mountainous country with castle rocks and purple peaks rising above the pines. The sky is brassy. There are patches of snow.

Along a line of telegraph poles leading toward a large hacienda, several bodies are hanging. These are dead Villistas, the people of Pancho Villa. In this case, they are all men. The bodies are twisting in the wind; ropes creak.

A Dorado—member of Villa's troop of bodyguards, the number of which may rise and fall from several to several dozen—takes off his cartridge belt, puts down his rifle and climbs a telegraph pole. Vultures flap away to settle again nearby.

It is a cold bright day in late winter. The Dorado is wearing a poncho, a sombrero and charro boots with heavy wool pants and a cotton shirt. The bodies hanging from the poles are wearing ragged clothing or else have been stripped. The Dorado puts his knife to the rope from which a body hangs by the neck.

The Dorado cuts the body loose and it drops to the ground.

MAIN TITLES START

Moving on toward the hacienda—

The courtyard inside the bullet-blasted walls contains bodies lying about. They are dressed in federal uniforms—tunics, tattered pants, billed caps. Some are barefoot. A few Villista bodies are laid out neatly along a wall. Some are women.

The door has been blown off the chapel. Children are playing. An old man sits beside the chapel, crying. Pigs are running around the courtyard.

Soldaderas—women and widows of the bodies on the telegraph poles and in the courtyard—are cooking a meal in iron pots. Some of them have infants slung on their backs. They are Villista women and women of the dead Federals, working side by side.

Dorados are cleaning out the hacienda store—the "company store" where the peons are kept in debt. Besides supplies, Dorados carry out the store's ledger books and dump them on the ground.

A Dorado with an axe is chopping down the Flogging Stake.

A 14-year-old girl, Isabel, chases a chicken for the pot. She is a fairly plain young girl, a Mexican-Indian, with a big-eyed face.

Several Dorados are rounding up cows from the pens.

EXT. HILLTOP—DAY

Below, people can be seen moving in the courtyard of the hacienda. But on top of the hill it is very still. A lizard creeps across a rock. Then a pebble rolls, and the lizard darts away.

A clump of brush is slowly pushed aside, and we see the face of Ambrose Bierce. He is 72-years-old, tall and lean and with a hard gaze, still handsome, with a white mustache and curly white hair. He smiles to himself and raises a pair of binoculars.

As the binoculars focus on the courtyard, through them we see a man walk up to one of the cooking pots, speak jokingly to a woman who ducks away shyly. The man scoops a handful of beans into a tortilla, which he rolls and begins to eat. He is wearing a rumpled brown wool suit, boots, serape and a flat-brimmed hat, with a rattlesnake band on it.

> BIERCE (V.O.)
> Pancho Villa . . . the Mexican devil. . . .

MAIN TITLES END

EXT. COURTYARD—DAY

Villa is a big man, six-feet tall, two hundred pounds, thick chested, who walks with a rolling, pigeon-toed gait. He has a thick mustache and reddish brown hair. In repose his mouth is usually open, giving him an adenoidal appearance. His teeth are strong and crooked and stained brown from the oxide in the water of Durango, where he was born 36 years ago.

Villa's most prominent feature is his eyes—light brown and friendly but capable of changing in an instant, becoming squinty and burning and ferocious. His sudden rages are such that observers compared them to epileptic seizures. Villa usually does not drink and often refuses to eat meat in an effort to control his temper.

But now he is chatting with the women around the cooking pots. One of them is the girl, ISABEL, who has caught a chicken.

> VILLA
> What a skinny little thing. Hardly a mouthful, eh?

He could be referring to the chicken, to Isabel or to both. The women take him to mean Isabel, and they laugh.

EXT. HILLTOP—DAY

Bierce lowers his binoculars for a moment.

> BIERCE
> The great devil Villa . . . We'll see how great
> a devil you are. . . .

THE SCREEN GOES TO BLACK

On the screen a legend appears. It says

CHIHUAHUA, MEXICO, ABOUT 1915

In the blackness we can hear moaning. Someone is praying.

> VOICE
> Hail Mary, Mother of God, be with me now . . .

> SECOND VOICE
> Shut up! You hear that?

A door is unlocked and thrust open. We see the blackness was the inside of a room where several men are being kept prisoner.

INT. ROOM—DAY

In the doorway stands Rodolfo Fierro, the leader of the Dorados. He is a Yaqui Indian, unusually tall and heavy-set for his race. Fierro is wearing ranchero clothes, a Texas hat, boots. Somehow the clothes don't quite seem to belong to him, but he is not uncomfortable in them. He is not the sort of man who would pay much attention to what he is wearing, as long as his clothes fit the weather.

FIERRO
It stinks in here. Open the window.

A Dorado comes inside and with a machete chops a thin wooden bar that held the wooden window shut. He pokes the window open. More light enters the room. In the distance through the window can be seen the hilltop.

Fierro pulls a list from his pocket and pretends to read it. Close-up, the list is an old receipt for 15,000 rounds of ammunition.

FIERRO
It says here we want you, don Alfonso. . . .
(He indicates a patrician hacendado, about 50, who rises stiffly. Don Alfonso is the one who had said, "Shut up!")
And you, Delgado. . . .
(Indicates the foreman, who had been praying)
And you, de Leon, little butterfly. . . .
(Fierro laughs and indicates a male secretary, a small, fluttery person)
. . . outside right now.

The prisoners file past Fierro. He notices a frightened teen age boy in a federal uniform in the corner.

FIERRO (CONT.)
And you wouldn't want to miss this, boy. This is your day to die.

The boy stumbles out with the others. Fierro follows them. As Fierro leaves the doorway, we see through the window a glint of light, a reflection of the sun on Bierce's binoculars.

THE BINOCULARS pick up the PRISONERS as they are marched outside.

EXT. HILLTOP—DAY

Bierce is watching through the binoculars. In the lens we see the four prisoners come out of the house and into the courtyard. Villa is still chatting with the women and pays no attention.

Bierce hears a click. Looking around, he first sees boots. Then looking up, he sees a grinning Dorado aiming a cocked Winchester at him.

> BIERCE (COMMANDINGLY)
> I demand to be presented to General Villa.

> DORADO (GRINNING)
> I am at your service, old man.

Scenes from "The Big Mamoo"

February 1986

Jonathan Demme is an important director, a wise and big-hearted man, and good company. We developed "The Big Mamoo" together, inspired by a nonfiction book by Jim Kunetka of Austin called *City of Fire.* Claire Townsend at 20th Century Fox, the executive for the project, was a dear friend and totally simpatico with us. David Axelrod and Ed Pressman were the producers. The angle Jonathan and I had on the story was that a bunch of very young, brilliant, and bizarre characters gathered on top of a mountain in Los Alamos and, working literally with screwdrivers and adding machines, managed to build a bomb that would change the world forever.

The more I learned about Fermi, Teller, Bohr, Oppenheimer, Groves, and the rest—reading their own books—the more remarkable the situation

Bud Shrake at Los Alamos, 1981. Photo by Claire Townsend.

became. Fermi spoke English like Jimmy Cagney, having learned it from the movies. Teller played the piano all night in the crude barracks shared by the scientists and their families with a belching, potbellied stove. Saturday nights the "eggheads" gathered in the lodge and got drunk on grain alcohol and put on dances and theatrical skits in drag. Pueblo Indians came to watch and dance with them. These were young people, and there were many sexual affairs. It was no secret that Kitty Oppenheimer, wife of the chief egghead, enjoyed sitting on the porch of her cabin nude in the dusk, having a cocktail and waiting for him to come home.

Driving to the first big atomic bomb test at Trinity, a carload of the top eggheads blew a tire, stranding them in a desert saloon since there were no spare tires. Earlier, a physicist was lit up and killed by radiation when his screwdriver slipped.

President Roosevelt speaks what I saw as the point of the movie when he says it is an ironic joke on Darwin that we are busily evolving ourselves out of existence, using the most brilliant of our people to do the dirty work.

This idea was not popular in the top office at Fox. We were told the atomic bomb was not the subject for black humor. Demme and I protested that the black humor was in your point of view—the details of the story were as true as a documentary.

Nevertheless, out on the sidewalk we went.

MUSIC: we hear the *Brahms Academic Festival Overture* played by a string quartet. Music builds and continues over as we

FADE IN ON:

THE UNIVERSE—

We are traveling through space with the sensation of incredible speed. Galaxies rush toward us. Suns, planets, moons, asteroids—worlds of ice and fire—zoom at us and pass terrifyingly close. We plunge toward a giant star— beyond which we see an eternity of stars. The giant star grows larger and brighter until it fills the screen with dazzling light. It is clear we are about to collide with this fiery star.

A legend appears:

PECONIC, NEW YORK
AUGUST, 1939

Brahms music rises to a crescendo as we hurtle closer into the giant star and

DISSOLVE TO:

CLOSE SHOT

ALBERT EINSTEIN. The famous scientist is examining a letter. We hear sea gulls, and the sound of surf. Einstein's lips move as he reads the letter to himself for a moment. Then Einstein looks up at two men who stand on the porch of a beach house on Long Island Sound. They are EDWARD TELLER and LEO SZILARD—young brilliant scientists, born in Hungary. Teller looks like a wild genius with bushy eyebrows. Teller and Szilard regard the seated Einstein with anxious respect as gulls swoop above the shore beyond the great man's summer cottage. Einstein wears slippers and a baggy sweater.

ANGLE ON EINSTEIN

EINSTEIN
"Dear President Roosevelt" . . . Hmmm . . . is dear how I should address the President of the United States? Like he is a cousin or an auntie I might write a letter to?
(shrugs)
Well . . . Several of you young men composed this letter, it's only for me to sign my name to it . . .
(a sharp glance at Teller and Szilard)
If this letter doesn't make me out too much of a son of a bitch . . . huh?
. . .
(reads)
"In the last four months it has become possible to set up a nuclear chain reaction in a large amount of uranium. . . . This new phenomenon would lead to the construction of bombs . . . extremely powerful bombs . . ."

Einstein puts down the letter and tries to light his pipe in the breeze. His matches keep going out. Teller steps forward with a Zippo and lights Einstein's pipe. Teller has a limp, the result of losing his right foot in a streetcar accident in Munich years ago.

EINSTEIN
Do you imagine a bomb the size of the Chrysler Building?

TELLER
(heavy accent)
We don't know what size this gadget might turn out to be, Professor Einstein.

Einstein weights down the letter with his tobacco pouch. He stands and walks to the railing of his deck and puffs on his pipe and looks out at the gulls and the water of the Sound.

EINSTEIN
I doubt such a bomb can be made. . . . But if it can be, . . . Ach. . . . If such a bomb can be made. . . . Well . . . if this horrible knowledge is to be put in the hands of man . . . Better we make this bomb before the Nazis do. . . .
(turns)
Do you have a fountain pen?

Teller gives Einstein a fountain pen. Teller unscrews the cap of the pen for him. Einstein pauses above the signature line.

EINSTEIN
What if your atomic chain reaction cannot be controlled? What if your atomic chain reaction hurls itself into a flaming holocaust that totally obliterates our entire planet?

TELLER
(smiles)
Our success will be announced to watchers in the universe by the glow of a new star in the Milky Way.

EINSTEIN
(chuckles)
... We'll be another mystery for astronomers from other galaxies to marvel at ... a million years from now they'll wonder what on earth we were doing ...

CLOSE—EINSTEIN SIGNS HIS NAME TO THE LETTER

CUT TO:

INT. WHITE HOUSE, OVAL OFFICE—DAY

PRESIDENT ROOSEVELT is reading the letter, while ALEXANDER SACHS stands by. Roosevelt studies the Einstein signature and looks up at Sachs.

ROOSEVELT
Fantastic. Incredible.

SACHS
Yes, Mr. President.

ROOSEVELT
A bomb made out of atoms?

SACHS
Two hundred of Germany's top scientists are working on an atomic bomb right now. They're far ahead of us—but fortunately Hitler scorns atomic research as a Jewish enterprise.

ROOSEVELT
What you're after is to see the Nazis don't blow us up before we blow them up?

SACHS
Precisely.

ROOSEVELT
What do Professor Einstein's eggheads want from me?

Sachs hands Roosevelt an already-written answering letter for the President to sign.

SACHS
Money.

Roosevelt examines the letter that orders funds for the Manhattan Project.

ROOSEVELT
This could be rather an enormous joke on that evolutionist, Darwin,— a bomb made out of atoms, the building blocks of life. Think of all the mothers and fathers working their asses off to send their children to the best schools? Think of the singing and piano lessons the children are taking? All the little girls in tights practicing ballet in front of mirrors? While we're busily evolving ourselves out of existence?

SACHS
Please think of Hitler, instead, Mr. President.

CLOSE—ROOSEVELT SIGNS THE LETTER . . .

[A later scene, on the way to the Trinity test site]

EXT. BELEN, NEW MEXICO, ROY'S CAFE—DAY

A Ford sedan stops in front of the cafe. The Driver jumps out and opens the doors for Oppenheimer, Groves, Teller and Fermi—and for Colonel Buddy Montana, head of public relations for the Department of War.

As the men step out of the car—the left rear tire goes flat with a loud hiss.

DRIVER
They wouldn't give me a spare tire at the motor pool—I told 'em who my passengers was, and they didn't give a damn.

GROVES
Stay out here and hitch us a ride to Trinity.

The five men enter Roy's Cafe, leaving the Driver to wander to the edge of the road—which stretches off empty as far as the eye can see.

CUT TO:

INT. ROY'S CAFÉ

Groves, Oppenheimer, Teller, Fermi and Col. Montana are drinking at the bar. The bartender is an FBI agent, dressed to look like a Mexican. But the bulge of his shoulder holster is unmistakable.

GROVES
You eggheads don't understand the public mind. We've got to have press releases ready. Listen to Colonel Montana—he's a specialist in snookering the public.

COL. MONTANA
Well, I wouldn't call the public relations game 'snookering the public.' But people are going to know something very big happened out here—and that's where I come in as chief of p.r. for the Department of War.

FERMI
I can dictate your press release.

TELLER
What would you say?

FERMI
(a pause)
A huge meteor struck New Mexico this morning and blasted the shit out of the whole state and all its citizens. Hunters and skiers planning to vacation in New Mexico, be advised it is now a crater and too hot to touch.

Col. Montana digs in his portfolio and brings out press releases.

COL. MONTANA
In fact, I do have a press release describing a celestial body smash-ing into New Mexico. I have prepared press releases to explain a total fizzle, a small embarrassing foop, a major explosion such as we hope for, the destruction of the State of New Mexico, the destruction of the Western United States . . . if the atomic bomb goes off bigger than that, the hell with the p.r. game, frankly.

TELLER
I'd make it 35 to one we don't blow up New Mexico. A thousand to one we don't blow up the whole world.

The FBI Bartender is leaning close to listen. He looks aghast.

OPPENHEIMER
The press release could say: "Even though the odds were 1,000 to one against them, the most brilliant men in history managed to obliterate the planet Earth today."

The FBI Bartender drops a beer mug on the floor.

ANGLE

The Driver opens the screen door.

DRIVER
I've got you a ride to Trinity.

The men toss dollars on the bar and go out. Fermi looks back at the FBI Bartender.

FERMI
Hey, pal, if I was you, I'd dig a hole. About six feet deep.

Fermi laughs and follows the others. The screen door slams shut behind him.

The Angels of Dien Bien Phu

From *Night Never Falls* (1987)

This is to me personally the most important book I ever wrote, and my favorite. Harry Sparrow is the fantasy me. He does what I desperately wanted to do—he writes a syndicated column, is a foreign correspondent appearing in major newspapers, travels to exotic places with unusual people, and wears a trench coat. Harry even lives in pretty much the same Chelsea flat Doatsy and I lived in when I wrote *Strange Peaches.*

But the real reason this novel is so important to me is it is the first long piece of prose I wrote after I had finally quit drinking booze and smoking cigarettes and taking speed and snorting coke. I mean quit for good. Until this book I couldn't imagine writing fiction without the release of tension that you get from liquor and tobacco. I wondered if I could write at all without a cigarette smoldering in an ashtray near at hand and without knowing there was a cold bottle of vodka in the refrigerator. Novelists hear voices in their heads that won't go away without being drugged.

It was hard to realize that fifteen years had gone by since I had written a novel. I was working in the movies most of that time, and staying up all night so I wouldn't miss anything. For several years I spent more time with Jerry Jeff Walker and the Gonzo boys than with my typewriter.

So I decided to test myself. I would write a novel that did not have the word "Texas" in it.

I elected to start it at Dien Bien Phu, where the western world should have learned a bloody lesson before Vietnam, but didn't. The enormity of the U.S. involvement in the Indochina War as far back as the 1950s, immediately after the Korean War, is staggering.

I did a lot of research for this book. I was never at Dien Bien Phu, of course. But while I was stationed at Fort Knox going through Officers Candidate School, our colonel made rousing speeches about Dien Bien Phu and predicted our class would leave its bones on Asian soil. However, I did go to the other locations in this novel, including the strangely eerie Algiers.

And when I finally sat down to write *Night Never Falls,* I used my faithful little Smith Corona Skywriter because that's what Harry Sparrow used.

The word "Texas" is not in this novel, but I did use the Alamo as a metaphor for Dien Bien Phu. However, I put that comparison in the mouth of a French Legionnaire.

The valley of Dien Bien Phu is the wettest place in all of northern Indochina. During the monsoon season—March through August—it is not unusual for eight feet of rain to fall. Five feet is the average. A storm that pours six inches of rain in an hour is common. French Union Forces captured the valley in November, during the dry season. They flattened and trampled the rice and vegetables. There was no stone or gravel in the valley. The French could not build masonry fortifications. There was no timber in the valley, either. The French tore down the houses in the villages to use the wood for construction. After the first week of the actual battle, loads of coffin wood from Hanoi, such as had come in on the ambulance plane with Harry, also went into shoring up bunkers. The dead were buried in shell craters or trenches dug by engineers.

Dien Bien Phu is not the name of a town. The words mean "Seat of the Border Country Prefecture" or "administration center." The name of the now-destroyed village where the administration center was now located had been Muong Thang. It was a Tai village. The Tais controlled the valley. The Xa tribe lived on the slopes. The Meos commanded the ridges and the highest mountains farther beyond. The yellow stucco building that had housed the French resident administrator was standing in perfect order when the paras of the FUF jumped in November. Now the yellow building on the hill known as Lola was flattened—only its wine cellar remained. A Chaffee tank was half-buried in the mud and rubble where the administrator's office had been.

In winter the temperature in the valley dropped to 30 degrees Fahrenheit at night, colder on the peaks. An exposed person could suffer and die from the wet chill. But with the monsoon rains came hot winds that blew seventy-mile-an-hour gales from Laos. When the battering of rain and wind paused, the heat and humidity in the valley became suffocating. FUF soldiers died from dehydration or exhaustion. Green flies, ticks and fleas flourished on the valley floor during monsoon. Within a short time after the Vietminh surrounded the valley and began their onslaught, another creature started to thrive: the maggot.

The Nam Yum flooded. Water poured into trenches. FUF troops at the southern strongpoint, called Isabelle, fought up to their knees in water and mud. Inside of every bunker the walls and floors oozed mud and the smell of sulphur and decay.

Harry emerged from the C.R. bunker on an early afternoon in the middle of April. In the three weeks he had been at Dien Bien Phu, Harry had changed in appearance. First to go had been the cordovan loafers—sucked off his feet and lost forever in a mudhole. Now he wore a pair of thick-soled paratroop boots Claudette Frontenac had given him. There were hundreds of empty boots around the hospital.

He had cut off his white linen trousers at midthigh and made them into walking shorts the color of a mechanic's apron. His suit coat and one good shirt were packed in a footlocker. A sniper's bullet had punched a hole through the crown of the Panama hat he still wore. Harry had heard a *theong!* and the hat had sailed six feet away. The sniper kept tracking him as Harry crawled after the hat. *Theong! Theong!* So close it seemed as if the sniper was letting Harry know he was being spared on purpose. Sick as he was with dysentery, Harry hardly cared about snipers and their bullets anymore. Harry had lost twenty pounds and had quit shaving. The thin, bearded face with bulging red eyes could have been that of a wino in a doorway in Soho.

Harry used his Haig Ultra pitching wedge to hold his Burberry up, like an umbrella above his head, as he stepped slowly into the slop. He also used the wedge for a cane, a scoop, a hoe, a hammer, a pointer, a scraper and a shovel. He even used it to stroke some ration cans and brass shell casings as he roamed the trenches. Harry could use the wedge as a bludgeon or a sword or, he figured, as a staff to tie a white flag on.

He lowered his wedge and Burberry and blinked. What was wrong? Harry smelled fried pork and diesel oil. Three weeks before, knowing the smell of fried pork meant burnt human flesh would have made him pause and reflect. Now he ignored the smells as he waded into the communications trench. He realized what seemed wrong: It wasn't raining. Heat rose from the mud carrying the odor of shit, but Harry had grown used to it now. Smoke and pungent cordite fumes made a haze below the clouds. The land around him was a steaming swamp. Nobody knew how many bodies lay under the mud.

By de Castries's accounting, the FUF could call on 3,000 fighting soldiers. Perhaps 6,000 deserters—most what de Castries called "Colonials," soldiers from Morocco, Algeria, Tunisia and Indochina—lived with trapped tribes in the caves. De Castries spoke of turning FUF artillery against the rats of the Nam Yum in their caves, but the ammunition was needed against Vietminh assaults. In the last twenty-four hours the FUF had fired 12,000 rounds of 105 artillery shells, half with the barrels cranked down to shoot directly into Communist troops swarming down the slopes. Incredibly, reinforcements kept parachuting in. A hundred volunteers—French and Vietnamese—jumped into Dien Bien Phu last night. Sixteen lived to see the dawn.

If Harry survived he knew he would never again underestimate the human capacity for courage, generosity, stupidity, or evil.

Harry was allowed to poke about the C.R. at will—unless Bigeard or Langlais was present. The paratroop officers were annoyed to have Harry there but could think of nothing to do with him. Besides, Harry was useful to them in a way. He played chess with de Castries and kept the colonel from bothering them for hours in a row. Playing chess with de Castries, Harry heard gossip and radio traffic in the command bunker. He couldn't write the information he learned in the bunker, but he would remember it for the future—if, indeed, there proved to be a future for him or for the world. The arms and munitions that were concentrated in this remote valley in Indochina were truly startling, even to Harry, who had seen the D-Day armada and the Patton armies.

Making notes of the lists of weapons used by both sides in the battle put Harry into a cynical mood, extreme even for a newspaperman trained to expect the worst from people. Reading his lists, Harry realized it was too simple to blame the arms merchants for this awful inventory of staggeringly expensive tools of doom. People must want to be armed to the eyeballs. The manufacture of weapons had become a very big business during World War II, but there was more to this lust for weapons than salesmanship. People loved weapons, they loved to fight and kill. The currency for weapons was human lives—but they kept crying for more. . . .

Reading the list of arms at Dien Bien Phu reminded Harry of his father's belief that the world would end in the year 2000. The atomic bombs at Hiroshima and Nagasaki had not dismayed Harry's father, nor would he join in the Civil Defense bomb-shelter panic that swept the United States. Colonel Edward Sparrow was not religious; he used New Testament prophecies only to help him make his point: The world would end in the year 2000. Harry's mother was the strong Catholic in the family. She was a spirited woman who went regularly to mass and confession; Harry's father played golf on Sundays.

He could explain why he knew the world would end in the year 2000. He believed it was universal knowledge. It had something to do with being alive in the year 1900. Everyone who was alive in 1900 agreed, Colonel Sparrow said. The special knowledge was passed along in the genes in 1900. The end was one century away. Nothing to worry about until 2000.

But this was 1954, forty-six years till the aviator's doomsday, and Harry wondered if his father hadn't been optimistic.

Harry was amazingly clear-headed. He swallowed two more Maxiton pills. Sergeant LeRuc had stashed an entire crate of Maxitons. He had been prominently mentioned in two of Harry's dispatches.

That afternoon, in the relatively quiet time before the evening bombardment began, Harry was headed for the underground hospital to see Claudette. Folded in an oilcloth packet inside his shirt was a batch of clippings that had been dropped by a Bearcat courier that morning. Included was his first dispatch—the eight-column headline angels of dien bien phu. Pieces written later—published with the i, harry sparow, standing boxed head—had come to the valley earlier, and Harry had begun to wonder if the first transmission had gotten garbled on its journey around the world.

But it finally arrived, along with another cable from Gruber that said worldwide playhot even epps pleased keep head down type faster. And then an addendum that Gruber had known would irritate Harry: london claim phibbs in thick of action. how? phibbs colorful interview with legionnaire says 5,000 nazi ss fighting dien bien. pls follow best gruber.

Harry figured Phibbs had gotten drunk with a French colonial soldier—could have been a Moroccan or Algerian or one of the African blacks—in Hanoi. The colonials hated the Legion. Harry knew there were at least two thousand Germans in the Legion at Dien Bien when Giap's assault began. Harry had heard Bigeard say, "If we had a division of those Nazi brutes, we would have taken up bayonets and won this fight by now." That was moments after Selchauhansen had led another successful counterattack from Lola. Radio reported to the C.R. that *bo-doi* bodies were piled six deep on barbed wire in the mud.

Harry heard harsh voices calling and looked up as a flock of crows flew across the valley. Every time the rain slackened, crows flew across the valley, their cries mocking the humans in the jungle and the mud below.

He found Claudette sitting on a pile of sandbags outside the hospital.

Wounded and dead lay in the mud by the entrance. Engineers and PIMs dug trenches to dispose of the bodies, but it had become a hopeless task.

Claudette's skin and uniform were caked with blood and mud. She was smoking a cigarette. Her face looked ashen in the ghostly aura that hovered around the hospital.

"What do you suppose I just did, Harry?" she said, her voice full of wonder. "Sit down, please. I need to talk."

"What's the matter?"

"We had thirty wounded for abdominal surgery lined up in there. All of them hopeless. The doctor asked me to pick out ten who were suffering the most." She dropped her cigarette into a mud puddle and looked at Harry. Her eyes were sunken and saw past him. In her despair, she moved him. He wanted to be a part of her, to console her. "So I did it, and we killed them."

"What do you mean?"

"The ten I selected got an overdose of morphine. We didn't have enough morphine to kill all thirty. So we killed the ten I selected, and the other twenty are dying now."

Harry reached over and took her hand.

"I tried to choose the ones who were afraid of death, who were fighting it." Claudette began weeping. Harry put his arms around her. He felt her body shuddering. "But the ones who were ready to accept death—they could make the transition on their own. They were ready to leave their bodies. The ones with faith, their spiritual guides were here with them. Some had already welcomed the peace that comes with death." She pressed her face against his shoulder.

"Where do you get a spiritual guide?" Harry said.

"They are here for all of us, to guide us, to comfort us. All you have to do is ask and then listen to your inner self."

Harry thought, this little angel has been heavy into the Maxitons.

"I'm sorry," she said. "You don't need to hear all this." Claudette stepped back, wiping the muddy tears. "I better go to work."

"Let me show you something," Harry said. He removed the angels story from the oilcloth packet.

"I didn't have time to interview you or Geneviéve before I wrote this," he said. "Had to get something off to the *Dispatch,* and this was the best thing I could think of that would get de Castries's approval. Hope you don't mind."

He watched her as she read the story. She looked puzzled at first at seeing her name in print. Then she began reading with urgency.

"They have information on Galard and you in the files at the C.R. The intelligence boys sent it," he said.

"This is very flattering, Harry," she said, reading the story, "but I don't deserve it. Geneviéve is the real angel. She stays on her feet for days and nights without sleep. She's amazing. What strength she's got. I must learn to be as strong as she is."

"You do what she does," Harry said.

"Why haven't you mentioned the other women? The Arabs? The Vietnamese? They do what we do, too."

"De Castries censored them. He says they're prostitutes."

"What a strange place to draw the line. A man who gives orders sending men to certain death and yet judges merciful women doing the work of God. If left to women, there would never be a war. And besides, in the Bible, Jesus didn't spurn prostitutes. What difference does it make what they are? If they are whores, they could go to the bordellos in the caves on the river. They're closer to being angels than I am, Harry. They didn't volunteer for this, but they're enduring it with responsibility," she said.

"I'll write about them after we get out of here."

"Get out of here?" she said.

"We got in. We can get out."

"Oh, Harry, don't treat me like a fool. I know what's happening."

She thrust the newspaper clipping back into his hands.

"You can keep it," he said. "For your scrapbook."

"I don't want the others in the hospital to see this story, Harry. It can only make things worse. Tear it up, please."

She turned and started toward the hospital bunker. There was something in the way her hips moved, her shoulders erect, that Harry found inexplicable and exciting.

"Are you in love with that Legionnaire?" Harry said.

Claudette glanced back at him. "Have you heard news of him?"

"He's alive."

"Praise God," Claudette said. She crossed herself.

"How did you ever meet him? A girl like you shouldn't know a thug like him."

Claudette's face brightened at Harry's jealousy. She looked at him with her head at an angle, hair cropped too short to dangle, as if she were studying a chess move, Harry thought, pleased at the picture of her looking at him that way across a chessboard. She might be able to play him a fair game. The physical desire he felt for her, sick as he was and stuck in hell, pleased him.

"He came to my apartment in Paris."

"He looked you up?"

"He knew my father. He came to talk about my father, console me as a friend of my father. He was wounded. I cared for him."

"Are you in love with him? Is that why you're here?"

Claudette gave Harry an impenetrable female look. He had no idea what she might say or if he should believe it.

"What a stupid question," she said.

"But what's the answer?"

"I know now I didn't come here because of him—not for his love—and not to find some part of my father. Or for my country to control this land. I didn't come here for any of the reasons that I thought I did. I'm here to help those that I can. Maybe I'm here to learn how to love. I see love all around me in the hospital. Not being in love but loving."

Harry watched her walk back into the hospital bunker. He shoved the clipping into the oilcloth packet. He smelled the breath of a hog, and looked up to see Pelwa.

Pelwa's left arm hung in a sling; his left hand was wrapped in a bloody bandage. With his unmaimed hand, he pulled the black SS cap onto his large skull.

"What are you doing chatting up the chief's girl?" Pelwa said.

"How bad are you hurt?" Harry said.

"Nothing much."

"Your hand mangled is nothing much?"

"The chief wants to see you, mister. Where have you been hiding? You afraid to come to Lola with me?"

"Let's go," Harry said.

"No sense you getting hot for that girl. No girl ever leaves the chief unless he's through with her, and he likes this one. No insult intended, mister, but you ain't in the same world with the chief when it comes to women."

"How would you know?" said Harry.

"Don't lose your temper with me." Pelwa grunted. "I don't know, mister, maybe you're the top stud in Chicago, America, but I bet you can't make a woman leave the chief. Come on, now. Let's take the 'Metro' over to Lola."

The network of trenches that laced the valley floor and low hills inside the amphitheater had become so extensive that Europeans called it the Metro. The trouble with the Metro, from Harry's point of view, was that you never knew where to get off; you could round a turn in a trench and be face to face with *bo-doi* in green uniforms and bamboo helmets. FUF and Vietminh lines had come close enough together that soldiers shouted insults and taunts and jokes back and forth.

A loudspeaker from Communist lines was booming as Harry waded with Corporal Pelwa through the slush and blood of the Metro. The message today was aimed at the Foreign Legion.

"Why are you dying for French imperialism, you brave soldiers of the *Legion étrangére*?" said the loudspeaker in French. "Throw down your arms and come over to us. We will send you home safely to Europe."

Pelwa led Harry into Selchauhansen's command post. Beside the entrance was a lone banyan tree. The command post was in the wine cellar of what had been the French resident administrator's house. The captain was giving firing coordinates on the radio when they entered. He wore his green Legion paratroop beret and a faded khaki jacket. Harry heard him asking for more flamethrower tanks. Leaning against a firing slit, the handsome Arab Ali Saadi was asleep standing up, stacks of brass bullet casings around his boots. Attached to the wall with medical tape, Harry saw newspaper clippings. Two of them were Harry's own stories from *The Paris Dispatch*, but most prominently displayed was phibbs: our man at dien bien phu. It was the Phibbs story about the 5,000 Nazi SS fighting for the Legion at Dien Bien Phu.

Harry guessed the man who called himself Selchauhansen was not much more than thirty years old. That meant he could have been no older than twenty when he became an officer in the Headhunters. When Hitler's Panzers invaded Russia in 1941, Selchauhansen would have been a boy of sixteen. At age sixteen Harry's dreams of the future involved playing shortstop for the St. Louis Cardinals. He turned twenty-one in his junior year at the University of Missouri when the Japanese bombed Pearl Harbor. Until December 7, 1941, playing the games of baseball and golf, starring on the swimming and diving teams in high school and college, dancing, drinking and the conquest of girls filled his life. He tried to please his father by winning prizes and maintaining decent grades in pre-law and his mother by going to mass with her at Christmas, Easter and Good Friday. He didn't make the varsity baseball team on the university level, though; he had good range at shortstop and a fair throwing arm, but curve balls were his fatal flaw at the plate. He won letters in high diving and freestyle swimming, and he worked for the campus newspaper, rising from general assignments to his own editorial column before Pearl Harbor. How different life must have been for the German.

Selchauhansen's green beret brushed the damp concrete beam above his head as he spoke into the American-made ANPRC-6 radio. Light from the petroleum-jelly lantern cast a dull gleam on the beret. Harry had expected to see an SS badge like the one on Pelwa's black cap. Coming into Strongpoint Lola, Harry noticed troopers wearing SS badges, caps and daggers mixed with their American-made World War II uniforms and steel helmets, and their French Legion khaki shorts and floppy campaign hats. But the badge Selchauhansen had pinned to his beret was the dragon and sword inside a circle: the universal mercenary symbol.

Looking at the man, Harry admitted it was reasonable Claudette could have fallen for him. There was a touch of the thoroughbred about him: long limbs, clean lines, intelligent eyes and a rich growth of reddish-blond beard. Harry's first impression of him as a mad monk was inadequate; the man looked like a modern Teutonic knight, glittering madness in his features. Imagine a black cross on his chest and a broadsword in his hands, and you understood why medieval Europe had feared the Teutons and popes had courted their favor. But Selchauhansen would at moments achieve a soft, feminine expression, a tenderness in the eyes and mouth that filled the onlooker with relief.

Selchauhansen handed the headpiece back to his radio operator and looked at Pelwa. "How's your hand?"

"Good as new," said Pelwa.

"Three fingers blown off this morning, and now he's good as new," Selchauhansen said, shrugging at Harry. "Sit down, Sparrow. I've been hoping you'd come find the truth to write. *The London Daily Mail* claims to have been here already."

"It would be hard to count how many scoops have come entirely from the *Daily Mail's* imagination."

"How is Claudette?"

"She's working at the hospital."

"I mean, how is she holding up?"

"She's okay."

"I want to thank you for helping me at the airstrip. I always repay a favor."

"Listen, whatever-your-name-is, I went through Poland in 1945. I saw what the SS did. I wasn't trying to help you at the airstrip. If it hadn't been for Claudette, I would have left you for dead."

"Oh, I'm not fooled about your reasons. But I am in your debt."

Harry said, "Why did you bring Claudette here? You knew what this was all about. If you care for the girl, why would you bring her here?"

"This is her war."

"Because she's French? Or do you SS bastards routinely punish the people you love?"

"Hey, mister, you shut your mouth," growled Pelwa.

"It's all right, Pelwa. Find us some coffee, please. And some tobacco," said Selchauhansen.

"*Jawohl, Herr Kapitän!*" Pelwa gave an exaggerated salute.

Harry opened his last pack of Chesterfields, gave one to Selchauhansen and put the pack on the map case between them.

"You may as well put your feet up and listen. You can't find your way out of here by yourself. I know you want to hear about the girl. I'll tell you. But first you have to listen to me. I will tell you how my Headhunters came here. I'll tell you what this battle is about. You will have a chance to write the truth. The only thing you mean to me is you tried to save my life. But your newspaper is important."

Harry nodded. There was passion in the German's voice.

"You were military age during the war, Sparrow. I guess infantry, maybe parachutes. You have the look of an officer," said Selchauhansen.

"I was a corporal, like Pelwa," Harry said.

The captain snorted. "There is no other corporal like Pelwa. What was your branch then? Armor?"

"I covered the war in Europe for *Stars and Stripes*," Harry said.

"You were a journalist even during the fighting?"

"I was where the fighting was, if that's what you mean," Harry said.

"Don't be offended, Sparrow," said the captain, "but no journalist can compare himself to a man like Pelwa. A journalist is an observer and a faker. Pelwa is right in the middle of the real stuff."

"Where do you think I am? Does this look like the Riviera?"

"Your press card is only a piece of paper; there are bullets flying here. But your press card wins you a dead officer's bunk in the C.R., doesn't it? I hear you play gin rummy and chess with the colonel. Is de Castries a good chess player?"

"Not bad. He's a quiet player."

"But forceful, they say. Let's see how good you are at chess."

Selchauhansen lifted a section of parachute silk that had been covering a mahogany chessboard and began to set up the ivory pieces.

Harry had learned to play chess from the third-base coach of the Cardinals in spring training in 1946. In the eight years since, Harry had followed the typical novice's road to the discovery that chess is unfathomable. At first he bought some books, learned fundamental rules and several openings. He learned chess language: *forks* and *splits, mates* and *checkmates, stalemates* and *draws.* He thought he could recognize patterns on the board. After two years he began to notice he was no longer improving. The good players kept killing him. And they weren't even good players compared to the bartender in The Cooper's Arms, who could beat any ten regulars simultaneously, blindfolded. And the bartender, good as he was, would have less chance against a grandmaster than Harry would have had in a golf match against Sam Snead. What hope did Harry have in chess? He lapsed into a style of play that used an established opening to a depth of six or seven moves, then he castled his king to the king side and tried to struggle into the middle game, hoping for errors by his opponent that were worse than his own. Harry had no prospect of chess brilliancy, not ever; he was discovering that chess was for few to be brilliant at. For players like Harry, chess was the conditioning of the logic circuits of the mind. Harry was impulsive; he wanted to be logical.

"I warn you, I am naturally gifted at this game," Selchauhansen said. "I am blessed. The first time I looked at a chessboard as a child, I could see all the squares and their importance. That's the secret to the game: Be aware of the entire board and understand the important squares. Do you want to play white or black?"

"White."

White made the first move. Playing white was like choosing to serve at tennis.

Harry made an opening of pawn to king four. The Legionnaire stroked his beard thoughtfully as his bloodshot eyes took in the board. Selchauhansen moved his black king's pawn two squares. Harry brought his king's knight out to bishop three. Selchauhansen replied with queen's knight to bishop three. Harry moved his king's bishop across to queen's knight five, attacking black's king four, a vital square. It was the Ruy Lopez, the opening Harry could play longest before the pieces started falling. Harry castled his king to the king's side on his fifth move. The moves went fast, the two men concentrating, not speaking. Selchauhansen's fifth move captured Harry's king's pawn with a knight.

"The Steinetz defense." Selchauhansen smiled. After that move, the captain relaxed. He had Harry sized up and the game won. "Do you mind if I continue my story? Can you think about your game with conversation going on?"

"I'm listening," Harry said.

"I was a farmer's son in Saxony in the thirties. I volunteered for the Elite Guard—the *Verfügungstruppe*. That's simply what one did, not a matter of choice. We were farm boys and boys who worked with their hands. When I joined the Elite Guard, one couldn't have a single filling in his teeth—that's how strict the standards were. You were proud if you got in. They changed the name of the Elite Guard to the Waffen SS and invited mobs of vicious hoodlums to join, but I was never one of them. I was always Elite Guard," Selchauhansen said. They accepted two canteen cups of muddy coffee from Pelwa. Coffee drippings made butterfly splotches on the sleeve of Selchauhansen's jacket, like the camouflage clothing the French parachutists wore. "The SS invented the camouflage uniform, you know. The French used to say we looked like tree frogs. Now they copy our style."

Harry scorched his lip on the rim of the metal cup.

"My father was a member of the Nazi party, of course. What big landowner wasn't? My family died in Dresden," continued Selchauhansen. "It's ironic. You Americans talk about war crimes and war criminals, but what you mean is you won the war and we lost it, so we are the criminals. What your bombers did at Dresden, dropping white phosphorous on top of a city that was already burning. . . . Well, that's the story of human history, isn't it? Punish the vanquished? The winners stage a holy inquisition and hang the losers. The French made me an offer: Join the Foreign Legion or be hanged as a loser."

"But the SS is different from being an ordinary soldier."

"I was the Elite Guard of the SS. Not, as I said, a Jew chaser. I was not at

Warsaw or the prison camps. We went to Stalingrad and back. I am a *Kopfjäger*. Do you know what that is?"

"A Headhunter," said Harry.

"We fought Marxist terrorists. The terrorists would blow up a hospital train and machine-gun wounded German soldiers. We would find the guilty terrorists and kill them."

"Or kill your hostages."

"Quite so. But we always announced our intention—who are the hostages, and what will happen and why. We set the terms loud and clear and showed no mercy whatsoever. But grabbing hostages and then killing them if you must is a moral thing, not a simple thing. It required examining the heart. It demanded careful consideration of the way one views the value of human lives in the course of history. I think I have learned the lesson my trials were teaching me. Check."

"Check?"

"Look at the board."

"Ah." Harry moved his king out of immediate danger from a black bishop. How could that have happened, he wondered. Harry had concentrated on his brilliant moves—setting up Selchauhansen for a knockout that would dazzle the self-proclaimed chess master—but he hadn't noticed an open diagonal into the heart of his position.

"Lesson?" Harry asked.

"The world has changed forever. Terrorism is the war of the future," said Selchauhansen. "In future, men will fight the military machines with terror. A few dedicated terrorists can bring down an empire that has no will—or way—to defeat them."

"They say the hydrogen bomb is the war of the future," Harry said.

"Pardon?" Selchauhansen studied the chessboard and fingered a small scab on the bridge of his nose. "The what?"

"The hydrogen bomb."

"I am talking about war. The hydrogen bomb is not war. The hydrogen bomb is total extermination of human life. Hydrogen war can't be fought— it's meaningless, everybody dies. War in future will be fought by terrorism. Individual against individual, idea against idea, hand to hand. The battle we are fighting at Dien Bien Phu is the start of Armageddon, the final war between good and evil. If you don't think evil is real and struggling to take over the world, you are very naïve. The devil is real. I have seen him."

"Listening to a morality lecture from an officer in Hitler's Imperial Guard is too much for me. Let's stow the good-and-evil crap. Your move."

"Check and mate in two."

"What? Oh, yeah, the knight again. I see." Harry knocked over his king, signifying defeat.

Letter: March 8, 1988, to Larry L. King, on Being "Sodbuster Two"

You probably don't know how hard it is to plow ground behind a mule. I didn't know until I found my hands on the handles of the plow, and Bill Wittliff started making grunting noises and flapping the mule's reins, and we bumped painfully and slowly through the hard clods of dirt, plowing rows for our big scene in *Lonesome Dove,* the CBS miniseries that won a lot of awards, but none for me.

The Suggs gang arrived at our sodbuster farm to kill us in the show. The script called for me to start running across the field, trying to escape. Upon hearing a shot, I was to fall down wounded so I could later be hanged and burned. I kept running. I heard no shot. My heart was pounding, my feet stumbled in the rows, I was winded. It was nearing dark and I could see my red Mercedes parked at the edge of the field out of camera range. Still I heard no shot. I was thinking I would keep running, jump in my car and drive away rather than do this scene again. At the last moment I heard it—the gunshot! I took a headlong tumble into the dirt, doing a convincing dying sodbuster, and the movie wrapped for the day.

Bill Wittliff later played a character called "Lobster Man" in a CBS movie that Gary Cartwright and I wrote. But he wasn't asked to do any stunts—only to play poker with the original Lash LaRue.

Dear Professor:

I realize that as a mere movie star who earned international fame in the roles of Town Drunk (*Kid Blue,* '73) and Motorcycle Cop (*Outlaw Blues,* '79), I do not hold a fig to you—a classical actor, singer and dancer of the legitimate stage.

But now I face the most demanding role of my long career and implore you to share with me the techniques of your craft. This could be Academy Award time, Professor.

Yes, I have finally consented to play the difficult part of Sodbuster Two in *Lonesome Dove.*

Billy D. Wittliff landed the role of Sodbuster One. But I felt that since he is also the producer, it was more professional of me to not threaten to walk over the small matter of One or Two. There are no small roles, as you know, only small actors. I am a bigger actor than most.

When first seen on screen, Sodbuster One and Sodbuster Two are plowing a field behind a team of mules. This will call for stumbling, cussing and sweating, all of which I did beautifully both as Town Drunk and as Motorcycle Cop.

But suddenly the vicious Suggs gang shows up and before you know it, Sodbusters One and Two are:

1. Shot

2. Hanged

3. Burned.

As of now, there is no dialogue except for screams.

However, at the right moment I intend to say:

SODBUSTER TWO
(proudly, courageously, but in tears)
The man whose life you are about to take—I mean mine, let Sodbuster One talk for himself—was once a child, just as you were. Listen to my tale from my humble beginnings right on up to date, and you will see it is a far, far better thing I do than I have ever done before. Strike not this ole gray head but smote if you must upon Sodbuster One, who is the very man who shot Jesse James in the back. . . .
(staggers, clutches heart)
Hark, I smell the sweet breath of the angels! Rage! Nay, rage not! 'Tis done! 'Tis done!
(sinks to ground, looks up)
Hey, Suggs! You got a match?

The first question I have is, how do you memorize your lines? I didn't have much trouble with my lines in *Kid Blue* ("Hey!") or *Outlaw Blues* ("You! You there! Stop! Stop! Get outta my way! Stop!" Harder than you might think)—but to memorize a syliloquoy, or spell one, do you read it while you squint and pinch your nose? I've heard that is the trick.

Should I transit into Shakespearean dialect after my famous stagger and heart-clutch, or should I sound more like Willie Morris?

My last line ("Hey, Suggs . . .") should be delivered like Humphrey Bogart in *Key Largo,* I think. Does it work for you?

I'm sure there are other questions about acting I haven't thought to ask. I can already cry on cue. I just think about the day my first wife's lawyer took all our money out of the joint account, and my $300 check for a new set of Wilson golf clubs bounced. I weep a little even as I write this some 25 years later . . .

You don't need to feel obligated to help Sodbuster One, but he thinks he is a student of acting and may need some straightening out.

One more thing. We are to be immolated on March 25–26. There is some urgency.

I will remember you on my way up. . . .

Backstories: Sodbusters One and Two

March 29, 1988

"Sodbusters" Bill Wittliff and Bud Shrake on the set of *Lonesome Dove*, 1988. Photo courtesy of Bill Wittliff.

HUMPHREY DEWITT [SODBUSTER TWO, to be played by Bud Shrake]— Heir to the fabled DeWitt estates that cover four counties in north England, young DeWitt killed the King's nephew in a sword duel over a disagreement at cards. He fled to America, bringing with him the first seeds of kiwi fruit ever seen in this country. Soon a prosperous kiwi plantation owner in Illinois, Humphrey fell in love with a psychotic beauty named Mary. They planned to be wed, but she jilted him in favor of a gangly lawyer who became President of the U.S. Heartbroken, Dewitt gave away all his wealth and land to orphans (Boys Town was named for him) and drifted south to Texas with nothing but a pocket of kiwi seeds, determined to make a new life—nay, an empire—on the frontier. In bearing and appearance, DeWitt would have been mistaken for Gary Cooper if he had lived another 60 years.

ANTOINE HOULIHAN [SODBUSTER ONE, to be played by Bill Wittliff]—
As a boy in Dublin, Antoine was rakish and debonaire while all his mates
were sods who punched him out frequently in the potato fields and church-
yard. After being caught and whipped by the priest for fondling himself during mass, Antoine joined the Royal Navy as a drummer boy. He jumped ship
in New Orleans, where he fell naturally into the gay life. His roots as a potato
farmer drew him to Texas, and he was dumbstruck with love at the first sight
of Humphrey DeWitt. Antoine has started to suspect he and Humphrey
are not growing potatoes on their farm but little green things instead. He is
about to challenge Humphrey when Suggs arrives. Think of Antoine as Dom
DeLuise with a brogue.

Letter: February 12, 1998, to Larry L. King, on Getting Older

I will always remember the pitying look I got from Celia Morris, wife of Willie at the time, when I excitedly congratulated her on the incredible luck of their dog Pete having leaped out the window six stories onto the New York sidewalk and survived unhurt.

Suddenly looking into Celia's eyes, I began to feel that I was the dog in this story and I was making my final trip to the vet.

Dear Yer Holiness Lionship [Larry L. King]:

In these uncertain times of anthrax and Saddam and the Pacific Rim financial genius turning out to be mainly another variation of the S&L scam, I want you to know you can count on your Clipping Service to send you glorious views of your ownself and kind of pissy views of pals, such as this brief essay on Willie's new book.

This makes twice again Willie has fooled me. I used to believe everything he said, like when he told me his dog Pete jumped out a sixth floor window in Gotham and landed on his feet unhurt.

A year ago he told me he had a new book called my dog skip. I didn't believe that until I saw him signing them in a tent at the Book Festival in Austin. Then he told me he had written a new book about the making of the movie the ghosts of mississippi. I thought, surely not. As we know, Perfesser, everybody who has been intimately connected with the making of a movie thinks there is a book to be written about the experience. And they're right. But the books are pretty much the same and usually turn out to be lesser works even than the movies they describe, and also almost nobody gives a shit about the writer's experience on the movie unless it is a tell-all about sex with glamorous stars of both sexes simultaneously.

But here is the ghosts of medgar evers. . . .

And Jap's book exposing all of us as drunken dope fiends is due out soon, the Guv tells me. Jap never mentions it, and I don't ask.

I have just finished a line-edit and a scribble-in-the-margins rewrite of the first 531 pages of my epic. I think I have about 100 pages to go. McMurtry has come out with two novels since I started this epic, and his new one, comanche moon, is 750 pages of print in a large size book! Makes my epic look like a novella.

Turning 30 hit me only in a romantic poet sort of way since we were all supposed to die pretty soon or else publish a major literary sensation. Turning 40 and 50 didn't hit me at all because I was too drunk to notice. I was sober at 60 but couldn't really comprehend it. Turning 65 definitely caught my attention, though it was only days before I was suddenly 66. I still don't believe the numbers. I think I am about 40 now, though the mirror disagrees and my social life is certainly different from what it was at 40, when we stayed up all night and were incredibly charming.

Yours in Christ. . . .

Showdown at the Colonial

From *Billy Boy* (2001)

Billy Boy is the story of a boy who is suddenly thrust into an adult world where he must make it on his own. He starts in the caddy yard at Colonial Country Club and encounters obstacles and characters that I grew up with in Fort Worth.

I did know Ben Hogan. I was in his presence many times and wrote about him in the *Fort Worth Press* and later in both Dallas papers. My first page one byline at the *Press* was my story of Hogan's triumphal parade in Fort Worth when he returned home from winning the British Open. I'm not sure Hogan knew my name, but he did recognize me enough to nod and say, "Hi, fella."

In this chapter Hogan carries on a conversation with his guardian angel, Hennie Bogan. This is not an invention of mine. Hogan really did believe that he had a guardian angel that first came to him when the little boy Ben saw his father shoot himself to death.

At 2:30 in the afternoon Harvey Penick put on a clinic at Colonial Country Club for 200 members who paid two dollars each to hear him talk about the golf swing and watch him hit trick shots for an hour on the practice range.

Penick did not teach group lessons, nor did he often leave his home at Austin Country Club. But he enjoyed doing exhibitions, and this was a benefit for the Texas PGA. He chose a left-handed club and hit it right-handed, and then a right-handed club that he hit left-handed. He turned the clubhead upside down and hit shots by spinning the club so fast in his fingers during the swing that the crowd could not see the clubhead squaring up to the ball. Penick brought out a steel ball attached to a length of chain that had a golf grip at the other end. He hit 100 yard shots with the steel ball as clubhead.

Using a rubber hose with a grip at one end and a 3-wood head attached to the other, Penick hit a dozen shots. The crowd was applauding. He placed one ball atop another with a bit of chewing gum. With his 7-iron, Penick hit the bottom ball 125 yards while the top ball popped up and fell into his hand.

At the end of an hour Penick explained what would be his final, climactic trick shot.

He placed two balls side by side.

"I will hit these two balls with one swing," Penick told the audience. "They will cross in midair, one hooking and one slicing."

"Oh yeah?" a voice yelled.

Ben Hogan staggered out of the crowd. His cap was pulled sideways. He had a loopy grin and appeared to be wobbling drunk. A wave of shock went up from the crowd. Muttering began. Hogan did a box step onto the tee. He was using a driver as a cane to keep his balance.

"Nobody can hit that shot. Not even you, Harvey," said Hogan, slurring.

"I've done it before, Ben."

"If you can do it, I can do it better," Hogan said. He tilted to the left as he walked toward the two golf balls. He managed to plant his feet. He waved his driver above the balls, took a big backswing and fell to his knees.

Bud Shrake and Harvey Penick at Austin Country Club, 1993.
Photo by Carrell Grigsby.

A few in the crowd laughed. The rest were too shocked and intimidated to laugh at Hogan.

"While I'm down here, toss me a ball, would you, Harvey?"

Penick dropped a golf ball in front of the kneeling Hogan. Blinking and wiping his eyes, as though finding the ball hard to see, Hogan twisted his cap again until the bill was over his right ear. He stuck out his tongue, clamped his lips on it and crossed his eyes.

Then from his knees Hogan swung his driver and hit the ball off the turf about 240 yards.

The crowd shouted and applauded. Hogan rose to his feet, pulled his cap around correctly and smiled. The crowd realized with vast relief that he was not drunk. He was pretending. This was an act Hogan had put on at exhibitions when he was younger, before he became a star. Today he did it to benefit the Texas PGA. The crowd laughed and cheered and clapped.

Hogan held up a hand to stop the applause.

"If you think that was a good shot, watch what Harvey does," Hogan said.

The slender Penick addressed the two golf balls.

Gesturing toward Penick's thin arms, Hogan said, "You will notice, ladies and gentlemen, that this shot requires great skill but no biceps whatsoever."

While the crowd was laughing, Penick swung his 7-iron and the two balls crossed in midair as he had said they would. The laughter turned into cheering and wilder applause. Hogan and Penick both took off their flat cotton golf caps and bowed.

"You got time to watch me hit balls, Harvey?" Hogan said.

Elvis Spaatz dispatched Chili McWillie and Ham T out to the range to act as security, keeping the crowd away from Hogan. Penick stood on one leg, leaning on his 7-iron, while Hogan began working his way through the bag, starting with his wedge. Elvis sent a canvas chair out to Penick after an hour, when Hogan was into his midirons. Penick sat in the chair and crossed his thin legs, showing his argyle socks and his new alligator golf shoes. Occasionally Penick would say a few words that the crowd could not hear at a distance. But mostly the great teacher watched in silence as the champion pounded golf balls down the range at Colonial. Hogan had often said he dug his golf game out of the earth, just as the old Scottish golf pros had said golf is a game of digging holes.

It was toward sundown when Hogan finished. It was that magical hour that falls across a golf course, when there is silence and peace and beauty and the shadows are reflections of another, better world that the golfer can feel the existence of. Hogan invited Penick to accompany him to the men's grill for a drink and a sandwich.

"Ben, I try to stay out of the men's grill at my own club," Penick said. "The men's grill is where the booze flows and opinions are stated and arguments start. It's a bad place for a club pro to be."

"The hell with em," Hogan said. "They're not going to start any arguments with me. Come on, I'd like to talk to you."

The champion and the teacher entered the men's grill and caused a brief hush in the room. There were card games being played at three tables. At other tables men added up their scorecards. Black waiters hustled through the room with trays of cocktails and beers.

At the round table in the middle of the room sat the Sandpaster foursome. They had been off the course for an hour and had downed several glasses of whiskey. Only Sonny Stonekiller was totally sober, as he sat with his glass of 7-Up over ice—the club champion, the all-district quarterback, handsome enough to be a magazine model. Chester Stonekiller, usually jovial, was in a dark mood, his big brown face like a sandstorm. Chester was drinking martinis. Mr. Titus, looking primly satisfied as he sipped his bourbon neat, had done all the arithmetic for their game. Dr. Sandpaster was relaxing with a tall scotch topped by a slice of lime. His purple glasses lay on the table, wisps of hair hung down to his eyes, his fingernails were growing long and clicked on the glass. Ira had come in with an 84. He was pleased because 84 had proved good enough to win a large amount of money from Chester, but Ira was a little distressed about Sonny. Three times Ira had seen Sonny fudge an inch when he marked his ball on the green. The first time, Ira wasn't sure he had seen it. The second time, Ira shrugged it off as excessive casualness. But the third time? Could it be?

Everyone at the Sandpaster table said, "Hi, Ben," except for Chester, who said, "What say, Hogan?"

"Fellas," Hogan said. He glanced sideways at Chester. Hogan looked across the table at Sonny but did not acknowledge him. Sonny sat back, sulking, and sipped his soft drink. A waiter showed Hogan and Penick to a table for two against the wall. The champion and the teacher ordered ice teas and club sandwiches.

Hogan was chewing his sandwich and drawing on a napkin his strategies for defending his championship in the upcoming U.S. Open in Detroit at

Oakland Hills with its sixty-six new bunkers and added length. Newspapers were calling the course The Monster. Penick was eating and listening, nodding now and then, impressed by the champion's confidence in a plan that called for many imaginative shots.

"Hey, Hogan," Chester said loudly.

Hogan ignored him and continued talking to Penick.

"Hey, Hogan," Chester said again. The room grew silent. Chester stood up, his prosperous belly filling his golf shirt, a martini in one strong brown hand and a cigar in the other.

"Chester, sit down," said Ira Sandpaster.

"Shut up, paleface," Chester said.

Chester took two steps forward, put both hands beside his mouth to amplify and shouted, "Hey! Hogan!"

"I hear you, Chester," Hogan said, and suddenly there was not even the tinkle of an ice cube.

"How come you won't ever play golf with my boy? You think you're too good for him?"

"Your boy doesn't play golf," Hogan said. "He just tries to see how far he can hit it."

"My boy Sonny can beat your ass, Hogan," said Chester.

"Your boy can't beat that kid Billy who caddied for me the other day," Hogan said.

"Sonny can't beat Billy at what? You don't mean at golf?"

Hogan raised a finger and beckoned to Elvis Spaatz, who was in the doorway. "Where's that kid Billy?" Hogan said.

"He just come back into the yard, Mr. Hogan," said Elvis.

"Well, go get him. Bring him in here."

"Billy can't come in here. Caddies are not permitted in this room," said Ira Sandpaster.

"Call a board meeting about it, Ira," Hogan said. "Get going, Elvis. Bring that boy here."

Billy had to run to keep up with Elvis as they went up the hill toward the clubhouse. Billy had caddied thirty-six holes that day, as he had done regularly since returning from Troy's funeral. Without Sandra Sandpaster to date, Billy had been saving his money, going with John Bredemus to the cafeteria at night and returning to his room to read books the older man passed along to him. Billy missed Sandra. He longed to kiss her. But he worked hard all day and fell asleep early with a book on his chest. When Billy arrived at the door of the men's grill beside Elvis, he first saw past the quarreling rabble at the Sandpaster table. His glance found Ben Hogan, whose head was tilted to the left and his eyes closed, as if listening to music. It flashed into Billy's mind that Hogan was conversing with Hennie Bogan.

Hogan smiled like Gary Cooper and nodded and opened his eyes.

"Come over here, Billy," Hogan said.

Billy heard anger from the Sandpaster table as he passed it, and he smelled whisky and cigar and cigarette smoke. He wondered what was happening. For a moment he thought of Bredemus, but he didn't know why. Billy walked over and stood beside the table where Penick sat with Hogan.

Hogan stood up, and it seemed the whole room took a step backward, forced back by the zone around him.

"Here's my proposition, Chester," said Hogan. "Your boy can't beat my boy."

"You're crazy as hell, Hogan," Chester said.

"They play four holes. Fifteen, sixteen, seventeen and eighteen. Stroke play. Your boy hits off the back tees and always drives first. My boy hits off the regular tees. I say your boy does not beat my boy."

"When?" said Chester.

"Tomorrow morning at ten," Hogan said.

"How much do we play for?" asked Chester.

"Chester, you're so rich, money means nothing to you," Hogan said. "Let's play for something real."

"Anything. You name it."

"If I win the bet, you and your boy both resign from this club at once and move to River Crest," Hogan said. He tilted his head to the left, listened and grinned. "You never come to Colonial again for any reason."

"But what will you lose when you lose?" asked Chester.

"If I should lose, I will resign from Colonial," Hogan said. "I'll never come here again, not even for the tournament."

"Ben . . . Ben . . . You can't do that, Ben . . ." voices pleaded.

"And to sweeten the pot, we'll play for ten thousand dollars," said Hogan.

"Make it twenty-five thousand," Chester said.

Hogan turned to Billy, who stood beside him, their eyes at just about the same level.

"First I better ask how you feel about this, Billy," Hogan said.

"Sir," Billy said, "I need to know what's in it for me if I win the bet?"

"You'll get a piece," said Hogan.

"What I want," Billy said, "is Sonny's junior membership with dues paid for a year."

Hogan laughed. "Good," he said.

"I'm the one says if it's good," Chester shouted. "And I don't believe in gambling against somebody who has got nothing to lose. If you want Sonny's membership, what will you bet against it, kid?"

Billy said, "I have six hundred dollars in cash I will put up. Every penny I have in the world." He looked at Sonny. "If I lose the bet, I swear I will leave Fort Worth and never set foot in this town again, and I will be out of your hair forever, Sonny."

"Like you matter. Don't flatter yourself," said Sonny.

"How about it, Sonny? Do we make the bet twenty-five big ones?" Chester said.

"Hell, yes," said Sonny.

"Ten thousand is mine," Hogan said.

Ira Sandpaster had been feeling disappointed in Sonny, on the basis of very little evidence, actually, but it was a feeling he had. A person who would even casually mismark his ball could never guide Ira to a 79, no matter how sweet his tempo. God would not allow it. Ira had not thought of Billy as being any kind of golfer—well, there were those shots he hit with Hogan and that notion that Hogan had taught him a secret—but if Ben Hogan thought the boy could play, Ira was inclined to think so. And there was the thrilling possibility of Chester Stonekiller resigning from the club. "I'll bet five thousand on Billy," Ira said.

Sonny looked at Dr. Sandpaster as if he had been betrayed.

"I'll cover another five grand," cried a fat man from the bar.

"Two thousand on Sonny," shouted someone from a card game.

"I got your two thousand," cried a card player from another table.

As the betting frenzy bounded back and forth in the room, Hogan said, "Will you stay over and referee the match, Harvey?"

"I'll be delighted," said Penick.

"I'll go with my boy and pull clubs for him," Hogan said to Chester. "I may read the greens for him."

"Who cares?" said Chester. "Sonny can beat that kid with one hand."

"He's got to prove it," Billy said.

"I can't wait to see you walking back to New Mexico, you country dumb-ass," said Sonny. "Me and Sandra will drive along behind you in her convertible and honk."

With Elvis Spaatz blocking for them, Hogan and Penick and Billy made their way through the room of agitated members, many waving wads of cash, shouting, some starting to push others. At the door to the pro shop, Hogan said to Billy, "You still have that 7-iron that belonged to John Bredemus?"

"Yes sir."

"You hit that club real well. I'll pick you a set of clubs that match it close as I can," said Hogan.

"I can get a set of clubs," Billy said, thinking of Bredemus.

"All right." Hogan tilted his head, this time to his right shoulder, listening for a moment, and then he looked back at Billy. "You're going to remember tomorrow all your life, Billy."

"Yes sir. I believe it."

Hogan turned to go. "Can I give you a ride back to your hotel, Harvey?"

"Appreciate it," said Penick.

"Mr. Penick," Billy said.

"I'm Mr. Penick's son, Harvey."

"Sir, I can't make myself call you Harvey."

"I'll have the car brought around," Hogan said. He walked out the door of the pro shop, past a number of caddies who were staring through the window.

"What is it, son?" asked Penick.

"Speaking of Mr. Bredemus . . ."

"Yes?"

"Could you tell me how he died?"

"Why, yes, I can," Penick said. "John had come through Austin and visited with me in May of 1946. He left in his new Ford and went to Big Spring, where he was remodeling the Pine Forest Country Club, doing new dirt work and planting. And he was suddenly struck down by a heart attack. A coronary occlusion. They said it was like he was hit with a hammer. He went down and was gone at the age of sixty."

Thoughts were racing through Billy's mind faster than he could review them. "You saw his body?"

"Yes, I saw his body. What is it, son? Are you some relative of John's?"

"No sir. I had heard a lot about him and admired him and didn't know he is dead, that's all."

"Play well tomorrow, Billy," Penick said and went to find Hogan.

The lights were on now in the growing darkness. Inside the men's grill the arguments were leading to violence. In the main dining room as the help set the tables and updated the menus, they were talking about the golf match, and one waiter made Sonny a ten to one favorite and began taking two-dollar bets.

Billy walked down the driveway in front of the clubhouse and saw the old black Ford waiting for him with a man in a tweed cap at the wheel. Cars were coming and going as people left after golf or arrived for dinner, but nobody seemed to notice the black Ford.

"Exciting day, Billy Boy?" said Bredemus.

Billy leaned down and looked into the large ruddy face with the broken nose and clear eyes and furrowed brow.

Billy said, "There's not a doubt in my mind that John Bredemus is dead. But there's not a doubt in my mind that you are John Bredemus. What are you? What is going on?"

"I'm hungry," said Bredemus. "Let's go to the Piccadilly."

From *Custer's Brother's Horse* (2007)

At Christmas of 2001 I flatlined in the hospital a few hours after surgery. I was dead for a while, then returned with a memory of what I saw while I was gone. As soon as I got home from the hospital, I started writing about an English novelist named Edmund Varney who was beaten to death by bandits on Christmas Eve, went into the afterlife, and later mysteriously returned to this life free forever from the fear of death and struggling to find the words to tell what he had learned on the other side of the curtain.

In the spring of 2002 I was at the opening party for the annual Dan Jenkins golf tournament in Fort Worth, and someone asked me the title of the novel I was working on. I said, "Custer's Brother's Horse." That was a surprise to me. All I knew at the time was that there was a young Confederate captain chained to a gallows in a prison yard in Austin, and Varney had just been chained up next to him. I knew that somehow the captain would wind up in Mexico, and Varney would return heroically to the afterlife. But I didn't know the horse would be a major character until the title popped out of my mouth.

I presented this manuscript as a Civil War novel, but to New York publishers, as my agent, Esther Newberg, explained, if the story takes place in Texas before 1900 and has horses in it, it is a "western."

In his mind Varney was back in Afghanistan. He was hearing drums and screams. His skull was throbbing and his stomach flopped like he'd drunk too much of that bloody fermented whatever the hell it was the Ghilzai head man served in that blasted bone cup that looked like his grandmother's knee. Varney had woken up from a concussion to find himself sprawled in the snow in a clearing surrounded by mud huts with rusted tin roofs made from British ammunition boxes. The wild Ghilzais were squatting on their haunches in the snow, clutching their knives and long rifles, smoking and laughing at him. He sensed now that his head was bleeding as it had been that morning in the village in the Hindu Kush less than a mile from where the British army and their women and children and servants were being slaughtered that very day on their retreat from Kabul, all killed, all fifteen thousand dead. Varney's fingers felt wet and sticky from touching his scalp, not at all a good sign.

He opened his eyes into a squint and peeped out, expecting he was going to see the bearded Ghilzai warriors capering in their pantaloons, their sheepskin cloaks scattering snow, swinging Varney's ruby amulet on its gold chain in a loop around their turbans and fur caps. But he saw cool gray smoke enveloping him instead. He heard voices cry out from somewhere in the smoke on the far side of wherever this was. One voice screamed, "Mother of Jesus, get away from me or I'll kill you." This sounded like what you might hear in Kabul, but Varney began to realize it wasn't smoke he was seeing, and these cries were not in the Pathan tongue but were in English of a sort, the slurred tones of the southern mountains, the flat drawls of the west. He began remembering that Afghanistan was long ago, maybe ten years or more, though it seemed less and was always near the front of his mind. He was among a different breed of savages now. He was in Texas.

"My God, this bloody fog is worse than London," Varney said. "Who would have believed it? Can't see the end of my blasted feet."

Varney tried to move his right leg and discovered he was chained. Behind him hidden by the fog Robin stood and watched. Varney grasped the chain in his strong right hand and yanked, but it rattled and held. He reached out with both hands and tugged again. Robin saw the swell of muscle in Varney's neck and shoulders. Varney dropped the chain. He licked blood off his upper lip. He touched the bleeding lumps on top of his head where the hair had gone thin, a patch of it missing.

Somewhere in the fog a voice yelled, "Please, I'm asking, will somebody help me?"

Another voice yelled, "You're in hell. What do you expect?"

Varney looked at the blood on his fingertips. His face had a patrician aspect, a heavy brow, a well drawn nose and chin. Robin was thinking this prisoner's head looked like a long buried bust of some ancient Roman senator, but the body was sturdy and blocky like that of a laboring man. Robin guessed the prisoner to be about fifty years old, about twice Robin's age. The prisoner's left earlobe was pierced by a green earring that looked to Robin like jade laid on silver.

Varney shouted into the fog, "If you think this is hell, you have sorely underestimated the devil. I've seen hell. I've been there and have returned. You arseholes are only in Texas."

The prisoner's accent sounded familiar to Robin, an upper middleclass

English preciseness like that of Robin's mother, who had been born in St. John's Wood in the north of London. After nearly thirty years in Texas, Varina Robin had maintained the sound of London in her accent. The rhythms of the prisoner's voice reminded Robin of her.

Varney looked down at his fist wrapped around the chain. "Hullo," he said, noticing another chain. He clutched the second chain in both hands and began to haul it in like a fisherman retrieving a net. Twelve feet away at the other end of the chain was Robin's right boot.

"What's this then?" Varney said.

The prisoner peered at Robin emerging from the fog so close by. Robin could see he was struggling to clear his mind from the blows that had been lavished onto his head by the Leatherwoods.

"Let me take a look at your wound," Robin said.

"Are you a physician, or merely morbidly curious?"

"I have some experience with wounds, but if you'd rather not, the hell with you."

"I've already been to hell," the prisoner said.

"I heard."

Varney studied Robin, looked him up and down with a curiosity that would have caused offense in almost any other circumstance. Varney's eyes were large and gray and somewhat protruding. At first his look was fierce, aggressive as a predator, but his gaze softened as a pain struck behind his eyes. This young man he was looking at seemed sincere. He was tall and blonde, wearing a gray hat and a tan uniform coat with two rows of buttons over a dirty cotton shirt, denim trousers and boots.

"Well then, please. Have a look at my nog. Awfully kind of you," Varney said.

Robin bent over and scraped away the sparse hair around the two lumps which rose like little purplish volcanoes from a clearing surrounded by gray thatched jungle. Blood had dried on the two lumps, but two fresher deep scratches were oozing on the prisoner's scalp high on his forehead. The prisoner's hair hung down over his ears until he combed it back with his fingers. Robin smelled whiskey on his breath.

"Santana Leatherwood raked your head with his spurs," Robin said.

"Pardon?"

"I'm surprised he didn't yank that earring out of your ear."

"This earring is protected by a powerful spirit."

"Do you remember how you got here?"

"I'm starting to, yes, up to a point. I was having a discussion with four Hittites on horseback and suddenly one of them belted me with a club and another whacked me with a shotgun barrel. But I don't understand why I now find myself chained to a gibbet in this bloody fog."

The prisoner rolled over, got onto his knees, gathered himself and stood up. He brushed his clothing with his hands. His knee-length jacket was filthy, bloody and ripped in places, but it was expensively tailored. His boots were scuffed and worn but made of fine leather by a master craftsman.

"Have you seen my hat?" Varney asked.

"You weren't wearing one."

"My satchel? My dispatch case?"

Robin shrugged.

The prisoner rattled his chain by shaking his leg.

"If I should snap this chain, what next? What lies around us concealed in this fog?"

"A stockade fence fifteen feet high," Robin said.

Varney swept the yard with his gaze, using his imagination to see through the fog and render a picture of his surroundings. He nodded. He said, "Well then." Varney looked at his chain and at Robin's chain. "This is quite an unexpected pickle. I must think this situation through. Do you have any tobacco?"

"No."

A dizziness struck him, and Varney said, "Sitting down sounds a proper idea." The prisoner traced along the gallows platform with one hand until he touched the wooden steps leading up. Varney tugged at his chain and found it was just long enough that he could sit down on the second step. The fog was beginning to fade. A crack of light showed in the east. Varney looked up at the hanging arm of the gallows. He said, "How many souls do you reckon have climbed these steps into the great mystery?"

"None yet. The Yankees just now finished building this gallows. The style in hanging around here is from a tree limb."

Varney touched fingers to his scalp and said, "What is your prognosis for my nog?"

"You've had a concussion but no fracture. You'll heal."

"Did you say someone put the spurs to me?"

"Santana Leatherwood left his mark on you. Those are good Mexican spurs."

The fog was lifting fast and the late spring sun began to light the prison yard. Other forms began to be revealed as the mist faded away. Men were rising, stretching, spitting in the dirt. Several were pissing against the fence. Varney saw there were about thirty prisoners inside the stockade. Tents and shelters had been erected by the prisoners. Blankets and bundles were strewn around the perimeter like an undisciplined military camp. But these were not prisoners of war, Varney saw. They looked to him like robbers, thieves, murderers, drunks, brawlers, degenerates, the failing and fallen. Varney searched with his eyes for the wretch who had been crying out for help, but he was silent now. The prison yard was circular, about seventy five yards across. The fence posts were logs planted in the ground end first, and there were two guard towers and a main gate.

"I don't see chains on any of the other chaps," Varney said.

"You and I have been set apart for special treatment."

Varney's face lit up with a wide smile that wrinkled the corners of his eyes.

"Then we must become chums," Varney said. "Edmund Varney is my name."

Varney wiped his right palm against his chest and then stuck out his hand. Robin was surprised at the strength of the older man's grip as they shook hands. The name sounded vaguely familiar, but Robin couldn't recall where he might have heard it.

"Jerod Robin."

"Tell me, Mr. Robin, why are we in chains?"

"Santana intends to hang us."

"Good Lord, why me?"

"You for stealing a horse."

"It was a misunderstanding. My embassy will be contacted."

"In Texas, horse thieves don't have any rights, Mr. Varney."

"Why you? What have you done to be hanged for?"

"I offended Santana Leatherwood."

"How did you do that?"

"I ran him through with a sword in battle in Tennessee."

Varney's white tufted eyebrows lifted. He scraped a handful of damp dirt and stood up from his seat on the gallows step. He scrubbed his hands with dirt in an effort to remove the dried blood. Varney grinned and said, "Worse and worse. Worse and worse." He dusted his hands and patted his pockets. He scowled. Varney searched his pockets more carefully. "Gone," he said. "By damn, it's gone."

Robin thought of his letter from Sweetbrush that was sewn into his coat.

Varney bowed his head wearily and pinched the bridge of his nose. The lumps on his head now appeared more like small blue eggs. The spur scars were red but had stopped bleeding. Varney looked tattered and his shoulders slumped. Then he shook himself. He raised his head and squared his shoulders. Robin was reminded of watching a bare knuckle fighter who gets up after being knocked down, gathers his wits and his courage and is game to continue the fight.

"How would I get in touch with this Santana Leatherwood fellow?"

"He'll be coming to see you soon enough."

"I am remembering now. The chief of the Hittites. You put a sword through him, eh? How Byzantine."

Varney paced to the end of his chain and back. He scratched the bristles on his chin. Varney again studied Robin from boots to hat with an intense curiosity that would have provoked a brawl if this had been Dutch John's. Robin looked like a prime young Scots-Irish southerner, a well-reared Celt on his way home from the war. Varney said, "Clearly you are a soldier." He paused. "You have the air of an officer." Varney squinted and sniffed. "You have the look and smell of a horse person. I can tell. I am a horse person myself. So you encountered this Santana Leatherwood in a skirmish and thrust him through?"

"It was more than a skirmish," Robin said.

"A battle then. What was it called?"

"Snow Hill."

"I haven't heard of it. When was this battle?"

"Last Christmas Eve."

"In Tennessee, you say?"

"In the Great Smoky Mountains along the North Carolina border."

"You were in a backwater affair. The battle at Nashville was in the middle of December. Sherman had gone from Tennessee long before Christmas Eve. The major fighting had moved toward the sea. With respect, Snow Hill must have been a skirmish."

"I was at Nashville. Then we went east to the mountains. That's where Snow Hill is. We judged our fights by how nasty they were," Robin said. "It was a battle."

"I do understand about war, my son," Varney said. "I did a career turn for Her Majesty's horse soldiers and the East India Company in India and Afghanistan in my younger days. Well, not so long ago, it seems to me."

"Is that what you call hell?" asked Robin.

"No. India and Afghanistan were hell some of the time and heaven much of the time, but they were merely a warm up for the real thing. My visit to true hell and my glimpse of true heaven came later. But I accept your definition of battle. Snow Hill was a battle that I never heard of. Am I correct in assuming you are going to tell me about it?"

"No."

"Later perhaps?"

"I don't see us having a later," Robin said.

"Last Christmas Eve you nearly slew the Hittite?"

"Nearly."

Varney paused and smiled at a memory.

"I was in Spain last Christmas Eve," mused Varney. "While you were fighting the Hittite I was in a cave in the Pyrenees."

"You get around," Robin said.

"Indeed."

Varney yawned. He drew in a deep breath. Robin noticed the creases in Varney's forehead and between his brows. From what Robin knew of London from stories his mother told, and from books in the library at Sweetbrush, he speculated that Varney might be a high born confidence man fleeing from a serious misadventure back home.

They heard the cry, "Bastards coming!"

Around the yard prisoners turned their heads to hide voices that began yelling, "Bastards coming!" The fog had thinned away. In Texas the weather would change quickly from cool and wet to hot and bright and dry. A guard in a blue Seventh Cavalry uniform pulled open the main gate. Little bow-legged Billy Leatherwood entered carrying a scattergun almost as long as he was. He stopped and talked to the guard and pointed toward Robin and Varney. Robin could see that Billy had put on a red neckerchief like those worn by his brothers in the collaborator Home Guard Company.

"Liiittle bastaaaaard comiiing!" a voice whinnied like a mule.

"You think that's funny? Making fun of people that way?" shouted Billy Leatherwood.

The Englishman said, "There's something familiar about that bandy legged chap."

"He's one of your Hittites. Coming for us."

"Ah yes." Varney raised an eyebrow and said, "Into the crucible then. I do wish I had my hat."

How to Live Forever (2005)

You would be surprised how many noted eggheads love golf. It is true that Samuel Beckett played golf all alone, thirty-six holes a day in Ireland, using two balls, while he was writing *Waiting for Godot.* Well, no wonder.

"How to Live Forever" is the goal of our society. Stephen Wright's observation—"My plan is to live forever. So far, so good"—is an underlying philosophy of our time. In this story Dr. Rupert Rimes faces up to eternity.

There are very few magazines that publish fiction anymore. There is really no venue for a story like "How to Live Forever," which is too long to be a short story but not long enough to be a novella. However, I think it is the right length to tell the tale.

The retirement party for Dr. Rupert Rimes was well under way at the home of his neighbor, Nobel Prize winner Dr. Albert Herkimer, on a wooded hillside that had a view to the east across the river. In the distance they could see the tower and the stadium of the University of Texas and the dome of the Capitol building. For thirty-five years Rupert had taught a course on the romantic poets Byron, Shelley and Keats that was overbooked with students lured by Rupert's flamboyant style of lecturing, but today that part of Rupert's life had ended.

"I suppose you'll do nothing henceforth but play that silly game," said Dr. Herkimer, who became a laureate for his calculations that proved there is intelligent life in a galaxy he had discovered. Dr. Herkimer rattled the ice cubes in his glass. "Your students will miss your stimulating lectures, Rupert. The popularity of romantic poets will wither and die while you bat that stupid ball around in the forest."

Rupert smiled. "You have overlooked something important in the universe by ignoring the game of golf, Herky. You're as bad as my wife. She thinks golf is foolish in the same way as heavy metal music, except for the walking."

"I do not understand the allure of golf, but then I haven't figured out totally everything in existence quite yet, have I?" said Dr. Herkimer.

They stood on the terrace near the hummingbird feeder while the party flowed around them. Dr. Herkimer wore a black cowboy hat on his thatch of white hair, and a jean jacket. He looked at Rupert through purple tinted glasses. The rambling old house was full of guests buzzing with cocktail chatter. Rupert saw his wife Cookie in the living room, looking pretty in white. She was talking to a swarthy man of middle age whose large brown eyes were intent on finding wisdom in whatever she was saying.

"The brown fellow with your wife, that's the guru Gama-Viji," said Dr. Herkimer. "He is visiting from Malibu to lecture our young people and increase his fan base. I am told his book *How to Live Forever* has been on the *New York Times* bestseller list for five years." They saw Cookie being distracted by friends, and Gama-Viji turned his intense, dark-eyed gaze toward the terrace as a waiter handed the guru another martini. Dr. Herkimer waved to get the guru's attention. "I hear Gama-Viji plays a wicked game of golf, if you can believe it," said Dr. Herkimer. "I picture him whistling into a flute while a cobra curls out of a straw basket, but I can't see the guru knocking out whaps from the earth with those sticks you people use."

Dr. Herkimer introduced Rupert to the guru and rushed off to shoo three guests away from the telescope on the terrace that was aimed at the upper windows of a downtown hotel.

"Such a pleasure to meet you, Dr. Rimes," the guru said in a voice that made Rupert think of oiled walnut. "Your charming wife says you are a devoted golfer, just as I am."

Rupert had not read a word of Gama-Viji's bestseller and had no idea how to live forever, except in the metaphysical sense, but if the guru wanted to talk about golf he had come to the right PhD. Rupert played golf once a week with an 18 handicap at Barton Creek Country Club, a short drive from home. He had been thinking he would use golf to fill the void left in his life without lectures to give.

"I'm not scoring very well as a regular thing, but I do intend to get better soon," Rupert said.

"I can be of great help to you," said the guru.

"Kind of you, but I believe I'd rather consult a golf professional," Rupert said.

"Dear man, for the first 20 years I played golf I struggled with a high handicap. No matter how many lessons I took, how many practice balls I hit, I couldn't seem to get better. Today I play at scratch all over the world. This is because of a very private, discriminating teacher who is currently living in London. After only one lesson from this man, I shot par at Sunningdale." The

Bud Shrake. Photo by Bill Wittliff, 2000.

guru reached inside his cashmere jacket, pulled out an alligator notepad and opened it. "This is my special gift to you on this special occasion."

The guru wrote down a telephone number.

"Your wife told me you are going to London on holiday. I will tell this teacher you will call. Believe me, Dr. Rimes, he will have you shooting par in one day."

The guru handed Rupert a piece of linen notepaper with the number on it.

"Please don't share this number with anyone. I can see you are skeptical, but I promise this teacher will make you a scratch player in one lesson if he decides to take you on. Of course I will put in a word on your behalf."

"What's his secret?" asked Rupert.

"You have heard the ancient wisdom—when the student is ready the teacher will appear. It is not for me to say what he might tell you."

Rupert thanked the guru and tucked the number away in his wallet. He had a low opinion of gurus. On the other hand Rupert had bought many books, gadgets and special clubs that promised instant dramatic improvement in his game, and hope always burned within him. Still—par golf in just one lesson? That was too much for even Rupert to swallow. At this moment the Chancellor spotted Gama-Viji and came loping across the floor with a goofy grin, and Rupert ducked away for another martini.

He didn't think about the teacher's phone number again until the drive home after the party when Cookie, who was at the wheel of their old Lexus, with the lights on bright to avoid hitting the deer crossing the road, asked what he and the guru had been talking about.

"Pure guru balderdash," said Rupert, who was into his deeply contented stage by then, humming the score from "Camelot."

Cookie Rimes was a busy professional photographer who specialized in weddings and in portraits of children dressed in white with wreaths of flowers in their hair. Five couples changed their wedding dates when they learned Cookie was going on holiday with her husband. Rupert and Cookie used all of their airline miles and flew first class from Austin to Dallas–Fort Worth, and then business class to London. They splurged on a limo from the airport and checked in at the plush old Stafford Hotel in St. James Place near the parks and the duck ponds. They had been to London often and had friends there. Rupert was a member of the Royal Poetry Society, where he had lectured on the romantic poets. Rupert was a crowd pleaser at the lectern. His friends included professors, poets, writers and theatre people. He played golf with them.

On the outer course at the Royal Mid-Surrey Golf Club early the morning after arrival, Rupert was confounded by the humps and hollows that had been laid out to suggest a Scottish links contradictorily set in a deer park. He had played at Royal Mid-Surrey in past years, but never as poorly. His companions politely blamed Rupert's performance on jet lag. At late supper that night after the theatre, leading comic actor Nigel Bloom stopped by the Rimes table at the Ivy. "Chap has dropped out of our regular two-ball tomorrow at Richmond Golf Club. I'd be pleased to have you as my partner. Pick you up at the Stafford at 10?" asked Bloom. Rupert had been thinking as he looked at his scrambled eggs that his problem that day had been in his wrist cock. Now he had it figured out. "Love to," Rupert said.

But Rupert's game was even worse at Richmond Golf Club. His cloudy expression made it clear Nigel Bloom was wishing he had invited someone else. Rupert swallowed his embarrassment, but he hated looking weak or foolish. While brooding over a cocktail in the men's grill after the round, Rupert remembered that the phone number the guru had given him was still in his wallet. The teacher answered and told Rupert to come straight over to an address in Hampstead.

A taxi delivered Rupert with his golf clubs to a white brick Victorian mansion on the edge of the Hampstead Heath.

"Please come in, Dr. Rimes," said the teacher, a handsome, graceful, middle-aged man with an accent that might be Swiss. He was wearing a white cashmere sweater with a blue silk shirt underneath, white cashmere slacks and soft black Italian loafers with white cashmere socks. A butler in full livery carried Rupert's golf bag onto the heath behind the house. The teacher watched Rupert hit six balls with his 7-iron. "I see," said the teacher. He led Rupert to the terrace, where the butler served drinks. "I must tell you that I adore romantic poets," the teacher said. "Keats lived not far from this very house, though he is buried in Italy, just where a romantic might wish to have it end for a poet, don't you think?"

Rupert said, "Yes, yes, but what about my golf?"

"Be at the first tee at Sunningdale Old course tomorrow at 9 a.m. We'll see what we can do," said the teacher.

Clubby old Sunningdale was one of Rupert's favorite golf venues in the world, two courses that were or had been golfing home to Noel Coward, Terrence Rattigan, Rex Harrison, Albert Finney, Hugh Grant, Arnold Fincher and many other show business and literary figures. Playing the Old course at Sunningdale put Rupert in mind of walking through a Sherwood Forest of pine and silver birch. Cookie was still sleeping when Rupert caught a dawn taxi for the thirty mile drive. He found the teacher dressed in plus fours and a cap, standing beneath the huge oak tree near the putting green and the Tudor clubhouse. The butler, now wearing a dark wool suit, picked up Rupert's golf bag.

"I brought Max to be your caddie. I trust Max not to give away our secrets, and he's a wonderful reader of greens," said the teacher.

The teacher pulled his own clubs on a trolley to the first tee.

"Do we just start right off with no warm up of any kind?" Rupert said.

"Dr. Rimes, you are a teacher so you understand that you as a student will learn the best by surrendering to me your entire attention."

"Right."

The teacher said, "Stand up tall. Tighten your navel. Lift your chin. Look into my eyes. Concentrate on what I am telling you." The teacher's eyes seemed to glow. Rupert stared into them. "Your hips are the motor of your swing. Your hips want to turn to the right and then turn to the left. Your hips want to turn and you must let them go. I want you to place your right thumb on the point of your right hip, and your left thumb on the point of your left hip. When you mash your thumbs against your hip points—your pelvis—this turns on your motor, and your hips will power your swing."

Rupert placed his thumbs on his hips.

"Your thumbs are the key that starts your motor. Now—do it. Mash your thumbs against your hips." Rupert felt his hips begin to tingle. "Good. Your motor is turned on. Your motor runs the power of your subconscious that knows how to do everything. Now you will hit the ball where you want it to go. Just select the correct club, pick out a specific target and trust your body to react in the unbelievably precise way it can when it is run by the intuitive mind."

Rupert quietly scoffed. This was hypnotism, nothing more than a parlor trick. But his hips were vibrating, and wanting to move. Rupert took his driver from the butler, looked down the first fairway and picked out a target. "That brown spot by the bunker," he said. The teacher nodded. Rupert swung the club with his usual motion, but something different and powerful happened. The ball flew 250 yards in the air, hanging high for what seemed a full minute, and came down within three feet of the brown spot.

An incredible rush struck Rupert, a burst of euphoria beyond any he had ever known. It was like an orgasm, but better. It was like the leap of his heart when a big trout struck his dry fly in a mountain stream, but better. It was like when his favorite basketball team hit a three-point basket at the buzzer to win the game, but better. In his life as a high handicapper Rupert had occasionally hit what he thought was a perfect shot and experienced what he now realized had been a minor league form of this ecstasy. The memory of each perfect shot had remained but the ability to repeat it had gone away. Now the teacher's hypnotic trick with the thumbs on the hips was producing perfect shots all around the springy turf of the Old course at Sunningdale.

Rupert hit one thrilling shot after another. His golf shots were not gargantuan, no 300 yard drives, but were perfect within his physical limitations. The butler read the greens and showed Rupert exactly where to putt. Rupert shot a five under par 65. He broke into tears of joy.

"Nice round. You are a good student," the teacher said as they walked up to the clubhouse from the eighteenth green. The teacher had a stylish swing and had shot near par. "Now Max and I must be running off to other business. Not that you're actually a business with me."

"But wait. How much do I owe you? I have traveler's checks."

"Dr. Rimes, you don't owe me a penny. Call me a poetry fan. I enjoyed our game."

"But I've got to pay you for this. This is wonderful."

"Please, Dr. Rimes. Just enjoy it," the teacher said.

Rupert felt himself trembling with euphoric energy as he watched the teacher and his servant walking toward the car park. They had gone around the Old course in three hours. It was high noon by the big clock on the slanting roof above the door of the clubhouse. There would be eight more hours of sunlight. Rupert craved golf like an addict craving a fix.

He turned back toward the veranda where golfers were sitting at tables with their sandwiches and ale. He saw Nigel Bloom at a table with two others. Nigel was laughing and gesturing with his hands forming the shape of a woman. They had an empty chair. Rupert noticed Nigel hesitate before inviting him to sit.

"Just for a nod, Rupert. We're off to play the New course in a few minutes. Waiting for a chap." Nigel introduced Rupert to a theatrical agent and to a solicitor.

"If he doesn't show, I'd very much like to take his place," Rupert said. Aware that this was what Nigel was fearing, Rupert wore his most charming smile.

Nigel shrugged and said, "Well, at least it's a four-ball, so you'd be playing your own shots when you can find them."

"I just came in from the Old course. Did a 65 this morning," said Rupert.

"What did you shoot on the back nine?" Nigel said, and led the table in laughter.

"Not worthy of you, Nigel, such an ancient joke," said Rupert. "The fact is, I have stumbled upon the secret of the golf swing. I am so grateful and happy that I am going to let you in on it. It's very simple. I press my thumbs against my hips, and that summons the power of my subconscious that knows how to do everything. There were times on the Old course this morning when I was invincible. When I can look 250 yards away at a three foot circle and hit the ball there because I say so is magical."

Rupert's speech on the veranda attracted a crowd of golfers who followed the foursome to the first tee of the New course, which was built in 1923. Like the others, Rupert was pulling his clubs on a trolley. He took out his driver, pushed between a novelist and an actor that he recognized from television, and stepped onto the tee.

"This is how I do it," Rupert announced to the crowd. "Observe the thumbs." He showed his thumbs to the audience and then pressed both thumbs into his hip points. "Dismiss it as a trick of self-hypnosis if you wish, but you will be astonished at what you see next. My target is the patch of dark grass near the left bunker way down there. Watch this."

Rupert took careful aim and made his swing. The ball popped off his driver in a feeble slice and hopped into a clump of heather.

The crowd around the tee gasped with shocked silence until Bloom, in the loud tone of a sports announcer, said, "And Rupert hits a flaming whoopsie into the coconuts," and then everyone but Rupert had a hearty laugh.

Something had gone terribly wrong. Rupert's hips had turned but only a little and he had felt no power. There was no tingle. His hearty confidence vanished. Rupert dropped his driver, bent forward and clutched his lower back with both hands. "Oh. Oh. I pulled something," he said. "You fellows better go ahead without me. I've had too much golf today. I need to find a chiropractor."

He heard them laughing as he limped away pulling his trolley. They howled like hyenas around a campfire. Nigel Bloom's laugh was more piercing than the others.

Cookie had spent her days visiting galleries and museums. At dinner that evening at an Indian restaurant, the higher intentioned Cookie tried to be interested in her husband's golfing tale. "Why don't you go back and see that teacher and tell him the problem instead of me?" she said finally. After dinner

Rupert and Cookie attended a new comedy by Arnold Fincher at the National, but Rupert couldn't enjoy it. Each time the audience laughed, he could hear Nigel Bloom and the fellows at Sunningdale hooting their heads off. "Flaming whoopsie into the coconuts" was seared into his brain like a neon sign.

Afterward as their taxi turned into the cul de sac in front of the Stafford, Rupert said, "Thank you, Cookie dear, I am taking your wise advice. I'll keep the cab and run up to Hampstead. I won't be late." The doorman opened the taxi door for Cookie. Getting out, she said, "It's already nearly midnight. Remember you have a meeting tomorrow at the Royal Poetry Society."

Lights were shining in the windows downstairs in the white brick Victorian mansion. The teacher answered the bell. He wore a white silk dressing gown and white pajamas with the collar turned up, and was carrying a cookbook.

"Everybody knows golf lessons don't last, but this is ridiculous," said Rupert.

He followed the teacher into the kitchen.

"This morning's round was just a sample of what you can expect if you enroll in the program," the teacher said, cracking eggs into a bowl and whisking them. "My offer is twenty-five more rounds of golf in which you hit the ball like you did this morning. Each round will have a guarantee of at best five-under par anywhere you choose to play."

"I'll take it," Rupert said.

"My price—"

"I don't care what it costs," said Rupert.

"My price is the day you complete the twenty-fifth round you die."

"Die?" Rupert said. "You mean, like a heart attack?"

"Well, something fatal. You will die and go straight to hell. My price for this program is your soul."

"What do you really want?" Rupert smiled. He took this reference to the Dr. Faustus legend as an attempt at humorous hyperbole, a way for the teacher to warn that he is exceptionally expensive, even for a guru. "Whatever would you do with my soul?"

"I am very serious. I am the best in the world at what I do and my price is dear. I want your soul—nothing less."

Thinking it over, Rupert asked, "Why only twenty-five rounds? I'll sell my soul twice for fifty."

The teacher stirred his eggs and did not smile. "One soul is all you get," he said.

Rupert was an irregular church goer, but he believed he had an immortal soul. Rupert and his soul were one and the same eternal package, with his body their disposable receptacle. But this teacher who stood before him in slippers pouring frothy eggs into a pan couldn't be the devil. This man in the white silk robe and pajamas with the tousled hair and the sleepy smile looked to be a guru's guru, more handsome and better dressed than the other gurus, with a warped sense of humor, but human nevertheless.

Rupert suspected he had figured out why the pressing of his thumbs onto his hips had turned him into a golfing machine. The device of hypnosis used by the teacher had unearthed the stored muscle memories of how Rupert had occasionally hit perfect shots in the past. The memory of every perfect shot since boyhood was stored in his subconscious somewhere. Golf was a constant struggle to remember things that he forgot over and over, such as the simple fundamentals of the swing. Golf instructors thrived on this flaw in the human brain. There was nothing supernatural about Rupert playing his very best and shooting a 65. Consciousness is not understood by science or philosophy. When the wealth of knowledge in his subconscious was freed up by the hypnotic trigger of the thumbs mashing the hips, Rupert could play the game with the best of them.

The great Bobby Jones had written, "Start your swing by pivoting your hips. Your muscles will recall the rest of the moves." That's what is going on here, Rupert told himself. Rupert had read a famous instructional book whose entire message was that golf is a game of confidence. This teacher knows how to make me believe in myself and be the best I can be, Rupert reasoned. Where is the crime in that?

The teacher flipped an omelet in a buttered pan.

"You must die sometime, anyway. Death is an inescapable part of the equation," the teacher said. "Hell is not really so bad as you may have heard. Most people are more concerned with staying out of hell than with going to heaven, but they're ill informed. Once they get there, many find they enjoy hell. You see lots of the best people in hell. We don't eat dead rats or walk on hot coals. Hell has got a bad reputation just because God never goes there."

"I hear my taxi honking," Rupert said, trying to sound jocular. "I believe I will give this a bit more thought. I hadn't counted on death and a trip to hell being included on the tab."

Rupert walked with dignity to the taxi. All the sudden he seemed to be the butt of everybody's jokes. Since he was a child on roller skates, his deepest fear was being made a fool of. As he slammed the taxi door, he thought he could hear the teacher laughing at him from the porch.

The Royal Poetry Society met in a brownstone in Mayfair. The topic for today was *After Yeats, the Wasteland,* but the conversation at the long table at lunch was about their Texas member, Rupert, and his thumbs on his hips. When Rupert entered the lecture hall he had caught Lord Brawley crudely aping Rupert's gesture on the tee at Sunningdale. During the lecture Rupert could see the story being whispered from mouth to ear through the hall. He heard a distinguished member from Oxford hiss, "Sixty five! Rubbish he did!" At lunch Rupert sat and poked at his shrimp cocktail and roast chicken and pretended to be a good sport. When he returned to the hotel, Rupert saw the bell captain mashing his thumbs on his hips and guffawing with the doorman.

Rupert and Cookie had reservations for dinner at a popular new Italian restaurant in Chelsea with two professors and their wives. The Rimes party was waiting on the sidewalk when Nigel Bloom sauntered out of the restaurant with a toothpick in his mouth. Nigel planted himself on the pavement in a parody of Rupert's golf stance at Sunningdale and dug his thumbs into his hips and bellowed, "Do the thumbs, Rupert! Do the thumbs and a table for six will open right up like magic!"

Rupert had the urge to take a punch at Nigel Bloom's glistening white teeth, but he froze as all around him people laughed. People he had never seen before were laughing at him and pointing. Being a buffoon was turning out to be the awful pain he had always feared it would be.

Smoldering with chagrin, Rupert sat at the desk in their small suite with a bottle of white wine he had ordered sent up from the bar and began to scheme his way out of the situation. It was imperative that he get rid of the preposterous-madman-on-the-first-tee-at-Sunningdale anecdote that had become the thing people were now thinking of whenever they thought of Rupert. His brilliance as a lecturer was being trumped by his foolishness on the golf course. What to do? As he tapped the pen against his glass, thinking, he had an idea that made him smile.

How about winning the U.S. Amateur golf tournament? That would give everybody something to remember him by—Dr. Rupert Rimes, distinguished authority on the romantic poets, also champion golfer. The U.S. Amateur was coming up in three weeks. He would have to get his handicap down from 18 to six to be eligible to enter. If he qualified and made it through the regional tournament into medal and match play at Winged Foot in New York, it would require a lot of golf.

Rupert put a pen to it on hotel stationery. He figured on 14 rounds to get his handicap down, two more at the sectional qualifier, then two in the medal round at Winged Foot. Once into match play he would have to defeat six opponents, including the 36 hole finals.

He added it up: twenty-five!

Rupert scratched his chin with the wand of the pen. If he decided to do this, he must insist on thirty rounds to have a safety net between himself and hell, just in case.

Suddenly he felt silly. He finished the wine in the glass, corked the bottle in its bucket of ice, snapped off the desk lamp and crawled into bed beside Cookie.

Pleading a bad back, Rupert turned down golfing invitations for the rest of their trip. He avoided his usual crowd, but could imagine them having a giggle at his humiliation. He went on long walks with Cookie and watched her snapping photos. They spent an afternoon sitting in lawn chairs under the trees in Green Park watching the ducks, swans and geese splashing in the ponds. They went to the theatre each night. But he could not push the divine rush of those perfect shots at Sunningdale out of his mind. He day-dreamed a segment of television news showing him modestly placing the U.S. Amateur trophy on a shelf in his study. Nigel Bloom could choke on that. Flaming whoopsie, indeed.

During the afternoon of their last full day in London, Rupert took a taxi to Hampstead and rang the teacher's bell.

Max showed him to a table on the terrace where the teacher had spread out his fly rod and kit and was tying dry flies in the warm sunshine, with a breeze stirring the flowers in the garden.

"I want you to realize that I know you are not the devil. But you are an enormously clever fellow. I don't know why you are playing this stupid game with me, but make it thirty rounds, and I'm ready to deal," Rupert said.

"Let me talk to the big boss," the teacher said. The teacher waved Rupert to a chair and picked up a mobile phone and punched the speed dial. Rupert heard the teacher say, "Yes, he is a prominent professor of poetry. . . ." The teacher smiled and looked at Rupert. He snapped the phone shut and said, "We have a special deal for you. Call it the professorial discount."

"What is it?" asked Rupert.

"I am empowered to offer you thirty-eight hell-rounds of five-under par, plus two hell-rounds of six-under par—a total of forty. You start a hell-round by pressing on your hips with your thumbs. If you don't press your thumbs on your hips, your own 18 handicap game is in play. I do not collect until you use your fortieth hell-round. If that round is never played, the whole service is free of charge."

"That was the big boss himself on the phone?" Rupert asked.

"The big boss gets mushy when we land a poet."

"Tell me the truth. What do you really get out of this? What's it going to cost me?"

The teacher inspected a freshly tied dragon fly and said, "In the long run, your soul is the only thing I want."

"Let's stop pretending you are the devil," said Rupert. "You are not even the big boss."

"True, there is only one Satan and only one God, but there are countless subdevils and undergods. I hold a rather high rank on our side. You'll learn the ropes when you come on board."

"And your side is what exactly?"

"Must I continue to spell it out? Each time you turn on your motor you will be affirming your covenant with evil. Your power will come from hell."

"You won't drop this hell nonsense?" Rupert said.

"No."

"But you do agree to forty rounds?" Rupert said.

The teacher snipped a bit of wire and nodded.

Rupert reasoned that no intelligent person could turn this down. Even if this teacher did have some sinister connections, there was no danger of death and hell if Rupert used his rounds prudently and kept a proper count. He would easily stop way before forty. Dr. Faustus in the legend had conjured up the devil with magic to bargain his soul for twenty four years of constantly gratified desires. In Goethe's epic drama for the stage, the devil approached Faust with the approval of God to test Faust's character with offers of sex, riches and power. For Rupert to dally with a golf guru—even an evil one—was an innocent situation compared to these. The teacher was smiling, apparently having fun with his devil act. This was how gurus amused themselves—at the expense of their followers. Rupert reminded himself that what counted, bottom line, was the hypnotism that would open his subconscious muscle memory of how to hit perfect golf shots.

"I'm meeting my wife for cocktails in an hour. Let's get on with this, shall we?" Rupert said.

The teacher guided Rupert into his office. It was an elegant room, done all in white, with cut fresh flowers and candles and tall windows looking out on the green heath. The teacher instructed Rupert to remove his shoes and kneel on the white llama carpet. Max entered and stood as a silent witness. The teacher placed a diamond pendant on a platinum chain around Rupert's throat. Rupert felt a sharp stab as the teacher pricked his finger with a silver needle. The teacher dabbed himself between the eyes with a drop of Rupert's blood, then pricked his own finger and smeared a drop of his own blood between Rupert's eyes. Rupert was reassured to see the teacher could bleed what appeared to be human blood. This hypnotism ritual was getting very creepy. He was trying to study the teacher's words and movements to learn how the hypnotism trick was done, but, as with all other magic tricks, Rupert couldn't figure it out. Max handed Rupert a pledge printed on a card that Rupert read out loud: "Satan, I submit to your authority. I place my faith in the power of evil. If I exceed the boundary of our agreement, you may collect my soul and carry me to hell where I will labor for your agenda forever." Rupert felt ridiculous but only Max was watching. The guys at Barton Creek would never hear about this.

As Rupert was on his way out, the teacher said, "The diamond pendant stays here, with me, Dr. Rimes."

"Sorry. I didn't notice."

"Have a nice career in golf," the teacher said.

"Will you be phoning to check up on me, or what?" Rupert asked.

"No, I won't be bothering you again—not until collection time."

"Then this is goodbye," Rupert said.

Rupert shook the teacher's soft white hand, waved to Max and hurried down the walk toward his waiting taxi. He thought he heard moans and wails from upstairs in the mansion. For the only time in his memory Rupert was glad to be leaving London.

Rupert and Cookie flew home to Austin. When the airport cab pulled up in front of their house they saw their 16-year-old granddaughter, a tall girl with short blonde hair, out in the road throwing a tennis ball for their Labrador to fetch. "What on earth is Rondelle doing here?" Cookie said, pleased to see her but concerned. Rondelle helped carry their bags up the steep driveway. She was a beach volleyball player in Santa Monica. She said, "Mom ran off to an ashram in Nepal with a rock drummer, and dad is stoned on the beach, so I thought I'd come live here for the summer."

"You're just in time," Cookie said. "I have a dozen weddings to shoot. I need an assistant."

Rupert slept around the clock and then drove to Barton Creek Country Club to begin his pursuit of the U.S. Amateur championship. There were a dozen men and three women in Rupert's irregular golfing crowd. He rounded up Reverend Billy Bird, oil wildcatter Jimmy Orr and former University of Texas football coach Darrell Royal, whose name was engraved in granite on the 90,000 seat stadium, to make a foursome at the Foothills, one of Barton Creek's four courses. What Rupert was about to undertake would require unimpeachable witnesses.

"Come on, Rupert, quit clowning around. We're holding people up," called Reverend Billy Bird.

Rupert was standing on the championship tee, some thirty yards behind the regular tee where the others waited. Rupert pressed his thumbs against his hips. His hips tingled with power, and his arms felt strong and whippy. A delicious surge of confidence swept over him.

"I'm playing from back here," Rupert yelled. He picked out a shadow far down the left side of the fairway as his target. Rupert swung and his driver made a clang that Royal said sounded like a hubcap falling off a speeding car. His ball flew 260 yards and landed in the distant shadow.

"I'd like all three of you to attest my scorecard today," Rupert said, getting into the cart with Royal. "I believe I'm onto something big."

That was the opening shot of Rupert's historic first five under par round at Barton Creek.

For the next seven days Rupert looped around the four Barton Creek courses compiling rounds of five-under par. Reverend Billy Bird witnessed all of them except one of the two on Sunday. In the men's grill in the Foothills clubhouse Rupert's table was constantly crowded with members and golf professionals who asked him over and over the name of his mysterious foreign teacher.

"Don't know his name," Rupert said truthfully. He kept the phone number and address to himself. "Ran into this fellow at Sunningdale. One lesson is all it took. I'm happy to show you how it's done."

Rupert would stand up and demonstrate, though not really touching his thumbs to his hips so as to avoid registering hell-rounds, or turning on his subconscious, whichever was happening.

By mashing their thumbs against their hips the others did improve their swings through encouraging their hips to turn. But nobody cut 25 strokes off his game overnight as Rupert had done. Reverend Billy Bird, whose televised ministry went out to 168 countries via satellite, limped into the shower room with large purple bruises on each hip from all the mashing, but he had never in his life broken 90.

Rupert stopped playing golf when his handicap fell to plus-two. He didn't want to waste hell-rounds on ordinary golf. He borrowed Rondelle from the photo studio, and they drove to San Antonio for the sectional qualifying tournament at Pecan Valley. Before the first round Rupert went to the practice range but quit hitting balls when he noticed other contestants looking curiously at the weakness of his shots. The thumbs on the hips didn't seem to work unless he was actually playing golf.

He saw Rondelle on the practice putting green talking to a handsome blonde boy and walked over to meet him.

"Grampaw, this is Charlie Cotton," she said. "He can show me how to read greens. Charlie is playing with us today."

Rupert recognized the name. Charlie Cotton was a 19 year old phenom, product of the junior golf school in Florida, now a freshman at Stanford. With Rondelle carrying her grandfather's bag, Rupert shot two rounds in 10 under par and finished second to Charlie by three strokes but easily qualified for the national tournament at Winged Foot. Still, Charlie had put a new thought in Rupert's mind—what if five under par wouldn't be good enough at Winged Foot?

Rupert, Cookie and Rondelle flew to New York City and checked into the Plaza Hotel. Rupert had phoned his old friend Billy Collins, the poet laureate, who played to a 16 handicap, and set up a dinner at Elaine's. Collins invited novelist John Updike, who was in town on business and wanted to meet Rupert, and playwright Arnold Fincher, both devoted golfers who scored in the 90s.

"I don't mind telling you, Rupert, we are all agog at the idea that you are a contestant in the U.S. Amateur," said Collins, whose bow-tie wagged as he spoke.

The toothy, patrician Updike said, "Oh my, yes. Competing at the highest level in golf is a thrill I can only imagine. If I had spent as much time thinking about writing as I do thinking about golf, I would have won the Nobel Prize by now."

Playwright Fincher told of his former friend and rival Samuel Beckett, who would play 36 holes a day in Ireland, all by himself, with two balls, pitting one against the other, while writing *Waiting for Godot*. "I believe Sammy would have given up all his literary prizes in a wink if he could have become a good enough golfer to play in the British Open," Fincher said.

Rupert's first sight of Winged Foot was an hour before his tee time for the first round of medal play. He and Rondelle pinned on their contestant badges, and she carried his bag to the first tee. By now he had entirely given up hitting balls on the range—a pastime he had once very much enjoyed, considering it a form of meditation. The quality of his practice shots was embarrassing for a contestant at this level and he didn't want the other players to watch him miss putts on the practice green.

He was paired with a car dealer from Reno and an airline pilot from Boca Raton.

"Excuse me, but you must be looking for the Senior Amateur, which is late summer in Minnesota," said the pilot. The car dealer laughed.

Rondelle stepped forward and said, "I've got a hundred that says my Grampaw will kick your butt, both of you guys."

Rupert had decided it was wrong for him to bet on a hell-round. It felt like it might be a sin to make money off his condition, whatever it might be. Rupert hugged Rondelle and said, "Darling girl, they are revealing their insecurity. Actually they are frightened that we are going to show them up, as indeed we are."

"All right then. Make them eat it, Grampaw," said Rondelle.

Rupert led the medal play with two rounds of 65. He marched through his match play opponents. Crowds began turning out to watch the professor and his granddaughter. A sports writer speculated that Rupert was using steroids. He smiled and waved to the gallery, enjoying his excellence.

The 36 hole final match was shown live on ESPN-TV. Rupert grinned into the cameras and said, "This is my ode to Byron, Shelley and Keats, and Cookie and Rondelle, of course."

The director picked up a shot of Rondelle leaning against Rupert's bag and trading smiles with his opponent, Charlie Cotton. The voice on television told viewers that Charlie and Rondelle had gone out on the other Winged

Foot course for a long evening with the explanation that he was teaching her to read the local greens. She conferred with Rupert on every putt. The final went to the last hole, where Rupert calmly sank a twenty footer for a birdie to win the championship. He knew he would make the putt, but it cost him a six-under hell-round.

On their return to Austin they were met at the airport by four television reporters with camera crews, two news photographers and three sports writers. For the cameras Rupert demonstrated almost mashing his thumbs on his hips, and showed how to turn them, but was careful not to switch on a hell-round. A reporter asked Rondelle if it was true that she and Charlie Cotton were romantically involved, and how she felt about her grandfather beating her boyfriend. She grinned and dodged the question.

All afternoon and into the evening friends dropped by the Rimes home to see the trophy. Cars parked along the narrow, winding road on the hillside all the way to the cedar house owned by Dr. Herkimer, who had gone off on a speaking tour of South America. When the last guest left, Rupert carried his trophy into his study and cleared a place for it on a shelf behind his desk. Looking at his reflection in the trophy as he polished it with his sleeve, Rupert was struck by a pang of conscience. He felt this may have been somewhat unfair of him—especially his six-under par hell-round that closed out young Charlie in the final. But Charlie had a rich future in golf. Who did Rupert really hurt? Certainly not the hedge fund manager he beat in the semis. Still, an inner voice warned Rupert that he should get out of the teacher's program now. Whether Rupert was hypnotized or was dealing with a guru from hell, either way it was time to quit. No more mashing the thumbs. He would go back to his regular game of shooting in the 90s with his pals. His sudden decline would be far less surprising to them than his sudden stardom had been. He would say he had been in the zone, and had now fallen out.

Cookie came into the study with a telephone in her hand. "It's the President of the United States on the line," she said.

"Hey there, Roopey, you ole polecat," said a voice Rupert had heard only on television. "I'll be in Austin for a few hours tomorrow. Let's tee it up at Barton Creek, you and me and the governor and Ben Crenshaw. Balls in the air at seven a.m. And bring that trophy with you. We'll get some pictures."

When he had hung up, Rupert said, "I'm playing golf in the morning with the President."

"I thought you didn't like him," said Cookie.

"That was before he phoned me," Rupert said.

On the first tee the next morning Rupert showed them how to do the thumbs on the hips. They tried it. "Makes sense to me. And you say you never need to practice?" said the President. Rupert shot a five-under par 66 from the back tees and did it with casual elegance.

As they posed for photos afterward the President said, "Ole Roopey is going to eat their lunch at the U.S. Open out at Riviera. He's a proud representative of Texas. He'll show them we're not all just a bunch of dumbasses down here."

Rupert went home for dinner to find Cookie opening cartons of takeout Mexican food and staring at the small TV on the kitchen counter. "What's this about you playing golf in the U.S. Open? Isn't that just for experts? What on earth is going on, Rupert?" she said. "Is this your second menopause? Are you having hot flashes again?"

"I might as well play in the tournament. It only takes four days. Apparently you haven't noticed, but I *am* an expert. I am the champion."

Cookie stayed home to photograph three weddings, but Rupert and Rondelle flew to Los Angeles on Wednesday morning and checked in at the Beverly Hills Hotel. Rupert wandered down to the pool to see if he recognized any celebrities cooking in the sun. Rondelle paged him, and he looked up from her call to find a fat man, oil glistening in his chest hair, waiting.

"Dr. Rupert Rimes, I am Luigi Black," the man said, shaking his hand. "I thought you would be at Riviera practicing." Rupert said no, he didn't practice these days. Luigi Black said, "Jack Nicholson, Sean Connery and I are playing at Bel-Air in an hour and a half. It would honor us to be joined by the amateur champion."

Rupert used another hell-round and shot a five-under par 65 at Bel-Air Country Club. "Here's to Rupert and his bloody thumbs," said Sean Connery, lifting a glass in the bar. Luigi Black said, "This is a movie. Rupert is a feature. Poetry spouting grandfather rises to the top of the golf world at an age when he should be on assisted living. You could play him, Jack." Nicholson said, "I could play him sixty. No older."

At Riviera the next morning, as Rupert was lacing his shoes in the contestant parking lot, Rondelle came running down from the old Spanish stucco clubhouse looking angry. "You're late!" she cried. Rondelle lifted Rupert's golf bag out of the trunk of his rented Cadillac. "I've never seen so many people."

Rupert and Rondelle hurried along in the tunnel made by police lines through the crowd to the first tee. Rupert punched his thumbs onto his hips and felt the power throbbing and looked out over the green fairways and trees of the Riviera golf course down in its valley with showplace homes on the heights. His heart soared. He said to Rondelle, "Hollywood, make way for the Rimes team."

Rupert was having a martini in the Polo Lounge Thursday evening, his 65 one stroke out of the lead, when a slender young man in an Italian suit and loafers with tassels introduced himself.

"Walpole from International Management. You have a fantastically lucrative future, Dr. Rimes. Please let me open the vault for you." Walpole asked him to sit down in the corner booth. Walpole tucked two hundred dollar bills into the maitre d's palm. They ordered vodkas on ice and Rupert acquired an agent. Rupert soon reached his stage of overflowing with jovial kindness, accompanied by sporadic humming, as Rondelle entered the Polo Lounge with her father, Randy, the surfing bartender from Santa Monica. Rupert knocked over his glass standing up to hug his son. "Good stick, Pops, you're piping 'em," said Randy.

Television and the press adored Rupert. After another five-under par hellround on Friday, his interviews went on for an hour inside the press room and another hour outside later. Rupert signed hundreds of autographs. He had a drink with a *Sports Illustrated* writer. He took Rondelle and Charlie, who was five strokes behind Rupert, to dinner at La Scala. From another table Luigi Black sent him a bottle of wine. Rupert signed more autographs. Back in his room at the Beverly Hills Hotel, looking down at the Gershwin house from his balcony, he phoned Cookie and woke her up. It was two hours later in Austin.

"You sound drunk. Aren't you playing golf tomorrow? What are you doing still up?" she said.

Rupert said, "I love you."

Cookie sat up in bed and smiled. She said, "I'm coming out there tomorrow right after I do the Rudman wedding in the morning."

Rupert found slipped under his door at the hotel a handwritten note from the guru Gama-Viji inviting him and Cookie to dinner on Saturday at the guru's Moroccan palace on the beach in Malibu. A Bentley limo was sent to fetch them. A tall bearded man wearing a gown and a saffron turban stood guard at the gate. Behind him the swooping curves of the roof were drawn against the sunset. A smiling Gama-Viji with intense dark eyes met them at the door. Over his shoulder the house opened into a wide view of the beach and the ocean.

While Cookie went on a tour of the house with the guru's personal assistant, Gama-Viji and Rupert took their martinis onto the terrace. Both men were drinking vodka on the rocks with three olives and a whiff of vermouth. The orange sun dipped into the sea, and a breeze smelled of salt and fish.

"Tied for the lead, indeed. My congratulations," said Gama-Viji. "No need in me asking if you made your deal with the devil, is there? How does it feel that after a distinguished career in academia, you become a worldwide celebrity by cheating at golf?"

"What do you mean cheating?" Rupert said.

"Is there a different way to put it when the game is rigged in your favor?"

"It's not rigged," said Rupert. "I am hitting all the shots, aren't I? They have people to total up the shots I hit. Television watches every step I take. Crowds gather around me and stare at my every move. How could I cheat?"

"He has fooled you into thinking you are hypnotized," the guru said.

"The teacher unblocked me and freed up my unconscious," said Rupert.

"He's smarter than you are. He wants your soul. I could name several famous people who have made deals with him. Our late friend Dr. Herkimer, for example."

"The teacher knows Herky?"

"Who do you think explained intergalactic mechanics to Herky? Who showed him there are things with brains living out there among the stars? Old Herky couldn't have thought of that on his own. Poor Herky. He's paying for his Nobel Prize as we speak."

"Herky's dead?"

"I'm sorry. I thought you knew. It was on the news that he had a stroke and died on the beach in Rio this morning."

Rupert scowled and looked out at the waves crashing into the sand.

"And now my bill is coming due," said Gama-Viji. "I'm about to sell my three hundred millionth hardcover. My new book *How to Feel Good About God* will be published next week and is already number one on Amazon. My manuscript of *What Is Life Anyhow?* is ready to go to the editor. I'm doomed.

I begged the teacher to take my money, take this mansion, take my fame, take it all back. I pleaded with him to let me return to my humble village in India. But he said it's too late. I'm terrified. I don't want to die."

"If you believe this guy is the devil, why did you give me his phone number?" asked Rupert.

"I was recruiting for him. I was trying to get on his good side. But I've learned he doesn't have a good side. I am sorry, Dr. Rimes. If there's still time for you to get out of your contract with him, I urge you to do it."

"You're crazy," Rupert said. "You're not selling hundreds of millions of books because of the devil. All you gurus are nuts. I know what I'm doing."

Gama-Viji gazed intensely at Rupert.

"The *Times* today speculates you are on drugs," the guru said.

"I am using my full capacity, that's all," said Rupert. "Tiger Woods had laser surgery on his eyes to improve his golf. I'm having a sort of surgery on my subconscious. What's the difference? It's the best of me that's on display now."

Rupert and Tiger Woods were the feature pairing the next morning and drew the biggest gallery in the history of golf. Knowing he had a six-under par round in the hell-bank if he needed it, Rupert played to the gallery. He quoted the romantic poets to them. The other pros had begun calling Rupert by the nickname Space Man, but Tiger called him Doc. Tiger was outdriving Rupert by eighty yards, but Rupert was hitting fairway woods onto the greens and making putts that he conferred on with his granddaughter. The crowd was cheering with growing enthusiasm for Rupert, the elderly underdog. It was a new experience for Tiger Woods to be rooted against. On the hugely long uphill final hole, Rupert was looking at an approach shot of 225 yards while Woods was only a short iron away from the green below the clubhouse. Rondelle handed Rupert the 3-wood, but an inner voice was telling him he felt immensely strong. He asked for the 5-wood. Rupert's ball bounced onto the front of the green, hopped three times and rolled into the cup for an eagle two and the U.S. Open championship by one stroke.

Rupert sat at his kitchen table in Westlake Hills with his agent, Walpole, looking at Rupert's photograph on the cover of the new *Sports Illustrated* magazine. They could hear Rondelle on the porch arguing with her father, Randy, who had come to Austin to take charge of what he called "site security." Fans and autograph collectors and media strays gathered out front on the narrow road. The ugly noise of bulldozers and crashing trees reached the kitchen from the direction of the old Herkimer house, which was being demolished so that the new owner, rumored to be a car dealer from Houston, could build a shiny steel and glass mansion on the once quiet hillside.

"Golfers all over the world are mashing their hips with their thumbs," Walpole was saying. "Many of them are claiming incredible results. Half a dozen books are being written by experts trying to explain why this works so well for you. Endorsement offers are piling up. We have assigned two staffers at IMG just to handle your mail. I'm hiring you a personal assistant to work here in Austin to filter your phone calls and keep your speaking dates straight. The moment you turn pro, you're a very rich professor. I see you on magazine covers and billboards and TV commercials. I see you on television, like head to head vs. Tiger for five million bucks to the winner. You're big time appearance money overseas. You play the majors. You're gonna need a jet. Leave it to me. What's that look on your face?"

"I'm thinking about quitting," Rupert said.

"I didn't hear that. You're just tired. Listen to me. We don't turn pro. Not yet. You win the British Open next week. You win the Masters next spring. The Rupert Rimes Grand Slam. Think what that'll be worth on graduation day."

They heard Cookie on the porch angrily saying, "That movie writer left the gate open. Prissy got out and is running down the road. There's twenty-seven pickup trucks down there wrecking the Herkimer house. Six old women are down by the mail box with cameras. They say they are Rupert's posse. That better not mean what it sounds like it means."

Rupert had checked and double checked his golf ledger that morning. He had five hell-rounds left. He could squeeze in the British Open with one hell-round to spare, but it was an uncomfortable fit. What if there was a playoff? "I don't know," Rupert said. "My back is bothering me."

"IMG has got the best back doctor in the world," Walpole said. "I'll fly him here."

Walpole excused himself and ducked out the front door with his cell phone at his ear, as Cookie came into the kitchen.

"Rupert, I've promised you will play in the fundraiser for diabetes research next week," she said. Rupert shook his head and gestured toward his lower back. Cookie frowned. "The diabetes people will be very disappointed. Margie Bird was telling me today that her husband and your other pals at the club say you have turned into a total butt. You act like you're too good to play golf with them any more. You don't even show up at the club for lunch any more. Rupert, if you are becoming demented—"

"Grandma," cried Rondelle through the screen door. "Prissy got run over. I think she's dead."

They flew to Edinburgh in the custom airliner sized jet owned by high tech billionaire golf fanatic Ludlow Jones, who was one of the thirty thousand members who actually attended Reverend Billy Bird's church in the flesh. On the plane Reverend Billy and wife Margie Bird played bridge with Rupert and Cookie while Ludlow Jones explained to Rondelle and Charlie Cotton how eventually an object the size of a candy bar can hold 5,000 movies. Randy smoked a joint, climbed into a bunk and went to sleep. Walpole talked on the phone in the rear of the plane for hours. Cookie laid down her cards and leaned back in her big leather chair and sipped a glass of white wine and said, "I can see now why you like this game of golf so much."

For the first three days of the British Open the weather was unusually calm and sunny in St. Andrews. Rupert hit the ball where his Scottish caddy, called Tip, hired by IMG, told him, and putted where Tip told him, and tied for the lead at 15 under par with Tiger Woods, Ernie Els, Sergio Garcia and Swedish pro Lars Klahhpolmen. Young Charlie from Stanford was three strokes back. Freed from caddying for Rupert, Rondelle rushed through the crowds to watch both men.

Saturday night in the dining room at the Old Course Hotel, Rupert stood and tapped on his glass with a spoon. He looked down at the faces of Cookie and his family and Charlie and the Birds and Walpole.

"The document, please," Rupert said.

Walpole grinned and opened his briefcase and handed Rupert a contract and a gold pen.

"You will testify, Reverend Bird, that this document is dated tomorrow night. Until then I am an amateur. After I win the British Open tomorrow, I turn pro and the heavens open up. Bonanza for everyone. Whatever my family wants, if money can buy it we can have it after tomorrow."

Cookie, Rondelle and Randy hugged Rupert and kissed him. Reverend Billy Bird led them in singing, "Jolly Good Rupert." Albert Finney, Sean Connery and Prince Andrew stopped by the table, made a show of punching their thumbs against their hips and loudly wished Rupert luck. The maitre d' delivered a magnum of champagne for Rupert with a note. The note said *I must see you at once. Outside. Your teacher.*

The teacher was wearing a light weight cashmere car coat and a Borsalino hat cocked toward his right brow. A misty rain was falling and the wind was rising off the North Sea. Rupert and the teacher walked down toward the Road Hole fairway. The teacher said, "I want to be sure you know that thirty-nine hell-rounds are used. Tomorrow will be forty, meaning it's collection day."

"No," Rupert said. "I've only used thirty-eight. I'm not in trouble with you unless there's a playoff."

The teacher reached into a coat pocket and pulled out a palm size computer. He punched a button and showed the glowing screen to Rupert. "Every time you mashed your thumbs against your hips to turn on your motor, it registered at the data base in hell. There it is. Thirty-nine. You can't argue with technology."

"Your machine is wrong."

"There could be a glitch in the system. Nothing is perfect, not even in hell. But it should be no surprise if a bargain with Satan doesn't turn out in your favor."

Rupert felt the rain pasting his hair to his forehead. "Let's get real here. What's your game?" Rupert said. "The devil is a metaphor, an explanation for evil—not a person you can call up on a cell phone. I admire your genius as whatever kind of guru you are, but tell me what you really want. A piece of the purse? I'll happily split the money with you."

"We made a deal. You could quit right now. Walk away. But I don't believe you will. People seldom do."

"What use would you possibly have for my soul?" Rupert asked.

"Your soul will be recorded in the Big Book as being on the side of evil. When my side reaches true dominance, say twelve to one, we will change everything, Rupert. We will overthrow God. My big boss will sit on the throne. In this contest between us and God, the souls of professors count for many more than one. Your soul is very valuable."

"If you're the devil, prove it," Rupert said. "Show me a glimpse of hell."

"We're making the world into a working model of hell," said the teacher. "Have you ever been to Tokyo? No? Nairobi? Well, you get the idea. Try to have a good night's sleep, Rupert. I'll be watching you tomorrow."

The teacher turned up his collar against the rain and walked into the blue evening haze.

While Rupert brushed his teeth and flossed in the bathroom, Cookie and Rondelle were watching the late news on BBC. "Oh, what a shame," Cookie called out. "Rupert, that charming man, that guru, he's dead." Rupert poked his head out of the bathroom door. "That Mr. Gama-Viji," said Cookie. "He drowned in the ocean at Malibu right in front of his home. It's such a pity. He always seemed so interested in everything."

Wind blew heavy rain against the windows in the middle of the night. Rupert got out of bed and went into the parlor. He felt fear crawling into him. Rupert recited a mantra to calm himself, but the words seemed hollow. He began to pray, but he told himself God didn't want to hear a complaint about a glitch in the devil's accounts receivable department. The fear grew into a stomach churning pain. His toes curled down. His hands trembled. The only logical explanation for what had happened to him is hypnosis, profoundly deep subconscious trickery of some kind, but who could dare depend on logic in such a crisis?

The enormity of what he had done was taking root in him. If the teacher was the devil's head of sales, then Rupert was a total phony—he didn't deserve those trophies, as the world would be about to see. But if the teacher was a perverted human guru and not actually a devil, then there was no reason for the terror Rupert felt. He hadn't cheated. He had hit his own shots, and he could do it again one more time.

It was still raining at gray dawn when Reverend Billy Bird knocked softly on the door. "I figured you'd be up," the Reverend whispered. "Cookie and the kid asleep? Close the bedroom door. I'll order us up a good Scottish breakfast. Ham and eggs and toast and hot tea. We've got to fortify you against this weather."

"I've had a horrible premonition that I might die today and go to hell," Rupert said.

"Nonsense. You've just got the jitters. Listen to me, friend. Hell is being in heaven and not liking it. You're on top of the world, Rupert, and it's about to get even better. You're going to go out there today and bring home that Claret Jug."

Rupert walked onto the first tee in a gray mist. He heard cheers and applause, but he felt alone and cold and petrified with fear. He reached for his hips with his thumbs, but he pulled his hands back. Why take the chance? Golf is largely in the mind. Rupert had already proved that. He would use his own game today. He would rely on the consciousness that won two major tournaments to come forth and play golf today. If it's mainly a matter of turning the hips, what's so hard about that?

He heard the starter announce *Dr. Rupert Rimes*. Rupert was frozen with fear and could barely push his tee into the wet earth. He wondered if hell could be worse than this fear? What was he so afraid of? Making a fool of himself in every living room and sports bar in the world? Letting his family and friends down? He watched a big drop of water fall off his nose and plop onto his hands that tightly clenched the club. He felt millions of eyes staring at him. There was no way out. He took a breath and swung at the ball.

The ball splashed along the ground for about a hundred yards. "Shake it off, Guv," said Tip. Rupert topped his second shot into the Swilken Burn, a ribbon of stream that crosses the course and flows into St. Andrews Bay. Tip squinted at Rupert and laid the ball out. The caddy handed Rupert a wedge. Rupert bladed the ball and it skipped back over the water onto the green. Tip scowled at him. Rupert took four putts for an eight. His playing companion, Lars Klahhpolmen, had picked up five strokes on him in one hole.

"The thumbs, Rupert! For God's sake, do the thumbs!" yelled Sean Connery, turning away in disgust.

"Air ye sick?" Tip asked.

"I'll be fine," Rupert said. He had a sudden idea that he would jump into a pot bunker and break a leg, but there was not a bunker handy now that he wanted one.

On the second tee, Tip pointed and said, "Ye want to take dead aim on that puffy cloud yonder." Rupert plunked a weak slice into the heather. "Air ye gonna do a single damn thing I tell ye?" Tip spat.

After four holes Rupert was thirteen over par for the day. Standing forlornly on the fifth tee box, he heard hoots of scorn and derision from the gallery. He was shaking with cold and soaked to the bone and miserable. He had ventured beyond fear into a startling new dimension of terror. He was alone, exposed and helpless. Everyone could see he was a sham, worse than a buffoon, and he was a pathetic coward as well.

Rupert took his driver from Tip, teed up the ball and slapped it scudding down the fairway. It hopped like a wounded rabbit and died after twenty yards.

"That's it! I quit!" Tip said. "I've got me standards."

Tip dumped Rupert's bag—the big new leather bag Walpole had bought him—on the tee and stomped angrily away into the crowd.

"You old fool, why you don't do your thumbs?" Lars Klahhpolmen said. "You are making me look bad."

Rupert sat down on his bag and buried his face in his hands.

"I'll carry your bag, Grampaw," Rondelle yelled. "Let go of me! I'll take his bag!"

Rupert looked up and saw Rondelle struggling with two security guards at the rope that separated the crowd from the players. He saw Cookie's worried face just beyond his granddaughter, with photographers and television cameras swarming around them, aiming their lenses at him on the worst moment of his life.

"It's no use," Rupert confessed. "I can't play golf. I'm a fraud. I shouldn't be here. I don't deserve those trophies. The devil made me do it."

"Pull yourself together, man," called a voice from the gallery. The teacher, wearing a gray suede cap and a black waterproof, pushed his way to the rope and leaned around a cop to be seen. "You're having a nervous breakdown." The teacher gestured at Rupert. "Get up, Dr. Rimes, and be a man. We're counting on you."

"That's him!" Rupert croaked into the microphone thrust at him by the BBC on-course reporter. Rupert pointed at the teacher. "That's the devil! He taught me to do this!"

Rondelle pulled away from the guards, ducked under the rope and ran to her grandfather. The BBC reporter stuck his microphone into the face of the teacher, who smiled winningly.

"Dr. Rimes is hysterical. He has broken down under pressure," the teacher said.

"You are his personal swing coach?" asked the BBC reporter.

"I'm a psychiatrist," the teacher said.

"Then Dr. Rimes is your patient?" asked the reporter.

Two officials from the Royal & Ancient Golfing Society scuttled onto the tee wearing blue blazers and gray slacks that showed their white socks. The referee tapped his watch and said, "You're on the clock, Dr. Rimes. Play on, or be penalized."

Lars Klahhpolmen had been gazing at the horizon. Noticing the officials, he scowled at Rupert and said, "Come on, Space Man. Do the thumbs. Let's get moving."

"Dr. Rimes has been to see me, yes," the teacher said to BBC. He turned to Rupert. "You've got to get hold of yourself. You're acting like a bloody fool."

"You don't believe he's the devil?" Rupert cried to the crowd. "I'll prove it to you!"

Rupert jumped up and mashed his thumbs against his hips. Instantly his hips vibrated with electrical power and burned with energy. He grabbed his driver from Rondelle. He glared at Lars Klahhpolmen and shouted, "I'll show you how to play golf, you Swedish meatball."

Rupert strode the twenty strides to his foozled tee shot. His ball lay in a slight indention in a bare stretch of fairway. Using his driver again, he bashed his next shot off the muddy ground with mind-blowing power—a mighty thwack!—and thousands of heads turned to watch his ball flying into the misty Scottish sky to fall on the perfect spot two hundred and sixty yards away. The crowd roared with amazement.

"Who but the devil could hit a shot like that?" Rupert yelled.

The crowd swept forward toward the distant green. Rondelle slung the heavy leather bag over her shoulder and marched with the sign carrier, the other caddy, Lars Klahhpolmen, the officials and the BBC reporter. Rupert lingered and looked for the teacher, but he had disappeared into the crowd.

Rupert's hips hummed like high wire lines, and he felt a rush of well being, a euphoric confidence. He had felt the familiar thrill when his thumbs turned on his motor. A sense of joy ran in his bloodstream. There was no joy greater than hitting the ball exactly where he wanted it to go. The crowd was chanting, "Roo-pert! Roo-pert!" Rupert birdied eight holes in a row, striding proudly beside his granddaughter. He declaimed verses from the romantic poets, to the noisy delight of the gallery and the television cameras and photographers.

The feeling took possession of him that he had learned to turn his own hips without any sort of spell—hypnotic or demonic—needed to open the flow of power from his unconscious. Rupert had conquered himself and this game.

On the last hole—with Tiger Woods standing nearby, squinting, arms folded, and the entire world watching on television—Rupert chipped his ball into the cup from the Valley of Sin and won the Open by two shots.

In front of the Royal & Ancient clubhouse, Rupert lifted the silver Claret Jug, the most precious golf trophy on earth, as his fans applauded wildly. He felt enthusiastic and jolly and without fear. He believed he had turned his own hips. He had hit his own shots. He was the master of himself. Golf is indeed a game of confidence. The teacher had served his purpose and was no longer needed. Rupert grinned into the cameras and announced, "Next spring I'm going to win the Masters and complete the Rupert Rimes Grand Slam."

Rupert led his entourage on foot toward a restaurant in the old town of St. Andrews for a victory dinner. Thousands of fans stampeded close around them, cheering like a football crowd, chanting Roo-pert! Roo-pert! Rupert's spirit soared as two stout red-haired lads wearing rugby sweaters swept him up onto their shoulders. Bobbing above the crowd, hearing his name bellowed by thousands of delirious voices, Rupert waved both arms over his head and clasped his hands in triumph.

As his bearers stepped off the curb, Rupert glanced down and saw painted on the pavement a sign that said *Look Right* and he thought *How perfect for me to win in the birthplace of golf!* just as the runaway red double deck bus plowed into the crowd.

Rupert became aware that he was standing on a sidewalk of a deserted street in a strange gloomy city late at night. Steam drifted up from sewer lids. This might be Manhattan that loomed around him in the dark, but there was something eerie about it. He saw lights that could mean a theatre district. He began walking toward the lights. A yellow taxi pulled up and stopped. "Get in," said the gaunt driver. Rupert got into the taxi and said, "Elaine's, please. Eighty-eighth and Second." The taxi sped away. They went across a bridge over a river. The dark city skyline fell away behind them. "Where are we going? Is this Queens?" asked Rupert.

The taxi entered a neighborhood of dark, two and three story buildings and stopped outside a bar that had lights in the window. "They're waiting for you in there," said the driver.

Inside a bartender was printing a menu in chalk on a blackboard behind the bar. The only other person was a woman with long dark hair, pretty in a sweet looking way, who sat in a booth. She wore a cloth coat with a fur collar. She smiled at Rupert and said, "I just got here myself. I was afraid I had kept everyone waiting."

Rupert slid onto the leather seat beside her. She snuggled against him. He tried to think who she might be. She seemed to be fond of him. "Where do you want to go to dinner?" she asked.

"All I remember is I was on my way to Elaine's," said Rupert.

"Famous last words," the bartender said, his chalk scraping on the blackboard. "Everybody who comes in here was on their way somewhere else."

"Why don't we just do Chinese?" the woman said.

A man pulled open the front door. He wore a black cowboy hat on a thatch of white hair, purple tinted glasses and a jean jacket. He walked to the booth and looked down at the woman. "Any news?" he asked. She shook her head. The man stuck out a hand to Rupert. "I think my name is Herkimer," he said.

Rupert replied, "I am Rupert somebody. What's going on here? What are we doing?"

"I don't know about you, but I am still waiting for an assignment," said the man in the cowboy hat. "What did you do before you came here?"

"I have no idea," said Rupert.

"Me neither."

The woman said, "I murdered my husband. I do remember that much. Otherwise, I'd be having dinner with him tonight."

The bartender turned and pointed at Rupert with a piece of chalk.

"You. New guy. Your review is on the board. You should take a look," the bartender said. "You need to know the evaluation before you go on to your next stop."

"What evaluation? What is this?" Rupert said. Suddenly he understood. "Am I dead? Is that it?"

"There's no such thing as death. You are in transition," said the bartender.

Rupert got up from the booth and walked to the bar. Printed at the top of the blackboard it said S-387925. Below the numbers were the words NEEDS WORK. And below that, the bartender had printed:

INTENTION IS EVERYTHING

"Between you and me," the bartender said in a confidential tone, "The fastest way to get this S off your soul number, get your soul G-rated, is to work on this evaluation. Try to get it right next time or at least better. No need for you to stay in hell forever, unless you just like it there."

"I'm in hell?" said Rupert.

"This is the transition depot," the bartender said. "The next bus to hell is pulling up out front just now. Get on it."

"How about me?" asked the woman in the booth.

"Yeah, there's no doubt about you. Get on the bus," the bartender said.

"And me?" yelled Herkimer. "I was here before either of them. I've got a S-designation. Why can't I get on the bus?"

"I think you're going to a different galaxy than them," the bartender said, as they saw the lights and heard the hissing of wheels outside.

The memorial service for Rupert drew a packed house of fifteen thousand to the basketball arena on the campus. Ten thousand more gathered outside around the television trucks that broadcast the event to the world. An opera star sang *Amazing Grace* with the university choir. Reverend Billy Bird delivered the eulogy—*Rupert: A Champion to the Very Sudden End.* Rondelle spoke emotionally of the life-changing thrill it was to caddie for her grandfather. She returned to the family section to sit with Charlie Cotton and with her father Randy, who wore a new Armani suit, and the softly weeping Walpole. Cookie was the final speaker. Her voice broke and she wiped away tears. She said, "Most people will remember him for his golf, but to me Rupert will live forever with his beloved poets."

The new steel and glass mansion on the old Herkimer property rose gleaming on a terraced hillside that previously had been covered with trees and had swarmed with deer. All the neighbors found in their mailboxes invitations to a housewarming at the mansion.

"I'm going to unload on that guy. He doesn't fit here in Westlake Hills," Cookie said to Rondelle as they walked along the road to the party. Other neighbors began arriving. Their mood was hostile, but they were curious. Cookie led the neighbors up the steps.

Before she could ring the bell the front door opened and a handsome, middle aged man wearing a black cashmere blazer, white silk shirt and slacks smiled and said in a European accent, "Mrs. Rimes, it is such a pleasure finally to meet you. I was Rupert's golf teacher in London. Please, everyone, come in. My house is your house." He gestured toward banquet tables laden with food and drink. Waiters in white uniforms were standing by.

The neighbors spread through the mansion and inspected its steel construction that was so different from other houses in the hills. They decided industrial steel made sense. Steel would endure. Cookie found herself admiring the house's clean lines, and the cantilever of the deck on the second floor with the view of the river and the city to the east. The teacher plucked a glass of white wine off a passing tray and joined her.

"It's a lovely vista from up here," the teacher said. "The blue sky, the river, the cedar covered hills—it reminds me of Greece, around Athens, with the great university on the horizon."

"What on earth possessed you to move to Austin?" asked Cookie. "You're a wealthy, sophisticated man. You could live anywhere you choose."

"I have some very important clients here. I need to be close to them," the teacher smiled. "I believe I can help that young fellow, Charlie, as long as I'm in the neighborhood. I'm sure that's what your late husband would want, if only he were here to witness for me."

The teacher whistled softly. From under the coffee table crawled a Scottish terrier. The pup licked the teacher's hand.

"How cute," said Cookie.

"He's very clever," the teacher said. "Already he has learned to do tricks to entertain my friends and clients—sit, beg, roll over, crawl on his belly like a serpent. I'm teaching him to run up and down this precipitous driveway to fetch the morning paper. It's too steep for me."

Cookie bent down and scratched the pup's ears.

"He has soulful eyes," she said.

The teacher smiled, "I'm so very fond of him. I hope you are not offended that I named him Rupert?"

At the sound of his name, Rupert barked.